DATE			
FEB 15 '89			
DEC 5 '90			
APR 26 '95			
MAY 24 '95			
NOV 6 '96			
NOV 27 '96			
JAN 20 '99			

EQUIVOCAL SPIRITS

EQUIVOCAL

SPIRITS

Alcoholism and Drinking in Twentieth-Century Literature

THOMAS B. GILMORE

University of North Carolina Press
Chapel Hill and London

© 1987 The University of North Carolina Press
All rights reserved
Manufactured in the United States of America

Library of Congress Cataloging-in-Publication Data

Gilmore, Thomas B.
Equivocal spirits.
Bibliography: p.
Includes index.
1. American literature—20th century—History and
criticism.   2. Alcoholism in literature.   3. Alcoholics
in literature.   4. Drinking in literature.   5. English
fiction—20th century—History and criticism.   I. Title.
PS228.A58G45   1987   810'.9'355   86-19355
ISBN 0-8078-1726-0
ISBN 0-8078-4174-9 (pbk.)

Chapters 1 and 5 of this book originally appeared
in slightly different form as articles in
Contemporary Literature (Summer 1982) and Twentieth
Century Literature (Winter 1982). A somewhat shorter
version of Chapter 3 first appeared in Comparative
Drama (Winter 1984–85).

Permission to reproduce quoted matter
will be found on p. 217.

*To my mother
and the memory of my father*

Contents

Acknowledgments

Any book thought about, researched, and written over a period as long as nine years naturally is indebted to many people, whose help it is now my grateful pleasure to acknowledge. The only concern diluting this pleasure is that, in the passage of so many years, I may have forgotten some names that properly belong here. To any such, I extend my apologies and my hope that they will charge me only with forgetfulness, not with ingratitude.

To Georgia State University and a number of my colleagues in the Department of English I owe a variety of thanks. Although the University System of Georgia has no sabbatical leaves, Georgia State has been generous to me with periods of relief from teaching duties; when I have combined these with summers free, as I have more than once been able to, I have enjoyed the benefits of a sabbatical in all but name. The periods of relief were with pay; and thanks to Paul Blount, former chairman of the department, and Clyde Faulkner, dean of the College of Arts and Sciences, I was aided by a couple of summer stipends in the early 1980s. Of special importance, because I was nearing completion of the book, was a stipend provided by Dean Faulkner in the summer of 1985. Throughout the whole period of reading and research for the book, which really continued until its completion, the assistance of Jane Hobson and her staff in the interlibrary loan office of Georgia State's Pullen Library was invaluable. Waino Suojanen, of the Department of Management, made useful suggestions for some of my earliest reading.

In my department, Tom McHaney and David Bottoms referred me to sources that I would otherwise probably have missed. John Burrison, having recently published an excellent book on Georgia folk pottery, gave me the benefit of his experience by answering a number of my questions about book publishing, in addition to furnishing the support of his friendship. Both Matthew Roudané and my old friend Gene Hollahan, whose knowledge of Saul Bellow surpasses mine, nevertheless gave encouragement to my chapter on *The Victim*. Victor Kramer read and commented on my Fitzgerald chapter, but of far greater importance to me has been his loyal friendship over a period of many years.

The Berryman chapter benefited from prompt answers to my queries by John Haffenden and by Alan K. Lathrop and Richard J. Kelly, both with the University of Minnesota Library.

My original interest as a scholar and critic is eighteenth-century British literature. Three scholars from that period were generously encouraging about my venture into modernity: John Sitter of Emory University; J. Paul Hunter, formerly of Emory, now dean of Arts and Sciences at the University of Rochester; and Donald Siebert of the University of South Carolina, whose support has heartened me even though we have never met except through correspondence.

Partly to reassure myself that my interest in the topic of this book was not uniquely eccentric, I decided to hold a special session at the 1983 MLA meeting. I was astonished to receive some twenty-five inquiries about doing a paper on drinking and alcoholism in modern American literature; attendance at the session was respectable; and three of the panelists chosen—Sonya Jones of Allegheny College, Nick Warner of Claremont McKenna College, and Martin Roth of the University of Minnesota—have been helpful and informative in ways that extend well beyond the session. Martin has read more than one chapter of the book; Sonya piqued my curiosity about Berryman by her own doctoral dissertation and enabled me to discover the interest of the University of North Carolina Press in my topic.

Although I withdrew it from consideration for publication by *Mosaic,* Dr. Evelyn Hinz, editor of that journal, was encouraging about the quality of Chapter 2.

This book is not academic in its inception, and I hope that neither its subject nor its style will restrict its appeal to an academic or intellectual audience. This hope is fostered by the encouragement and interest of a number of friends who do not inhabit the groves of academe, among them Father Damian, of the Monastery of the Holy Spirit, and Virginia Davis, whose interest was particularly important because it came early. Virginia Ross deserves special thanks as the only person who read and commented on all my chapters as I completed them; she has dwelt long enough in the academic groves to hone her excellent native intelligence, and may yet reenter them.

I am greatly indebted to Sandra Eisdorfer, senior editor of the University of North Carolina Press, whose encouragement and criticism alike were always clear and forthright, and who first enabled me to see my book as a whole.

The various chapters have gone through so many drafts, handwritten and typed, that they fill a large shelf. Among the departmental assistants or secretaries who have had a hand in the typing (and I may be forgetting some of the earliest) are Brenda Coker, Rhonda Gargis, Marianne Ruelle, and Cindy Webnar, the last of whom also became a friend and shared a strong interest in my subject with me. The typist who gave the book final shape with amazing speed, accuracy, and unfailing good humor is Barbara Harris.

The two friends and critics who have most thoroughly read and commented on the book are Bob Ryley, of the City University of New York, and Tom Garst, of Cornell College. Bob, also a panelist in the 1983 MLA special session, unerringly spotted my worst illogicalities and stylistic vices. Tom wrote page after page of detailed comment, unearthing many obscurities and opacities; although sometimes diffident and self-doubting, he was invariably incisive and never dead wrong. Old friends the most.

It is a little melancholy to think how many hours of the childhood and adolescence of my three sons, Owen, Miles, and Frank, I have spent working on this book. But as they have grown to young manhood, they have also grown more appreciative of my work, to the point that they now boast to people about it even before publication. Owen, the oldest, even volunteered to read and criticize the Introduction, thus preventing several infelicities. My niece, Colleen Hannah, expressed gratifying interest in my progress.

My mother, Sarah Tegler, takes great pride in this book and provided substantial material help at the time when I most needed it.

How can one do justice in a few words to the complex network of support furnished by a marriage of thirty years? My wife, Virginia, has been consistently a patient listener and critic. Even more important, she has possessed the healthy self-reliance and independence simply to leave me be, with love and caring, for the long and otherwise lonely stretches that I needed for the book.

Abbreviations

Two works frequently cited have been identified by
the following abbreviations:

AA
*Alcoholics Anonymous: The Story of How Many
Thousands of Men and Women Have Recovered from Alcoholism.*
1939. 3d ed. New York: Alcoholics Anonymous World Services,
1976.

12 & 12
Twelve Steps and Twelve Traditions.
New York: Alcoholics Anonymous World Services,
1953.

EQUIVOCAL
SPIRITS

Introduction

Probably some readers will sense how profoundly personal this book is: the experiential suffering and knowledge in which it is grounded at its deepest levels are the kinds that, as Kirby Allbee puts it in Saul Bellow's novel *The Victim*, can only be gained "the hard way, the way you pay for with years of your life." To say more would be to say too much, except to add my heartfelt gratitude for being among the few who have been able to pass beyond their suffering and use it as one means to secure and enlarge their knowledge.

In many dozens, probably hundreds, of works of modern literature, heavy or alcoholic drinking is important in ways or for reasons almost too numerous to mention: a drunken character, a pivotal drunk scene, a theme or subject, or something as elusive as mood (the way in which the characters' frequent but mechanical drinking, for example, contributes to the feeling of total emptiness in Anthony Powell's *Afternoon Men*). In spite of this importance, one might almost say the ubiquitousness, of drinking in modern literature, mine is the first booklength study of the subject.

There have, of course, been other approaches to it, but nearly all of them seem frustratingly peripheral or brief, supplying little more than starting points for a study of the subject. Many of these works are biographical. I would not belabor them in any simplistic fashion for committing the "biographical fallacy." Their deficiency lies rather in their apparent failure to realize that without his work the drinking or alcoholic writer is of no more intrinsic interest than a skid-row derelict or a drunken truck driver, and that for this reason his work should have primary focus, even when (as in a couple of my chapters, on F. Scott Fitzgerald and John Berryman) the work is also used as a window to a new understanding of the writer. More accurately, I am often trying to show how two separate subjects, the writer's drinking and the work in which he writes about drinking, can shed light on each other. In contrast, most previous comment on a writer's drinking is merely that—inert, unconnected with his writing. At its most superficial, this can consist of scarcely more than catalogs of the names of modern writers who drank heavily or alcoholically (this important distinction is often blurred), sometimes recorded in an appalled or deploring tone. Apart from a kind of head-shaking or implicit "tsk tsk" at the expense of some celebrated writers, it is hard to see the point of these lists.[1] Any sort of argument is an improvement over name-dropping; some critics have suggested or attempted to demonstrate that the prevalence of alcoholism among modern writers indicates their peculiar susceptibility to it. This is Alfred Kazin's implication in 1976 when he notes that "of the six American Nobel Prize winners in literature," three—Lewis, O'Neill, and Faulkner—were alcoholic drinkers "for great periods of their lives" and two—Hemingway and Steinbeck—"were hard drinkers."[2] Donald W. Goodwin, using Fitzgerald as his example, is perhaps representative of those arguing that writers are indeed more often the victims of alcoholism than are members of other occupational groups.[3] Yet Donald Newlove, himself a writer and a self-confessed reformed alcoholic, vigorously disputes this thesis: "Booze is not an artistic or occupational problem: there are as many drunken sanitation workers, brain surgeons, priests and car thieves as there are drunken writers, printers, actors and ad men."[4] At the least, the argument remains inconclusive; much more evidence, of a detailed and specific kind, needs to be adduced. Even if the writer's greater susceptibilities could be established, however, one might still be inclined to ask: So what? How does this fact affect his writings? Valuable though he is at questioning or exploding some insufficiently investigated claims about a connection between drinking and modern writers, Newlove also reveals the hazards of an attraction to generalizing about alcoholic writers combined with a skimpy attention to their work. Of the John Berryman who achieved sobriety near the end of his life, Newlove speculates that a possible reason for his suicide was his realization that "starting fresh meant that a massive part of his work so far was self-pity and breastbeating. This was the last mask he couldn't rip off, it was like tearing the beard from his cheeks. Too, too painful. Too much invested."[5] This idea may derive from the prominence that Alcoholics Anonymous gives to self-pity as a fault of the alcoholic. In reality, however, my Chapter 7, which, like all my other chapters, pays close attention to the writer's work, suggests that at least in the poems concerned with drinking (and I believe in the poems as a whole) Berryman's self-pity is only a relatively minor strain, one among many. In short, when biographical generalizing about drinking writers slights or ignores their actual work, it can be virtually as pointless as listings of heavy-drinking or alcoholic writers. The result is neither good biography nor good literary criticism; there will be too many exceptions or complexities ignored, ways in which the writer's work fails to conform to any single preconceived theory.

One might hope that full-dress biographies of drinking writers would deal more satisfactorily with a writer's complexities, including his drinking problem and its relationship with his work. Although I cannot claim familiarity with all biographies of modern writers, as far as I know, this particular hope has never been fulfilled. This failure is the more regrettable because if, as is sometimes said, alcoholism is a total illness, with far-reaching effects that are not only physical but also psychological and even spiritual, it would have important effects on the writer's work that a literary biographer could ill afford to neglect. Nevertheless, judging from two biographies of alcoholic writers chosen at random (I am unable to say whether they are representative of modern literary biography), such works do largely neglect the subject or evince some ignorance of alcoholism. Until the last fifty pages or so of his recent biography of James Agee, Lawrence Bergreen has only two brief passages that focus entirely on Agee's drinking. Thereafter, the references increase, reflecting the worsening of Agee's alcoholism in his last years; but from the brevity of these references, the lack of sustained attention to Agee's drinking, and the failure to connect it with his writing, it is easy to see that Bergreen regards the subject as unimportant.[6] The failures of Rae Jeffs in her biography of Brendan Behan, who died of alcoholism at forty-one, are perhaps more disturbing because she senses the importance of Behan's affliction and in fact devotes many pages to accounts of his drunken behavior, which was at times violent. She became acquainted with him as one of his editors in his later years and was involved in helping him to tape books, a method that embarrassed him but that he acquiesced in because he needed the money and his publishers wanted to capitalize quickly on the fame he had achieved. Ms. Jeffs seems at times not quite fully to grasp the most likely reason for this method: Behan was by then too sick and shaky from alcoholism for the intense concentration and effort required by writing.

By expressing her view that Behan needed mostly will power or "perseverance" to overcome his problem, and by manifesting her impatience with him when he failed to exercise it, Ms. Jeffs more glaringly exposes her ignorance of the nature of his illness.[7] Lois Wilson, the wife of Bill Wilson, cofounder of Alcoholics Anonymous, has said of her husband during his drinking years that "he had plenty of willpower to do anything in which he was interested; but it wouldn't work against alcohol even when he was interested."[8] Some AA members have a cruder version of this: If you think that will power can overcome alcoholism, try using it the next time you have diarrhea.

In works primarily biographical, then, the drinking of writers has been handled inadequately and unsatisfactorily. In literary criticism that gives priority to an author's work, attention to the subject of drinking has been no more satisfactory. Here the fault has been less in ignorant treatment than in something close to complete neglect. The reasons for this are perhaps not immediately apparent. One of them, however, might be connected with the fact that until recently drunkenness was in many ways a taboo subject, an unmentionable disgrace that often led families to pack a drunkard off to a sanatarium, where his confinement sometimes became permanent, or to quarter him in a remote part of the house, an attic or a basement, as actually happened to one woman alcoholic of my acquaintance: sodden with alcohol and feeling the shame of her drinking as keenly as did her husband, she no more thought of protesting her virtual imprisonment than he thought of lifting it; only by a nearly miraculous concatenation of events did she live to become sober. This kind of attitude toward drunkenness could explain the general neglect of the subject by biographers as well as literary critics and also another rather striking phenomenon common in the reaction of both to drunkenness: the tendency to ignore its harsh reality either by transforming it into something else or by rationalizing it—seeing the Fitzgeralds' romantic gaiety in the 1920s instead of Scott's increasingly ugly alcoholism, or claiming that Jack Kerouac drank alcoholically because he was exiled to the edges of American life.[9] Heavy drinking and its results can be just as disturbing in literature; this may be the main reason why, to borrow Martin Roth's term, the subject has been "invisible" to critics.[10] There are doubtless a number of reasons why *The Victim* is the least popular of Saul Bellow's novels, including some puzzles inherent in the work and the generally higher regard for his later novels, beginning with *The Adventures of Augie March*, as being more characteristic of Bellow. But almost certainly one quality that has put off critics and readers is the pervasive grimness of *The Victim*, the distaste and even dread aroused by the plot of an apparent skid-row bum harassing another man and threatening to pull him into the depths with the lowest of the low. Any other Bellow novel—any other novel—looks almost jolly beside this story of drinking in its most wretched, degraded aspect.

There are probably at least two other reasons for the neglect of drinking in literature by critics. If Frank Lentricchia is right, literary criticism has, since the late eighteenth century, progressively narrowed the concerns it considers appropriate for critical investigation;[11] some such tendency could easily rule out drinking or alcoholism as legitimate interests except for sociologists or physicians. Another and more obvious reason for the neglect is that literary critics naturally attend to what they know best, which is not alcoholism. Thus Stephen Spender's long introduction to *Under the Volcano*, a major critical essay on Lowry's symbolism and his literary antecedents, dismisses in a page the centrally important subject of the Consul's alcoholism and how it shapes his vision.[12] Thus Daniel Fuchs, in a recent book on Bellow, dilutes a short section on *The Victim* by comparing it to a story by Dostoevsky rather than concentrating on the crucial matter of how Leventhal responds to Allbee as a drunken failure.[13] These examples of neglect could be multiplied almost indefinitely.

I have been demonstrating in some detail the need for my book, the void it fills. To repair the demonstrable neglect, *Equivocal Spirits* always focuses primarily on an author's work and always pays close attention to its details. Unlike all previous approaches to the subject, moreover, it is interdisciplinary in two important ways. It looks carefully at the places where biography and literature intersect when each of these illuminates the other, as in the chapters on Fitzgerald and Berryman. Otherwise, as in the chapters on John Cheever's stories, *The Iceman Cometh*, *Brideshead Revisited*, and *Under the Volcano*, the focus is more nearly exclusively on the literary work: that the authors were heavy or alcoholic drinkers is important mainly as it adds authority to their depictions of drinking. In another respect, however, my book is much more persistently and thoroughly interdisciplinary, joining literary analysis with scientific knowledge of alcoholism. Although I believe that literature can contribute much to an understanding of the complex nature and causes of heavy or alcoholic drinking, and perhaps even more to arousing and shaping our emotional responses to the problem, I also believe that a mastery of the scientific knowledge of alcoholism, which is impressively large and still developing, is indispensable both as a foundation for studying literary representations of the illness and as a means of accurately appreciating the distinctive contribution that literature makes. From this conjunction the book repeatedly if implicitly poses two broad questions: What new light can scientific knowledge of alcoholism provide for the student of literature? And how does literature confirm, intensify, dramatize, augment, or occasionally even challenge the adequacy of this scientific knowledge? The various answers to the first question can best be seen in the chapters of this book; but because its primary concern is with literature, some attempt to answer the second question should be made now.

Works of literature are intrinsically more dramatic and emotionally intense than scientific studies, in which these elements would be out of place. Almost anyone realizes, for example, that alcoholism can disrupt and poison domestic affections, but John Cheever fleshes out such a truth with emotional intensity. Of the writers considered here, Cheever most squarely challenges the adequacy of scientific definitions of alcoholism, which often refer to the drinker's inability to discharge his social responsibilities as key evidence of his illness. In a few of his stories, Cheever implicitly asks whether it is legitimate to define or judge alcoholism by the criterion of social responsibility and even whether alcoholic defiance of the dictates of society is not a greater good than conformity to them. Such questioning of received opinion may itself be an expansion of knowledge. Another kind of addition comes from a detailed confirmation or validation of existing knowledge, as provided in Eugene O'Neill's *The Iceman Cometh*: of Vernon Johnson's distinction between an alcoholic and a drunk and of several important perceptions of Alcoholics Anonymous. As is true throughout the book, of course, there is a two-way traffic in knowledge: Johnson's distinction and Alcoholics Anonymous facilitate a more accurate understanding of the characters of O'Neill's play.

The two chief ways in which literature augments scientific knowledge of heavy drinking or alcoholism have yet to be mentioned. These are (1) literature's ability to recognize and preserve the complex humanity of the alcoholic and (2) its awareness that often the root cause or effect of the illness of alcoholism is spiritual. I am, to be sure, naming two of the chief strengths of literature regardless of its particular subject. With certain exceptions, such as satire, literature is usually interested in complex individuality rather than in norms or types; and as it has evolved, modern science is secular, leaving spiritual concerns to other modes of inquiry, literature among them.

An excellent example of the differences between scientific and literary knowledge can be found in the way in which these two modes treat alcoholic hallucinations. Anyone interested in an extensive look at the scientific approach can begin with the sources cited in my footnotes to the chapter on *Under the Volcano*. Primarily, these studies categorize: by the images of the hallucinations, by their subject matter, or in some other fashion. Even when the major attribute of the hallucinations is their fullness of development and there is no rigorous attempt at categorization, what is remarkable about them is the way that science detaches them from their source for scrutiny. If the hallucinator is mentioned at all, it is with only the most rudimentary strokes: Patrick F. (often, alas, one of those drunken Irishmen), age fifty-nine, hod carrier, with a long history of drinking and hospitalizations for treatment of alcoholism. The contrast between this kind of sketch and the representation of the Consul in *Under the Volcano*—the most fully developed and inward depiction of an alcoholic among the various works I treat—could not be greater. "Patrick's" hallucinations, as recorded by science, could usually be anybody's; but the Consul's are an integral part of his complex humanity (perhaps even the most important part) as well as the richest product of his vivid imagination.

Good literature firmly resists stereotyping of the alcoholic. It instead portrays a figure divided, like most of us, not into two tidily comprehensible parts but into a welter of jarring emotions. Whether he is winning or losing the struggle with his alcoholism, it is the ability of literature to convey the multifarious complexity of the struggle in a fictional character (the Consul) or a real person (John Berryman) that satisfies—much more than the traditional view of Scott and Zelda Fitzgerald partying their way through the 1920s, setting a glamorously romantic example for society, and somehow coming to grief only because of Zelda's insanity and the Great Depression. Zelda's story is not considered here; but I do revise Scott's in a way not only more honest than the romantic view of him but also more complex. Even though his alcoholism and his strong tendency to deny it wrought havoc in his life and career, partially spoiling some of his potentially best work, his very attempts at evasion can be complexly instructive about alcoholic deviousness. And, in some of his best stories, the painful experience of prolonged alcoholism coupled with an intermittent ability to be honest about it resulted in sharply incisive diagnoses of the illness. Just as literature rejects monolithic portrayals of the alcoholic, so at its best it refuses the explanation of a single cause for the illness, especially a cause outside the alcoholic, such as society or the sacrifices demanded by artistic creativity. Fitzgerald was brought low by an illness about which he could not or would not be honest, not by the crash of 1929. Donald Newlove rightly ridicules the belief that Jack Kerouac was driven to drink by American society. In my chapter on Berryman, I reject a similar assumption about his drinking, as well as a corollary assumption that this illness fatally flawed his poetry.

The perspective of science on alcoholism is almost always the same: diagnostic, analytical, objective. But the perspectives of literature are varied, at least some of them suggesting that the disease of alcoholism is more a question of perspective than an ascertainable fact. When the angle of vision is largely interior, there is little doubt about the fact of alcoholism—that of Lowry's Consul, for example, or John Berryman. In his short story "The Sorrows of Gin," however, John Cheever seems primarily interested in presenting the indeterminacy arising from different perspectives on drinking; finally, it is impossible to know whether the Lawtons have a drinking problem. Similarly, in *The Victim* Saul Bellow is concerned less with the problem of alcoholism than with the problem of perceiving it. Ultimately, he raises and answers a metaphysical question: How reliable is our knowledge when based on observation deeply colored by emotion? Put so baldly, the question has an obvious answer: Not at all reliable. But, as usual in literature, the working out of the answer—in this case the tense frictions of a relationship between Asa Leventhal and the supposed drunk, Kirby Allbee—holds the greatest fascination. Driven by disgust and fear, Leventhal's fear of being dragged down to Allbee's skid-row level, we may totally misperceive reality—even something as apparently fundamental or seemingly verifiable as whether or not a man is an alcoholic. To say "we" is not unwarranted, for though *The Victim* is realistic enough on one level, on another it is allegorical. Leventhal embodies the fears of everyone in a society obsessed with success, in which failure is the equivalent of hell. As his name suggests, Allbee is not some piece of unspeakable gutter filth but Everyman—our counterpart, our brother.

Of the writers included in my book, Bellow and Cheever are the ones who raise the most searching questions about the scientific approach to alcoholism—not, finally, so much because they object to stereotyping (although Cheever certainly does, in "A Miscellany of Characters That Will Not Appear") or because they find one or another concept of alcoholism inadequate. Rather, *any* such concept reduced to a label or name, "alcoholic," and applied to a human being is an outrageous denial of his full, complex humanity. It is "packaging," the term used by Schlossberg, the old humanist and touchstone character in *The Victim*, to protest any simplification of human beings and their relationships. This is probably why Bellow leaves open the question of Allbee's alcoholism. As Keats's idea of negative capability suggests, the best course for literature may be to raise provocative uncertainties.

The second major contribution of literature to an understanding of alcoholism is to focus on its spiritual dimensions,[14] a task that science is not equipped to undertake. "Spiritual" should certainly not be reduced in meaning to "religious"; any good definition of the term would be capacious, including many elements of the irrational and the emotional. In realizing that literature is better than science at conveying what drunkenness or alcoholism feels like—its terror, its pitiableness, its degradation, its ludicrousness, occasionally even its glory—we are recognizing its ability to capture spiritual qualities.

Some reasons why writers drink are naturally suggested in their work; in a broad sense, these reasons are often spiritual. In Cheever's "The Scarlet Moving Van," the alcoholic character Gee-Gee, whose nickname derives from "Greek god," drinks in large part to escape the humdrum realities of suburban living. To step beyond the works dealt with in this book, James Dickey's poem "Bums, On Waking" indicates some important spiritual means provided by alcohol for escaping or dissolving ordinary reality. Of the bums, Dickey asks, "Who else has died and thus risen?"[15] The answer, of course, is Christ. In their wanderings, their extreme dislocation, and the befuddlement of their alcoholic blackouts, never knowing where they will awake or to what, the bums possess an enviable, almost Christlike power of self-resurrection, removed from the limitations of sober reality and thus able to experience a daily renewal of wonder at the strangeness of life, as if waking to it for the first time. These are qualities that most writers would prize, and some have sought them through alcohol. A poem by Raymond Carver, "Drinking While Driving," shares with Dickey's the sense of renewal supplied by alcohol, of imminent release from dullness: "Any minute now, something will happen" is the last line of the poem, and that something promises to be more exciting in its unpredictability than what the driver has been experiencing.[16]

Clearly, though, these poems of Dickey and Carver share another, more important view: alcohol is the source of inspiration or the courage to take risks. No one needs to be told of the hazards of drunken driving, and anyone who drinks so heavily that he blacks out and wakes up not knowing where he is—a rather common experience among alcoholics, not just bums—is obviously setting his life at risk. Hence the appropriateness of the title of my book, Equivocal Spirits: alcohol, which in some uses seems to be a life-renewing force, is always potentially and sometimes actually a destructive force. When heavy drinkers themselves or when representing characters who are, modern writers seem particularly interested in exploring that borderland where the renewal of life, by extending the limits of ordinary perception or experience, impinges on destruction or death. Because to some extent these writers reflect or shape the values of their society, a character like Allbee may be emulating them in his use of drinking for authentic risk-taking. As he puts it at one point, he wants to get off the merry-go-round, to test his mettle by hitting bottom.

My chapter on alcohol and comedy is important to the book because it indicates the one domain in which drinking is unequivocally good. As in Don Marquis's The Old Soak (1921), lengthy satiric portraits of heavy or alcoholic drinkers are possible; but when a satiric element is absent or at least subordinate to the focus on a largely sympathetic protagonist, drunkenness is usually restricted in comedy to a scene or scenes of renewal: drinking provides an eruption into a better world or self (Lucky Jim) or a means of learning the truth, sometimes astringent, about oneself (Jake's Thing and Keep the Aspidistra Flying). When the traditionally affirmative aspects of comedy are uppermost, alcohol as "spirits" seems to cooperate with some other sort of benevolent spirit. As William James fervently puts it, "Sobriety diminishes, discriminates, and says no; drunkenness expands, unites, and says yes. It is in fact the great exciter of the *Yes* function in man. It brings its votary from the chill periphery of things to the radiant core. It makes him for the moment one with truth."

James, however, ominously adds that these desirable effects are attainable from drinking "only in the fleeting earlier phases of what in its totality is so degrading a poisoning."[17] They are attainable only before drinking hardens into the disease called alcoholism. When Thomas Mann salutes "that creative, genius-giving disease . . . that . . . springs with drunken daring from peak to peak," we need to realize that his speaker is the Devil.[18]

Any inquiry into the spiritual qualities of drinking, then, soon encounters their profoundly equivocal, almost paradoxical character. Even though Allbee seeks authenticity, a testing of his true self or worth by means of heavy drinking and falling to the bottom of society, his final appearance in *The Victim* seems to strike a note of inauthenticity. Although Allbee's quest involves risk-taking, the endangering of his conventional self, and in fact seems radically to alter this self in some ways, the usual result of alcoholic drinking, as AA has discovered, is the escalation of fear rather than the courageous confrontation or use of it—a proliferation the more harmful precisely because the alcoholic can avoid facing it by submerging his awareness of it in drink. If Cheever's godlike Gee-Gee triumphantly escapes the usual penalties and sorrows attached to alcoholic drinking, Cheever provides "The Scarlet Moving Van" with a foil character, Charlie Folkestone, who is not so fortunate. If the Consul's alcoholic drinking in *Under the Volcano* is the chief source of his vivid imagination, the novel also reveals the exorbitant price he must pay as his drinking increasingly becomes a form of dark, demonic possession. It is as if the Consul and some other alcoholic characters somehow cannot see that using a physical means, alcohol, to achieve spiritual ends or powers may corrupt or pervert those ends.[19] The excitement of escape and the hope of renewal sometimes end in the dull slavery of addiction. Nevertheless, much of the literature about alcoholism achieves great value when it directs our attention to the duality or equivocality of the spiritual dimension of drinking. When *Brideshead*

Revisited conveys the paradox that the disease of alcoholism can ultimately mean salvation, it is exploring territory far beyond the ken of science. Three other matters should be dealt with in this introduction. Although a few critics have been skeptical of the methods and efficacy of Alcoholics Anonymous,[20] it has by now won widespread recognition for being the leading repository of theoretical and practical knowledge of alcoholism—both of its nature and of how to treat it. Still, in view of my extensive reliance on this knowledge throughout my book, some readers may welcome the persuasion of some testimony to the extremely high regard in which AA is held. Among many possibilities, I shall cite only three striking instances of this testimony. Nowadays, many large companies or corporations have in-house programs of alcoholism therapy for their employees, nearly all of them claiming high rates—often 70 percent, 80 percent, or more—of recovery.[21] Administrators of these programs also sometimes claim that their success rate is based on the strength of an employee's fear of losing his job if he should not participate fully in treatment, and that this is the strongest possible motivation for his becoming and staying sober. Another element, seldom explicitly acknowledged but just as important, affects this high rate of success: virtually all of the company therapies borrow heavily from AA. When the in-house program terminates, usually after a few weeks, the recovering alcoholic is advised to enter AA or, if he has already done so, to continue to follow its program and to attend its meetings. A second example of the impressive influence of AA can be found in the many hospitals whose therapy for alcoholism is fundamentally an intensive series of AA meetings and an urging of patients to practice the AA program. This pervasive use of AA by hospitals has generated some resentment among the AA membership, who believe that the fancier private hospitals and the insurance companies without which their prices could not be sustained are colluding to charge huge sums (nearly $12,000 a month, for one example, and sometimes the hospitalization is even longer) and to make fat profits for a mode of treatment that AA itself offers absolutely free. As a final example, if imitation is one sort of testimony to success, AA has been remarkable in the epigones it has spawned—Overeaters Anonymous, Gamblers Anonymous, Narcotics Anonymous, Cocaine Anonymous, and Neurotics Anonymous, doubtless together with other progeny whose existence has escaped my notice. All of these organizations, I believe, simply adapt the language and principles of AA to suit their purposes, which are largely the same as AA's: to understand and arrest an addiction. Because of its highly respected knowledge of alcoholism, then, I have thought it entirely appropriate that my book should draw more extensively on Alcoholics Anonymous than on any other extraliterary source. At the same time, and as AA itself readily admits, no single source has a monopoly on knowledge of alcoholism, so I have also used a variety of other scientific sources.

Although there seems to be no irresistible logic demanding one arrangement of chapters rather than another, a few reasons for my ordering can be given. I have grouped first those chapters of relatively restricted subject or scope: alcoholic hallucinations (*Under the Volcano*), alcoholism as a spiritual illness (*Brideshead Revisited* and *Under the Volcano*), a dramatized anatomy of alcoholism and a distinction between alcoholics and drunks (*The Iceman Cometh*). Chapters 4 and 5 are similar in the sense that the writers treated therein, Cheever and Bellow, searchingly question or challenge the concept of alcoholism, chafing at it as a stereotype, raising doubts about its scientific objectivity, disputing the stigma usually attached to it, skeptical about the very validity and usefulness of the concept. Chapters 6 and 7 pay significant attention both to the alcoholic author's life and to his work, attempting to demonstrate their relationship and the ways in which each can illuminate the other. The eighth and last chapter counterbalances to some extent the essential seriousness of the others by indicating that even heavy drinking can on occasion be a constructive, liberating force.

Finally, it might be well to say a little about my reasons, simple though these are, for choosing the modern period, for selecting certain writers and work and for excluding others. Because a good many twentieth-century writers have been heavy or alcoholic drinkers, someone with a flair for the catchy generalization could, I suppose, dub this period the Age of Literary Alcoholism, just as (with the same flair) one could call the Romantic period the Age of Literary Opium Addiction. Whether such generalizations could stand the test of historical scrutiny, or whether they really amount to anything when the complex effects of individual addictions are carefully examined, is another matter. If any credible historical argument can be made for the modern period as one of cultural alcoholism, it might begin with the hypothesis, though limited to America, that Prohibition was a catalyst for heavy drinking in some circles because it made such drinking seem, in the same circles, admirably audacious and defiant. The argument might then proceed by reflecting on whether it is something more than coincidence that some of the most penetrating works about alcoholism begin to appear at about the time of the repeal of Prohibition or shortly thereafter: Dorothy Parker's "Big Blonde" (1930), Fitzgerald's "Babylon Revisited" (1931), O'Neill's *The Iceman Cometh* (written in 1939), Charles Jackson's *Lost Weekend* (1944). But my book undertakes no such argument, which might well prove inconclusive. And when one considers the lives or works of such later writers as John Berryman or Richard Hugo, it becomes impossible to maintain that the heavy drinking of writers or its incisive exploration in their work began and ended with Prohibition and its immediate aftermath.

I make no apologies for excluding from my book such a sentimental chestnut as *Days of Wine and Roses* or the voluminous work of Charles Bukowski, which seems to be at the farthest possible extreme from *Days* but which I nevertheless take to be another species of sentimentalism thinly overlaid by its macho trappings, the sentimentalism lying in Bukowski's assumption (exemplified by heroes who are always about the same) that drunken defiance of philistinism is the only proof needed of superiority to philistinism. I do regret the exclusion of a number of works definitely deserving of study; among these I would mention the poems of Richard Hugo; Brian Moore's *The Lonely Passion of Judith Hearne* (1955), a masterful study of the shifts and evasions of a woman alcoholic trying to deny her problem; and William Kennedy's *Ironweed* (1983), whose alcoholic protagonist should be seen as a figure resembling an epic hero. Doubtless others not mentioned also deserve inclusion. I can only say that there are limits to the patience of every reader and that, if I have erred, I have tried to do so by stopping short of these limits and leaving the reader sighing for more, rather than cursing my prolixity.

Ultimately a writer pleases others by pleasing himself. Thus my primary criterion of choice has been my keen interest in the works considered here. I have sought to avoid works whose portrayals of alcoholism replicate or seriously overlap each other. I have included at least one extended treatment of each modern literary genre, novels, plays, short stories, and poems. Some famous writers who are reputedly heavy or alcoholic drinkers have produced no work of great interest on the subject; these I have naturally excluded. On the other hand, a writer has not had to be verifiably alcoholic for inclusion; Saul Bellow certainly is not, and although at some periods of his life Evelyn Waugh was certainly a heavy drinker, I am not convinced that he was alcoholic. To have selected only the work of alcoholic writers would have meant rejecting *The Victim*, one of the major studies of the indeterminate character of alcoholism, even raising doubts about the validity of applying the concept to human complexity. To have worked from the assumption that only writers who are certifiably alcoholic can write perceptively about alcoholism would have belittled the power of observation and imagination.

ONE

The Place of Hallucinations in *Under the Volcano*

ost critics of *Under the Volcano* have concentrated on its density of symbolic meaning and its relationship to other modern literary masterpieces.[1] These focuses are necessary, but they may have led critics to overlook one of the most salient and distinctive features of the novel: the fact that the hero is a drunkard,[2] one with such monumental thirsts that other drunkards of literature (one might think of Don Birnam in *The Lost Weekend*, because Lowry feared that its nearly contemporaneous success would undermine his own) seem pale and timid by comparison. No one has fully appreciated Lowry's almost breathtaking audacity in forging a modern Everyman or Dantesque figure from a man with a uniquely gargantuan craving for alcohol. Nor has anyone sufficiently noticed the importance in the novel of a result of such excesses, a result that is well enough known to observers of alcoholism but that, to other readers, may be one of the strangest characteristics of the story: its hero's numerous and vivid alcoholic hallucinations.[3]

The frequency with which Lowry employs hallucinations of varied types and for varied purposes distinguishes his novel even from other stories about alcoholics. For example, instead of being repeatedly subjected to hallucinations, as Lowry's Consul is, Birnam, of *The Lost Weekend*, several times escapes from his alcoholic miseries into nostalgic memories of childhood. His one genuine and fully developed hallucination, that a bat is attacking and devouring a mouse, is vivid and horrible but also brief and sharply set off from the rest of the novel.

Lowry was interested in conveying the awe and wonder, the pity and terror that alcoholism could arouse if its victim was a person otherwise intelligent and noble. The hallucination became one of his chief vehicles for reaching these effects as well as a major expression of his imagination. Appreciation of Lowry's imagination is enhanced by contrast with Jack Kerouac's *Big Sur* (1962), in which the protagonist's hallucinations are confined to less than twenty pages near the end of the novel and are scarcely enough to compensate for over two hundred pages of apparently structureless, slice-of-life observations. The continual mingling and blurring of hallucination with reality, their frequent overlapping or indeterminacy, are one source of the great richness of texture in *Under the Volcano*, a fecundity like the riotous jungle growth that Yvonne and Hugh press through on their way to Parián. This mingling and indeterminacy aid in the depiction of a more compelling and complex protagonist than Don Birnam or the hero of *Big Sur*. If the Consul is as certainly fated as Birnam by his alcoholism, the considerable suspense generated by his story lies not in our ignorance of what will happen but in the ingeniously imagined, increasingly hallucinatory ways in which it will be brought about.

Another source of suspense or tension in *Under the Volcano* is our sense that the Consul is engaged in a struggle of almost epic significance against dark, demonic, terrifying forces that are in large part represented or bodied forth by hallucinations. More heroic still, the Consul struggles not so much to avoid succumbing to the hallucinations as to make sense of them. Birnam's intelligence, though acute, is applied to less titanic aims: mainly to finding the means, financial and physical, to go on drinking. It is not surprising then that Lowry, in his extremely long and important letter to his eventual publisher, Jonathan Cape, the letter that persuaded Cape to accept *Under the Volcano* without change, expressed resentment and exasperation at the comparisons that Cape's editorial reader had repeatedly made between his novel and Charles Jackson's. For all his self-doubts and insecurities, Lowry thought his book incomparably better. He was right, largely because of its hallucinatory power.

That Lowry himself recognized the importance of hallucinations in *Under the Volcano* is demonstrated in his letter to Cape. He was pleased that Cape's editorial reader found "the mescal-inspired phantasmagoria," the Consul's "delirious consciousness," impressive, objecting only to the reader's complaint that these effects are "too long, wayward and elaborate."[4] Lowry added that, when he undertook to revise the novel, it became "a spiritual thing."[5] This apparent connection of the squalor of alcoholic hallucinations with spiritual matters suggests one characteristic quality of Lowry's mind: its tendency to blur distinctions or to combine ideas or categories usually kept discrete. On various occasions, for example, the Consul hears voices that he terms his "familiars." At one level these are auditory hallucinations, which some scientists regard as more common among alcoholics than the visual kind. These voices, however, are sometimes also Lowry's versions of good and bad angels; consider the novel's epigraphs from Bunyan and from Goethe's *Faust*, and several allusions within the novel to Marlowe's Faustus, in some respects an even closer analogue to the Consul. If, as Douglas Day maintains, *Under the Volcano* is "the greatest religious novel of this century,"[6] the authority of its vision derives to a great degree from the soil of the alcoholic hallucinations. In this juxtaposition of the sordid or debased with the exalted, similar to that which Yeats explored in "Crazy Jane Talks with the Bishop," Lowry was adept at perceiving correspondences.[7]

Though mostly in sources not familiar to the student of literature, records of actual hallucinations are abundant. There are, to be sure, many different species of hallucinations. For example, there seems to be wide agreement that alcoholic hallucinations differ from drug-induced hallucinations, which (at least in the early stages of drug use) often consist of recurrent geometric patterns or designs and vivid colors with either a neutral or a pleasing emotional effect.[8] In contrast, the typical alcoholic hallucination can perhaps best be described as paranoiac, involving schemes or plots of persecution, threats of violence, or the perpetration of violence, sometimes leading to the death of the hallucinator-victim.[9] Some rather specific variants of these recurring delusions are also common: for example, according to a survey of 382 hallucinating alcoholics, no less than 48 believed that hostile gangs or the police were pursuing them.[10]

We have no way to determine, of course, exactly how much of *Under the Volcano* portrays alcoholic hallucination actually experienced by Lowry. It can scarcely be mere coincidence that an important element of the novel—the recurrent motif that the Consul is being spied on, which turns into full-blown police persecution in the last section—bears so striking a resemblance to a common type of alcoholic hallucination. Moreover, although Lowry almost certainly spent some time in jail in Oaxaca, Mexico, in late 1937 or early 1938, several of his letters explaining his incarceration and the events lead-

ing up to it—the details in some instances found their way into the
novel—sound so overwrought that they can only be regarded as
largely the product of hallucinations. Lowry's major biographer,
Douglas Day, acknowledges that the police must have been aware of
Lowry because of his flagrant drunkenness, surely a more likely reason for his jailing than the claim in his correspondence (later partly
incorporated in the novel in the police confusion of Hugh with the
Consul) that he was mistaken for a Communist friend. Day rejects
this claim as "pure romance" and regards Lowry's stories of ruthless,
mysteriously malevolent police persecution as "almost certainly exaggerated." This is an excellent assessment.[11] The paranoiac exaggeration probably took the form of hallucinations. If we realize that
these were later transferred *mutatis mutandis* to the novel, we may
better understand why several explanations of the Consul's fate, especially in the final section, are not quite convincing. Hallucinations
remain ultimately intractable; they cannot be reduced to rational
intelligibility.

That Lowry transfers to the novel some of his own hallucinations
is not in itself remarkable. It is the uses to which he puts hallucinations—some probably experienced, others perhaps wholly invented,
still others perhaps a combination of experience and imagination—
that call for further comment and evoke admiration, for they are one
of the most striking manifestations of Lowry's genius.

Most hallucinations recorded in medical or scientific works are
evidently the fruit of mediocre minds: in spite of the lurid or sen-
sational circumstances giving rise to them, they make rather dull
reading. Not so the Consul's hallucinations. In the closing section of
the novel he sits in the Farolito tavern, sinking into despair. He is
faced with the prospect of hallucinating, whether or not he continues
to drink; nevertheless, he seems incapable of anything less than an
arresting vividness. The following passage seems to be almost a synop-
tic reprise of hallucinations he has frequently suffered: "his room
shaking with daemonic orchestras, the snatches of fearful tumultuous
sleep, interrupted by voices which were really dogs barking, or by his
own name being continually repeated by imaginary parties arriving,
the vicious shouting, the strumming, the slamming, the pounding,
the battling with insolent archfiends, the avalanche breaking down
the door, the proddings from under the bed, and always, outside, the
cries, the wailing, the terrible music, the dark's spinets."[12]

Even this passage, as close to being abstractly typical of alcoholic hallucinations as any to be found in the novel, possesses a couple of distinctive touches. Though the "daemonic orchestras" and "insolent archfiends" may be strictly metaphorical or slightly humorous (or both), they may also be fleeting signs of what almost every other hallucinatory passage in the novel confirms: that even the most seemingly simple hallucination is endowed with moral or spiritual overtones. Just after his arrival at the Farolito, the Consul has what seem to be a couple of auditory hallucinations. Unlike the common run of these, which are merely persecutory, the Consul's are packed with moral meanings or hints: "the place was not silent. It was filled by that ticking: the ticking of his watch, his heart, his conscience, a clock somewhere. There was a remote sound too, from far below, of rushing water, of subterranean collapse" (p. 337). The Consul and the reader know why he should have a bad conscience; he has run off from his brother and his former wife after some particularly vicious words to them. And the rushing noise may be from the nearby barranca, the ubiquitous ravine symbolizing a kind of cloacal hell into which the Consul's body is finally hurled. The phrase "subterranean collapse" thus hints physically or literally at the barranca and metaphysically or morally at the Consul's spiritual condition. The use of hallucinations to convey moral meaning or significance will receive more extended treatment later, as will another of their qualities also evident in this passage: they usually have contact with or basis in reality. That is, there may actually be a clock ticking somewhere in the bar, and there certainly is a barranca, though whether it is the source of the rushing sound in this passage is left problematical.

The hallucinations, then, are ordinarily placed in some nonhallucinatory matrix, seen as connected with or emerging from reality. This is one means that Lowry discovered for naturalizing the device, for making it believable. To gain the same end he had other means as well. One function of the first section of the novel is to establish Mexico as a land whose scenes are objectively surreal or hallucinatory, a land in which even the Consul's friend Jacques Laruelle perceives the birds as "something like monstrous insects" and in which, he reflects, "you would find every sort of landscape at once, the Cotswolds, Windermere, New Hampshire, the meadows of the Eure-et-Loire, even the grey dunes of Cheshire, even the Sahara, a planet upon which, in the twinkling of an eye, you could change climates, and, if you cared to think so, in the crossing of a highway, three civilizations" (pp. 13, 10). In such a setting the Consul's hallucinations will seem less bizarre than they might otherwise.

All of the main characters, in fact, respond to Mexico as if it had a hallucinatory strangeness. On her return to the Mexican street where she has lived, Yvonne, the Consul's former wife, registers most of its scenes as if they were novel and disturbing: for instance, a shanty "with its dark open sinister bunkers" from which their servant "used to fetch their carbon" (p. 63).

If Yvonne's perceptions seem only slightly hallucinatory, some abrupt visions of Hugh, the Consul's brother, have the horror of the genuine thing: "Something like a tree stump with a tourniquet on it, a severed leg in an army boot that someone picked up, tried to unlace, and then put down, in a sickening smell of petrol and blood, half reverently on the road; a face that gasped for a cigarette, turned grey, and was cancelled; headless things, that sat, with protruding windpipes, fallen scalps, bolt upright in motor cars" (p. 248). For any reader who might have missed the resemblance to hallucinations, Hugh reflects that these grisly images were "like the creatures, perhaps, in Geoff's dreams." As we become acquainted with Hugh, we see that he differs from the Consul in his concern for the world of contemporary reality; he seeks a role in the Spanish Civil War. Yet, by means of Hugh's visions, we begin to realize that the Consul's hallucinations may be an almost normal response to a world on the verge of mass carnage. Indeed, Hugh and Yvonne "hallucinate" frequently enough (in the sense of having visions or hearing sounds without an easily identifiable source in the natural world) that the phenomenon comes to seem not a symptom of alcoholic madness but a valid way of seeing.[13]

The hallucinatory is so naturalized in the novel that it is, paradoxically, humdrum reality that turns grotesque, a crude travesty or parody of itself. Consider Quincey, the stereotyped American neighbor of the Consul, and the unnamed, old-school-tie Englishman who comes upon him lying drunk in the road. Though the Englishman is a version of the good Samaritan, the dialogue between him and the Consul (pp. 79–81) is close to a Terry-Thomas caricature; the thoughts running through the Consul's mind while he lies alone in the road (it is amazing that he is capable of any thought at all) are more sensible and rational than the conversation. To some degree, then, sober reality is so intolerably thin that it travesties itself. Intoxication, or hallucination, becomes a way to pierce this buffoonery, to discover important truth and seize its complexity.

Quincey and the Cantabrigian also attest to Lowry's comic power. He may have been justified in his recurrent complaints that readers of *Under the Volcano* did not adequately appreciate these powers,[14] which are sometimes manifest in his ability to use hallucinations for comic effect. Because this means that the Consul is occasionally able to laugh at a major cause of his suffering and terror, such comedy affords further evidence of his heroism. Anyone well versed in the alcoholic hallucinations of medical records can recognize this as a refreshing contrast to their usual dreariness.[15]

One element in the preposterousness of Quincey is his supposition that hallucinations consist of the popular clichés of snakes and tigers and even pink elephants (p. 135). The Consul's jest that he expects (Henri) Rousseau to come riding out of his garden at any moment on one of those tigers is completely lost on Quincey (p. 132). Not long after his chat with his unenlightened neighbor, the Consul, as if in a hammy but clever enactment of Quincey's low opinion of him, takes a swig of bay rum, smacking his lips over it and remarking to Hugh, "A charm against galloping cockroaches anyway. And the polygonous proustian stare of imaginary scorpions" (p. 174). The Consul is able to wrest comedy even from mostly serious or grim material. In the studio of his friend Laruelle he notices a couple of pictures, both dealing with drunkards, both of a hallucinatory vividness and with obviously allegorical meaning. In the first, "harpies grappled on a smashed bedstead among broken bottles of tequila, gnashing their teeth. No wonder; the Consul, peering closer, sought in vain for a sound bottle." In the second, which foreshadows the divergent fates of Yvonne and the Consul himself, a group of drunkards is seen tumbling "headlong into hades" while the sober are ascending to heaven. The Consul notes wryly that the "females were casting half-jealous glances downward after their plummeting husbands, some of whose faces betrayed the most unmistakable relief" (pp. 198–99).

The most unusual comedy perhaps occurs in that section (XII) that most thoroughly incorporates the themes, plots, and moods of alcoholic hallucinations. It is unusual because it is unexpected in this increasingly somber and portentous section, and because in this section the mingling of hallucinations and reality reaches its baffling height. The resulting comedy is, in Lowry's words, "macabre," with "a certain gruesome gaiety" that is hard to describe any more exactly (pp. 363, 354) but that is certainly at a vast remove from the joyful, liberating comedy of *Lucky Jim*. Just after the police seize him, the Consul sees something that appears to be a kind of comically sympathetic reflection of his own condition, the more startling for its incongruity in this context: "it was only the uncontrollable face on the barroom floor, the rabbit, having a nervous convulsion, trembling all over" (pp. 370–71).[16] Thus the gathering gloom is several times alleviated by rays of humor. An old woman who tries to warn the Consul against the police at the same time seems to be one of his persecutors because she plunges her hand into his pocket as if in search of money (p. 367). The figure most successfully blending macabre humor and deadly seriousness is the pimp, a symbol of love degraded to lust (one of the Consul's sins in this final section) and the animate symbolic counterpart to the barranca, the Consul's cloacal retribution and hell. After intercourse with the pimp's prostitute, Maria, the Consul encounters her master, "an incredibly filthy man sitting hunched in the corner on a lavatory seat, so short his trousered feet didn't reach the littered, befouled floor" (p. 352)[17]—a vision so grotesquely disgusting that at first it can hardly be credited except as hallucination. Like other hallucinatory images in this section, however, the pimp proves to be real enough. Though he is one of the Consul's most insidious persecutors by pretending to be his friend, the pimp manages to stay within the bounds of comedy by a relentless mutilation of English.

It is no small proof of his heroism that the Consul, almost to the end of his life, maintains enough detachment to extract comedy from situations whose blurring of hallucination and reality is increasingly terrifying. The tension or struggle between hallucination and reality in his perceptions further bespeaks his heroism. In the Consul we see a man delivering an exact scientific discourse on the name and identity of a red bird spotted by him and Yvonne when, scarcely a moment later, he is assaulted by a hallucination that the trees are shaking or dancing to a soundless music (pp. 74–75). His never knowing when or how suddenly a hallucination will descend on him, and his refusal to accept this state without struggling to resist, distinguish, or comprehend it, help to ennoble him. At times when we might expect him to surrender to hallucinations most abjectly or incoherently—or simply to pass out, as when he is lying drunk in the Calle Nicaragua—he instead holds an incisive interior monologue on the relations between himself, Hugh, and Yvonne (pp. 77–79).

The Consul is not always so triumphantly in control. Before his final rejection of Hugh, he envisions him "advancing as if to decapitate him" with a razor (p. 303). The Consul responds with great anger, which he knows to be baseless because he can identify his vision as hallucination; yet it leads to the harsh words and, in turn, to the rupture needed as an excuse for him to go to the Farolito. Even when he succumbs to hallucinations or their effects, we see him not so much as a drunkard bringing them on himself as a pitiable victim of demons or furies beyond a control that he usually attempts to exert. The pathos of his flight from Hugh and Yvonne is heightened by their discovery that he has left, in a tavern they visit in their search for him, a fragmentary poem about another flight—not from them but from apparent hallucinations of pursuers, "eyes and thronged terrors" (p. 330). In this poem, as in the novel as a whole, the Consul wages a valiant and moving struggle against such forces of irrationality and terror.

The fear and pity elicited by the struggle are also the product of a frequent, almost pervasive ambiguity in the novel between hallucinations and reality. If this ambiguity appeared to result primarily from the Consul's drinking, it might seem a weakness or confusion more contemptible than pitiable. Usually, however, the ambiguity seems to lie in the nature of things, sometimes appearing to be simply an aspect of an extraordinarily rich and animated metaphorical texture in the novel. Even in the last section, the Consul has a few moments of calm in which he can register impressions as if they were objects in a Dutch still life. Yet even here the figurative language portends the hallucinatory terrors to come: "a cry down the street someone being murdered, brakes grinding far away a soul in pain" (p. 353). Earlier, in Quincey's garden, just before asking Dr. Vigil (perhaps not altogether seriously) what he can do for a case of delirium tremens, the Consul casts "a suspicious eye . . . at some maguey growing beyond the barranca, like a battalion moving up a slope under machine-gun fire" (p. 138). There can be little doubt that the maguey is real, but if its resemblance to a battalion is merely

Hallucinations in *Under the Volcano*

figurative and not partly hallucinatory, why would the Consul eye it with suspicion?

In a country represented by such strange and abundant phenomena as a madman garlanded with a bicycle tire, a bus driver carrying pigeons under his shirt, a bald boy wearing earrings and swinging on a hammock, and a procession of buses to different exotic destinations appearing simultaneously from a single road in the country (pp. 224, 232, 240), it should not be surprising that even Lowry's major biographer will not pretend to decide whether a pair of fawns being slaughtered for a hotel dining room or a vulture sitting in a wash basin—both details mentioned by Lowry in his correspondence, and both included in an unsent letter written by the Consul to Yvonne (pp. 36, 88)—are hallucinated or real.[18] If the foregoing ambiguities are not particularly unsettling, some others are. After conjuring up a vision of drinking in Parián in terms of the tritely hallucinatory imagery of mirages, the Consul suddenly finds the reality surrounding him in his garden to be so richly and vividly reanimated as to border on hallucination: "from above, below, from the sky, and, it might be, from under the earth, came a continual sound of whistling, gnawing, rattling, even trumpeting" (pp. 139–40). This juxtaposing of two types of hallucination suggests that only an augury of death (Parián has already come to have this meaning) can galvanize the Consul— and then only in a hectic, almost hallucinated way.

Hallucination and reality pile up in layers, sometimes becoming as complicated in their relationships as rock formations in a terrain with a long history of violent geological upheaval. A relatively simple instance, but with a twist of surprise, occurs in the Consul's garden: after listening to his "familiars," those auditory hallucinations mentioned earlier, the Consul sees in his path not the hallucinated snake we might expect, but a real one—and with at least faint symbolic overtones of the serpent in Eden (pp. 126–27). At other points the relationship becomes more tortuous. In Quauhnahuac, near the beginning of the expedition to Parián, the Consul pauses with Laruelle before some Diego Rivera frescoes in which native warriors are dressed as wolves and tigers. As he gazes, these figures appear to the Consul to merge into "one immense, malevolent creature" (p. 212). Not much later, with a mysterious continuity having resumed the comparatively undisturbing hallucinatory quality of art, those animals or some like them appear as murals in a Quauhnahuac tavern, El Bosque (the wood). By this time, in their context and because of numerous other allusions to Dante, they may remind us of those beasts that block Dante's direct route to Mount Purgatory as *The Divine Comedy* opens.

In general, the further along we are in the novel, the more complex and problematical is the relationship between hallucination and reality. Section X begins with a new and foreboding development: the Consul is for the first time drinking mescal, which he has already associated with his doom. Almost immediately following this disclosure is the first really long passage whose character remains irresolvably ambiguous. It involves a memory (perhaps a remembered hallucination) of a time when, after drinking all night, the Consul was supposed to meet a woman, Lee Maitland, at a train station. There are suspiciously improbable circumstances. The woman never appeared; even her reality is somewhat doubtful ("Who was she?" asks the Consul in retrospect). The trains that pass through are described as "terrible . . . shimmering . . . in mirage." The clickety-clack noise they make is repeatedly emphasized, as it might be in an auditory hallucination. Finally, at evening, "the next moment" (as though an alcoholic blackout had filled the intervening time), the Consul recalls himself "in the station tavern with a man who'd just tried to sell him three loose teeth." On the other hand, there are entirely plausible naturalistic details in the recollection: as the Consul waited in the early morning, "the dehydrated onion factory by the sidings awoke, then the coal companies. . . . A delicious smell of onion soup in sidestreets of Vavin impregnated the early morning. Grimed sweeps at hand trundled barrows, or were screening coal" (pp. 281–83). Are we dealing with remembered hallucination, remembered reality, or some inextricable combination of both?

Such complicated interweaving of hallucination and actuality, with an increased uncertainty about the identity and time of the latter, recurs in the same section. The Consul, dining with Hugh and Yvonne in a Tomalín tavern, suddenly (that is, after an apparent blackout) finds himself seated on a toilet, from which vantage point he alternately reads from a tourist brochure about Tlaxcala and listens to the continuing conversation of Hugh and Yvonne, to which he makes an occasional contribution. Or so it seems at first; but if the preceding is an accurate description of reality, it soon appears that the overheard bits of conversation are not merely from Hugh and Yvonne but from various times and people; and then it appears that we are dealing not only with remembered reality but with remembered and current auditory hallucinations, these shifts and confusions all developing in the space of a few minutes (pp. 293–301). Perhaps it is no coincidence that the tavernkeeper of this section is named Cervantes; *Under the Volcano* is as adept as *Don Quixote* at mingling hallucination or fantasy with reality, and the two stories, by means of their ambiguities, raise perplexing and not always answerable questions about the validity of conventional distinctions between sanity and insanity, reason and imagination, fantasy or hallucination and reality.[19]

The indeterminacy of reality and hallucination is nowhere else as extensive as in the final section of *Under the Volcano*. The problem there is not so much to follow what is happening (though this is not always easy) as to account for it. As is common in alcoholic hallucinations, persecution and violence seem to occur for no adequately credible reasons. Virtually without warning, the Consul copulates with a prostitute, Maria. Though this is part of his doom because, at the level of allegory, it is a betrayal of his love for Yvonne and may even be a kind of symbolic murder of her, it seems also the stuff of hallucination because, at the level of reality, the Consul's sudden access of lust while in a state of extreme intoxication is unconvincing.[20] The fornication seems the first step in executing the persecutory plot of the typical hallucination, with Maria leading the Consul into the progressively greater darkness of the back rooms of the Farolito, rooms the Consul had earlier thought of as "spots where diabolical plots must be hatched [and] atrocious murders planned," past "a sinister chuckle" and "two men . . . drinking or plotting" (pp. 200, 347–48). The several policemen who later begin to threaten him he regards as "phantoms of himself" surrounding him in his "delirium" (pp. 361–62)—that is, they are at least as much hallucinatory as real. And the motives for persecution are more those of alcoholic delirium—flimsy pretexts for malignity—than of believable reality. Finding an unsent cable of Hugh's on the Consul's person, a cable that contains a cryptic reference to Jews, the fascist police seize on this as a reason to vilify the Consul as a Jew; but in fact any excuse for their bullying would serve just as well. The ambiguity especially of the final section, then, is appropriate for a novel in which the spiritual fate of the central character is left uncertain.

Ultimately some of the ambiguities are partly resolved. However tenebrous the episode with Maria, she is unequivocally instrumental in the fall of the Consul; however phantomlike the police, resembling the persecutors in alcoholic hallucinations, one of their number murders the Consul. However exciting or challenging the ambiguities between hallucination and reality, this effect is transcended by one of greater importance, the most stunningly innovative use to which Lowry puts the hallucinations in the novel. Though there are some differences among those who have described or defined hallucinations, nearly all agree on one key element: their falsity or unreality.[21] But Lowry makes the hallucination perhaps his chief vehicle for moral implication and for the prophecy or discovery of truth. Here again, perceiving an analogy with *Don Quixote* may be helpful. Both works suggest that imagination, insanity, or hallucination offers a surer route to more important truths than does reason or sanity. Early in the novel, in an unsent letter to Yvonne, the Consul acts as a prophet when he records the fear that he will destroy himself by his imagination (p. 40). Because, for the extreme alcoholic, hallucinations can be a major expression of the imagination, we see that the Consul's hallucinations prophesy reality on the cutting edge or "final frontier of consciousness" (p. 135).[22] Moreover, particularly in the last section of the novel, they *become* truth or reality.

How may this strange metamorphosis be explained? Richard Cross, in a penetrating comment on another Lowry protagonist, Ethan Llewelyn of *October Ferry to Gabriola*, notes that the most likely reason for the fire that destroys Llewelyn's house, inherited from his father, is his feeling of repressed rage toward his father combined with a sense of unworthiness and damnation resulting from guilt over that rage. These feelings, by some magical transference from a psychological condition to material reality, cause the conflagration.[23] Similarly, perhaps one could account for much that happens in *Under the Volcano*, especially in its final section, by realizing that the Consul so longs for his own destruction that, with the aid of an immense quantity of alcohol, he hallucinates the various means to this end: the threats, the police persecution, the confused violence, even his own murder. Simultaneously and mysteriously, as in a kind of self-fulfilling prophecy, the hallucinations become actuality.

A complementary explanation of the metamorphosis originates in a comment Lowry once made to a friend, Norman Matson, in a Parisian bistro: "I find places like this, dark small places . . . everywhere. . . . Sometimes I think I first imagine them, see them in a nightmare and then find them actual and existent in the world."[24] If nightmare and hallucination are practically synonymous for an alcoholic like Lowry or the Consul, Lowry evidently meant that his hallucinations always have some duplicate in the real world. But it seems from this remark that somehow the hallucination is the antecedent or higher reality, necessary for the invention or birth of a more mundane material reality. That is, if Lowry couldn't hallucinate these "dark small places," they wouldn't exist. Of course, the very phrase suggests the Farolito. An actual Farolito or some similar Mexican tavern or taverns may have furnished embellishing details for Lowry's descriptions in *Under the Volcano*, but the seminal concept was almost certainly in one or more hallucinations.

Prior to the final section of the novel, there are some simple examples of the use of hallucinations as prophetic symbols. Glancing into a public garden at one point, the Consul sees what he terms the routine hallucination of a figure "apparently in some kind of mourning . . . head bowed in deepest anguish" (p. 130). Very few of the hallucinations are merely routine. Whatever the identity of this anonymous figure (who may be the Consul himself), he is quite clearly grieving for a loss of Eden, an expulsion from paradise, the gardens of *Under the Volcano* repeatedly assuming this symbolic association.

A somewhat more complex prophetic symbol involves a sunflower. There is no reason to doubt its reality as a natural object, but the Consul fantasizes or, as it were, hallucinates the significance that he attributes to it. He first complains to Dr. Vigil that this flower, growing behind his house, watches him with hostility and hatred; later he comments to his brother that it stares at him "fiercely . . . . Like God!" (pp. 144, 179). This last is one of the novel's echoes of Marlowe's Faustus, who in his last minutes, in a moving and profoundly serious parody of Christ's Passion, agonizingly implores, "My God, my God, looke not so fierce on me."[25] It is understandable that the Consul, whose descent into the darkness of hell has already begun, should imagine that a symbol of God's light and goodness is judging him.

A still more complex prophetic hallucination is the Consul's picture of his soul as a "town ravaged and stricken in the black path of his excess. . . . the light now on, now off . . . the whole town plunged into darkness, where communication is lost . . . bombs threaten" (p. 145).[26] Actually, this ramified image is both prophetic and retrospective: if it looks toward the Consul's destruction and the Quauhnahuac cinema's power failure in Section I, it also looks back, in its hint of a plague of locusts, to the carapace of a locust that the Consul has recently found (p. 133). More important, however, is the tendency of this hallucination, like many other passages in the novel, to invest the Consul's fate and soul with a universal importance. In a novel in which the Spanish Civil War hovers in the near background because of Hugh's presence, in a world poised on the brink of global destruction (as Lowry well knew, writing and rewriting his novel during World War II), the hallucination's imagery of a destroyed town, lost communication, and bombs can stand for any of thousands of pictures of razed towns or cities, perhaps, more specifically, for the infamous and symbolic instance of Guernica. In any event, Lowry can be extremely skillful, as he is in using this hallucination, at bringing us to see the Consul not as an isolated individual but as suffering the fate of Everyman in the late 1930s. Essentially the same imagery reappears intensified, with the Consul at its center, in the final hallucination of the novel: "the world itself was bursting, bursting into black spouts of villages catapulted into space, with himself falling through it all, through the inconceivable pandemonium of a million tanks, through the blazing of ten million burning bodies" (p. 375).

Because *Under the Volcano* is at one level an allegory, it frequently exhibits characteristically allegorical fluidities or overlappings of identities; these should not surprise us, a basic assumption of allegory being that all characters are merely different facets or aspects of a single, prototypical mankind.[27] In an allegory of cosmic sweep, there is usually one character who comes closer than any other to being a prototypical Everyman. In *Under the Volcano* this is the Consul, and hallucination helps to show the links between him and the other characters.

Hallucinations in *Under the Volcano*

Perhaps the first time the term *hallucination* appears is when the Consul notices an "object shaped like a dead man . . . lying flat on its back by his swimming pool, with a large sombrero over its face" (p. 91). Though he wishes it would "go away," he is little disturbed by his vision, which is so fleeting that no significance attaches to it. Undergoing several metamorphoses, however, this hallucination becomes one of the most important prophetic symbols in the novel—a prophecy, indeed, of the Consul's own death. The sombrero covering the face connects this vision with a nearly dead man, not hallucinated but discovered by the roadside as Hugh rides a bus with Yvonne and the Consul to Tomalín, a stage on the Consul's journey to his own destruction in Parián. The bus stops; Hugh notices that the man lies with his arms stretched toward a wayside cross twenty feet distant, an apparent suggestion that he yearned for but failed to achieve salvation. He is linked not only with the poolside apparition but with an Indian on horseback whom both Hugh and the Consul had seen that morning (p. 246). The Consul's reaction to the man, badly wounded and obviously in need of help, is strange—unaccountable, in fact, if we miss the allegory. Though his wish to avoid becoming entangled with the authorities has a certain plausibility, his inordinately strong fear of helping, his refusal to be the good Samaritan, implies a refusal of brotherly compassion which is necessarily, in allegory, also a rejection of self. This is only one of the Consul's moral and spiritual rejections, but it is important, for with it the pace of rejection seems to intensify. This train of events begins with a casual, fleeting, seemingly meaningless hallucination beside the Consul's pool.

Increasingly harsh and cynical because of his mounting desire to escape from Hugh and Yvonne (again, allegorically and morally, to strip away more of his humanity) and to drink self-destructively in Parián, the Consul picks a quarrel with Hugh in which he criticizes his desire to help the wounded man, whose right to die he defends (p. 309). The Consul's argument may seem to have some cogency as part of his larger attack on Hugh as a globetrotting busybody and brummagem savior. In asserting the futility of compassionate action, however, the Consul is exposing his accelerating rejection not only of the world in general but also of those closest to him, for this section of the story ends in his flight from Hugh and Yvonne—a final severing, as it turns out. The Consul experiences several types of suffering for his rejection of Yvonne, one taking the form of a particularly gruesome hallucination. Looking from the Farolito toward the jungle path by which he has arrived in Parián and by which Hugh and Yvonne, in Section XI, attempt to follow him, he sees "some unusual animals resembling geese, but large as camels, and skinless men, without heads, upon stilts, whose animated entrails jerked along the ground" (p. 341). The last image, at least, makes sense as a representation of Yvonne's death, trampled by the horse belonging to the dying Mexican—a death for which the Consul is in more than one way responsible. The next thing he sees is a policeman leading a horse up the path.

Not only does the Consul fail to grasp any meaning in this hallucination; after the brief interval of lucidity in which he sees the policeman, he also fails to see the even greater significance of a second hallucination in which the face of a beggar reclining outside the Farolito is changing to that of Señora Gregorio, another tavernkeeper in the novel, "and now in turn to his mother's face, upon which appeared an expression of infinite pity and supplication" (p. 342). The Consul, of course, is much in need of pity; and his mother may be supplicating or beseeching him to understand the vital meaning of the extraordinary shifts of identity registered by the hallucination. These may indicate that, because we are all essentially one person, we need to practice love and pity if only for our own salvation. Instead of heeding this lesson, the Consul chooses, albeit with fitful misgivings and twinges of conscience, to continue on the path to hell. Therefore phantoms or hallucinations that are also real, ghosts of a younger self or of better days, appear to accuse or reject him: the policeman referred to as the Chief of Gardens is recognized by the Consul as an image of his former self (p. 359); a tavern patron who looks "like a poet, some friend of his college days" (p. 360), pointedly snubs him. Morally, these rejections may represent punishments for the Consul's rejection of Hugh and Yvonne, and of his own better self.

Even though the end of the novel is highly problematical in meaning, it may afford hope of redemption for the Consul, an arrest of the slide through rejection to damnation.[28] This, too, is presented largely in the form of a hallucinatory reverie that may be the most intricately kaleidoscopic of any in the novel. Just before his life ends, the Consul may find the answer to his prayer to be released from the "dreadful tyranny of self" (p. 289). He seems at last to heed his mother's supplication and compassionately to acknowledge that we are all one by experiencing the extremes of pelado (or Barabbas) and Christ, atoning for his neglect of the dying Mexican by entering his identity as well: "Now he was the one dying by the wayside where no good Samaritan would halt" (p. 375).[29] These identifications begin proliferating when the Consul asks: "the policemen, Fructuoso Sanabria, that other man who looked like a poet, the luminous skeletons, even the rabbit in the corner and the ash and sputum on the filthy floor—did not each correspond, in a way he couldn't understand yet obscurely recognized, to some faction of his being?" (p. 362). The police, the Consul's "phantom" persecutors, assist the spread by their questioning, unable to decide whether the Consul is a Jew, pelado, Englishman, or "Norteamericano" (p. 372). But the process only achieves its culmination with the Consul's last reverie, in which he also appeals strongly for Yvonne's forgiveness. Although the Consul's body is treated as offal, because even the trees pity him (p. 375) the novel ends on a note of hope for the salvation of his soul. Like much else, this last important development, appropriately enough in a novel about an extreme alcoholic, centers on a hallucination.

T W O

Brideshead Revisited
Sebastian's Alcoholism as a
Spiritual Illness

One indication of how Evelyn Waugh will approach the alcoholism of Sebastian Flyte in *Brideshead Revisited* is revealed by differences between otherwise strikingly similar settings in this novel and in Waugh's *Handful of Dust*. The settings are two virtually indistinguishable nightclubs: the Sixty-four, at 64 Sink Street, in *Handful*, and the Old Hundredth, at 100 Sink Street, in *Brideshead*. Both clubs are rendezvous for male members of the British upperclass when on a spree.

In *Handful*, in a passage that has no counterpart in *Brideshead*, Waugh offers a genially ironic tribute to the club's ability to survive a generation of obviously well-justified police and even parliamentary investigations into its violations of the law.[1] The drunkenness of its two visitors, Tony Last and his friend Jock Grant-Menzies, is not disturbing. Indeed, the most disturbing element of the scene may be that the men are not drunk enough to shed their genteel stuffiness and thus take an appropriately harsh revenge on Tony's wife for her infidelities. Their petty harassment—a few telephone calls in the course of the night—is nullified the morning after by Tony's apology, which reassures Brenda that she can continue her adultery with impunity. The total effect of the scene may best be described as that of a liberation that fails to occur. As its epigraph from *The Waste Land* implies, *Handful* is populated by mannequins that no amount of drink can endow with authentic vitality.

If the scene from *Handful* can be viewed as incipient comedy aborted, the similar scene from *Brideshead* is a good deal more foreboding. As Sebastian, Charles Ryder, and Boy Mulcaster pull up in front of the Old Hundredth, their attention is drawn to a man near the doorway; although he is a kind of conventional, stage-prop drunk, his muttered remarks—"Keep out, you'll be poisoned," "You'll be robbed and given a dose"[2]—accurately predict the fact, if not the nature, of an impending misfortune. Mulcaster, anxious to impress his friends with his familiarity with the club, attempts to exchange civilities with its proprietress, Ma Mayfield, although he does not at first recognize her; bored, she does little more than repeat "Ten bob each" in a mechanical way that is faintly sinister. Once his party is seated, Charles notices two prostitutes approaching whom he labels, because of their faces, "Death's Head" and "Sickly Child" (p. 116). These omens narrowly miss fulfillment, for when an extremely intoxicated Sebastian later drives away from the club with his friends and the two women, he almost has a "head-on collision with a taxi-cab" (p. 117) and is jailed. In the highly atypical clamor of his denials of drunkenness, and in his desire, upon release, to go abroad rather than return home or to Oxford, we glimpse Sebastian's awareness of a sudden change for the worse in his life, the end of innocent, carefree drinking.

The scene at the Old Hundredth and its aftermath, then, are early signs that Sebastian has developed a serious affliction and that Waugh will treat it seriously. At this point we can have no idea how complex and ambiguous Waugh's treatment will become. The complexity derives in large part from Waugh's twofold view of the illness: the first might be called naturalistic, realistic, or psychological; the second, spiritual. The two views are present almost from the beginning of Waugh's examination of alcoholism, and their coexistence through much of the novel gives that examination an unusual richness and depth. Eventually, however, the spiritual aspect of Sebastian's alcoholism seems to assume paramount importance for Waugh. Ambiguity arises from a double view of even this aspect: although he may never completely cease to regard Sebastian's drinking as a fault, Waugh increasingly presents it not as an ordinary weakness but as a kind of *felix culpa,* a necessary trial and preparation of Sebastian for a better world. With the eventual ascendancy of this view, the cogency of the novel is undermined (at least as a study of alcoholism) by the diminution of both its complexity and its ambiguity. Or perhaps it would be more accurate to say that Waugh's interest in providing a full, credible picture of alcoholism was ultimately supplanted by more compelling interests.

In spite of a family and a great personal charm that make Sebastian one of the most sought-after young men in English society (during his first year at Oxford, his rooms are filled with invitations from London hostesses; p. 31), he possesses several prominent traits that are not only sharply incongruous with his advantages but that, according to some studies of alcoholism, greatly increase his probabilities of developing it. His volatile moods, his pronounced insecurity and immaturity (symbolized by the Teddy bear that he takes with him to Oxford), and his deep-seated feelings of inferiority deserve to be noted.[3] More than one observer has pointed out a crucial and sometimes insuperable difficulty in attempts to define an alcoholic personality: one cannot always tell whether the characteristics in question preceded and caused the drinking or resulted from it.[4] Although it is true that alcoholic cause and effect may often be tangled, Waugh enables us to see more clearly than in real life that the above-named characteristics definitely precede Sebastian's alcoholism and probably contribute to it. On his first visit to Brideshead, Charles observes that Sebastian almost sneaks him in and out, introducing him only to his nanny and avoiding a sister whom they could easily have met. Charles finally asks Sebastian whether he is ashamed of him. When Sebastian expresses the fear that his family will steal Charles from him (p. 37), it must come as a surprise, because neither Charles nor the reader has yet encountered that family's other members. It becomes clear, too, that Sebastian is not referring omnisciently to the struggle for Charles's loyalties that later occurs between Sebastian and his mother. He states the fear quite simply: although charm is one quality that Sebastian clearly possesses, he nevertheless thinks he is doomed to lose Charles, to his family collectively or to any individual member of it. A person so insecure about his most outstanding strength is likely to discover some extreme means of relieving his pain.

Because low self-esteem borders on self-hatred, another trait often ascribed to the alcoholic, it is not surprising that Sebastian evinces this even while his own alcoholic drinking is still relatively new. The vehemence with which he scourges himself may be rather startling: at home for Easter during his second year at Oxford, Sebastian, who stays drunk most of the time, at one point says to his houseguest, Charles, "If it's any comfort to you, I absolutely detest myself" (p. 135). This seems an overreaction: Sebastian has neither done nor said anything truly detestable; engaged in solitary drinking, he has largely kept away from other members of the family. Similarly, after his arrest for drunken driving and his release from prison, Sebastian's reactions seem excessive: where a more conventional young man, such as Boy Mulcaster, would dismiss the incident as a trifle, Sebastian says to Charles, "I might go abroad . . . . I'd sooner go to prison. If I just slip away abroad they can't get me back, can they? That's what people do when the police are after them" (p. 121). Assumptions of derangement or hypersensitivity will scarcely explain these reactions. The explanation probably occurs during Charles's first extended visit to Brideshead. Although Sebastian has hitherto seemed casual about his Catholicism, Charles is set straight at this time; and Sebastian is unquestionably in earnest when he claims to be "very, very much wickeder" than his friend (p. 86). His Catholicism sets such extremely high standards of conduct that Sebastian feels his departure from those standards more keenly than any non-Catholic could. The worse his drinking becomes, the more acutely Sebastian suffers from the widening gulf between his values and his drunken behavior. According to Vernon E. Johnson, an unusually perceptive student of alcoholism, this conflict between values and behavior is exactly what defines the alcoholic and separates him from a sociopathic or skid-row drinker.[5]

As Sebastian's alcoholism progresses, Waugh offers many glimpses of symptoms often agreed to be indicators of alcoholism: Sebastian's increasing tendency to drink surreptitiously (p. 130) or alone; his preference for low company in pubs during his second year at Oxford (p. 108);[6] his drinking to achieve the oblivion of blackouts (p. 159); his trembling hands (p. 134); his neglect of his appearance (p. 152). Sebastian's desire to flee the consequences of his arrest for drunken driving, a desire that expands and intensifies as the mortifications of his drinking accumulate until it drives him over parts of three continents, is often referred to in Alcoholics Anonymous as the typically alcoholic fantasy that there is a "geographical cure" for this illness. Waugh also depicts quite fully the alcoholic's marked tendencies toward manipulation of others and the invention of excuses or rationalizations for his drinking.[7]

At least one of Sebastian's apparent excuses—"If they treat me like a dipsomaniac, they can bloody well have a dipsomaniac" (p. 156)— is not merely a rationalization; for if Sebastian would have become a dipsomaniac regardless of the treatment of which he complains here,

this treatment may abet it. Alcoholics Anonymous believes that alcoholism is a family illness.[8] Alcoholic irrationality may so thoroughly
pervade the family that one of its members may, for example, try
pouring the alcoholic's liquor down the drain. Although the actions
of Lady Marchmain, Sebastian's mother, are much more elaborately
contrived than this example—at various times in the novel they involve her enlisting or attempting to enlist the aid of Charles, Rex
Mottram, Mr. Samgrass, and an Oxford priest to report on, curb, or
stop Sebastian's drinking—her motives are not appreciably different,
nor are her results. The alcoholic determined to drink can always
find a supply. Moreover, in ways that she fails to see, Lady Marchmain may even be enabling Sebastian to drink. As Charles tries in
vain to explain to her, her surveillance, by threatening his freedom,
provides Sebastian with an additional motive for desiring alcoholic
escape (p. 144). Samgrass's role also indirectly encourages it by letting Sebastian know that he will be rescued from any troubles caused
by his drinking. This protection fosters the emotional immaturity
and its concomitants—irresponsibility, defiance, and rebellion—
sometimes cited as being among the gravest liabilities of alcoholism.[9]

There are reasons to suppose, however, that Waugh would have
been dissatisfied with any analysis of his treatment of Sebastian's alcoholism that failed to move beyond naturalistic symptomatology or
psychology. In its cruder or more obvious manifestations, Waugh
probably looked on psychology as no more illuminating than the response of Julia, Sebastian's sister, to his alcoholism: "It's something
chemical in him." Charles rightly reflects that this "cant phrase of the
time" was just "the old concept of determinism in a new form"
(p. 129). Similarly, a reductivist psychology can appear to say that a
person with Sebastian's qualities must become an alcoholic. But if, as
Anthony Blanche suggests, the knowledge of the psychoanalyst is important for understanding the Marchmain family, he mentions another skill that ultimately seems even more important: that of a "diabolist" (p. 53). This strange term requires a recognition of Anthony's
motives and limitations. At this point in the story he is, in a sense,
competing against the Marchmains for Charles's allegiance, and for
this reason alone he is generally catty about them. In addition, Anthony is incapable of coming any closer than "diabolist" to defining
the Marchmains' essentially spiritual quality. The alcoholism of
Sebastian is, for Waugh, primarily the sign of some spiritual impov-

erishment or malaise. This added spiritual dimension makes it a more complex and mysterious illness than a determinist or behaviorist could ever acknowledge.[10]

Two facts of Sebastian's family are extremely important for an understanding of the deep spiritual division that his alcoholism reflects. Lord and Lady Marchmain have long been separated; and his father has abjured, seemingly for good, the Catholic faith. It is no doubt with his father in mind that Sebastian refers to himself as "half-heathen" (p. 89). Although one of Sebastian's excuses for drinking is to escape the control of his mother—and although it may even be true, as his father's mistress suggests, that Sebastian hates his mother (p. 102)—his other half remains loyal to her religion and God. Sebastian's self, as sundered as the former union of his mother and father, perhaps seeks and finds in drinking some relief from this pain.

Another, more subtle reason for Sebastian's alcoholism may lie in an inheritance from his father. Both Cara, the father's mistress, and Lady Marchmain note their similarities. Cara observes that "Sebastian drinks too much" and that Lord Marchmain "was nearly a drunkard when he met me" (p. 103);[11] Lady Marchmain asserts that, in fleeing her, Sebastian is repeating the pattern of his father (p. 137). The inherited spiritual malaise, however, lies beneath these resemblances; it can be described as an ignorance of how to love. Lord Marchmain, says Cara, misdirected to his wife a type of love that "it is better to have . . . for another boy than for a girl," a romantic friendship. Although his relationship with Cara prevents his developing into a drunkard, she emphasizes to Charles that Lord Marchmain does not love her; their relationship is founded on companionship and sex, "that one thing that no man can do for himself" (pp. 101–3). Improving on his father, Sebastian builds a romantic friendship with Charles. As Cara defines it, this is only a step toward mature love, "a kind . . . that comes to children before they know its meaning. In England it comes when you are almost men." The friendship is terminated partly by Sebastian's alcoholism, partly by Charles's involvement with the rest of his family. Without paternal example, Sebastian is left to grope his way toward some higher order of love, but he learns much more readily to dull the pain of emptiness with alcohol.

The medicine, however, becomes itself a "soul sickness" (*12 & 12*, p. 46) and aggravates the isolation or loneliness it is supposed to ease.

Sebastian's older brother, Lord Brideshead, commonly referred to as
Bridey, once explains that he drinks seldom and reluctantly because
for him alcohol does not promote what he regards as its chief end: a
feeling of "sympathy between man and man" (p. 93). For Sebastian,
the more his drinking inflames and augments his self-hatred, the less
his desire to achieve any such sympathy. It is not just that he wishes
to drink alone; both by his own preference and by the consequences
of his alcoholism, he increasingly is alone, a common outcome as alcoholism advances (pp. 127, 129–31, 149, 168).[12] This isolation is
conveyed by images and hints of coldness, as much internal or spiritual as physical, that largely replace the warmth and gaiety of Sebastian's first year at Oxford (e.g., pp. 104–5, 121).

Sebastian at last slips the leash of his various keepers and leaves
England—for good, as it turns out. Charles, learning of his where-
abouts from Anthony a year or more after last seeing Sebastian himself, locates him in Morocco. Dispatched to bring him home because
Lady Marchmain is dying, Charles is unsuccessful; Sebastian himself
is in a hospital, too sick to travel. There are signs, however, that he is
beginning to effect a recovery from his spiritual illness. Although
Sebastian has not stopped drinking at the time of Charles's visit, we
find out from Cordelia, another sister who visits him later, that he
had almost quit during his period of living with Kurt, a German who
is forcibly sent home and then commits suicide rather than become a
Nazi. The implication is that if Sebastian and Kurt had continued
living together, Sebastian might have recovered fully.

The crucial elements in this recovery are much like those designated as necessary by the program of Alcoholics Anonymous: an end
to isolation and withdrawal; a recommitment to society; and in particular a willingness to escape "the bondage of self" by helping fellow
alcoholics to recover.[13] There are differences, of course: Kurt is no
alcoholic, and one person hardly constitutes society. But his need for
help is great—he is starving when Sebastian finds him (p. 214) and
has a badly infected foot that will not heal. His need matches Sebastian's equally great need to be of service to someone, which he could
never fulfill in his family (p. 215). Most important, in his relationship with Kurt the fundamental part of Sebastian's spiritual recovery
is his learning for the first time a complete and deeply satisfying form
of love. Kurt is so unattractive—his face is lined, his teeth tobacco
stained and "set far apart," and he speaks "sometimes with a lisp,

sometimes with a disconcerting whistle, which he covered with a giggle" (p. 211)—that even Sebastian realizes that no one likes him (p. 214). No one, that is, but Sebastian, whose love is self-effacing charity manifested as a desire to perform homely duties for Kurt, most touchingly illustrated when he is out of the hospital and insists that it is his job to bring Kurt's cigarettes to him (p. 216).

With Kurt's death, Sebastian's recovery is stopped. According to Cordelia, who sees him last and whose report is part description, part prediction of the remainder of his life, he has become and will continue to be a periodic drunk. Even this occasional intoxication might have been ended had Sebastian been allowed to become a missionary lay brother; Cordelia informs Charles that he was denied this privilege by a monastery near Carthage (pp. 304–5). In the end, however, Sebastian's drinking is to be viewed not as a misfortune but as a blessing, and it is in revealing this view that Waugh most radically departs from any scientific depiction of alcoholism.

Sebastian's ethereal beauty and his surname, Flyte, suggest that his restlessness is not so much a longing to elude his mother's control or alcoholic escapism (though it contains both of these elements) as it is a quest or pilgrimage in search of his truer destiny, his otherworldly home. Much other evidence in the novel, direct and indirect, bears upon or supports this hypothesis. Neither Sebastian's family nor his society has any place for him; he cannot fit, at least not without becoming much less attractive. His father, though generally sympathetic, is seriously flawed and remains rather shadowy despite Cara's attempts to sketch in his details; Sebastian's mother unintentionally becomes his enemy and persecutor; the eccentric Bridey, though penetrating at times, has his own preoccupations and can spare little attention for his younger brother; Julia, closest in age to Sebastian, regards his drinking with impatience and contempt; and Cordelia, sharing something of her brother's sweetness or purity and having a willingness to forgive his drinking, is much younger and ultimately follows a different path. On his first visit to Brideshead, Charles is struck by what seems to the reader, in retrospect, an uncanny prescience on Sebastian's part: he does not say "'That is my home,' but 'It's where my family live'" (p. 35). In his society Sebastian is equally out of place or homeless. One can scarcely wish that he were different when one takes stock of the people who are at home in the world: Samgrass, oily and obsequious; Rex Mottram, a thoroughly vulgar freebooter; Boy Mulcaster and his sister, Charles's wife, representing the vacuous aristocracy; Hooper and the unnamed "travelling salesman, with his polygonal pince-nez, his fat wet hand-shake, his grinning dentures" (p. 139); and Anthony Blanche, whose strengths are verbal vitality, shrewdness, and honesty but whose honesty and shrewdness are seriously limited by envy of Sebastian's appeal and an inability to comprehend its source. As his last name may suggest, Anthony is a blank or cipher, still another version of the type of modern worldliness or emptiness, busily registering "who's in, who's out" among the "packs and sects of great ones." (If the Flytes were an obscure, working-class Catholic family, Anthony would take no interest in them.) Charles Ryder, the narrator, is, apart from Sebastian, the most attractive male character, but he too suffers from the sterile modernity that afflicts the rest. Although he is strongly drawn to the Marchmains and, unlike Anthony, dimly perceives the source of their magnetism (p. 303), Charles long clings to his agnosticism and exemplifies the limitations of aesthetic humanism, for which reasons alone his friendship with Sebastian was destined to founder.[14]

The dissimilarity between all of these characters and Sebastian makes his own appropriate path extremely difficult to discover. One might say, not altogether metaphorically, that he does not so much find it as drunkenly stumble onto it. In so doing, he makes certain renunciations that bring him toward wholeness. He leaves behind his heathen, pagan, or Arcadian self (p. 127). It is part of the mordancy of Waugh's comment on a despiritualized, wasteland Europe that Sebastian achieves this metamorphosis in the realm of the infidel, though it is perhaps also significant that the apparent end of his pilgrimage is Carthage, vividly commemorated by Augustine,[15] and that his wanderings carry him toward the Holy Land.[16] He renounces the aesthetic—with its roots in materiality and with himself, for a time at Oxford, one of its treasured artifacts—for the ascetic. The common object of both these movements is spiritual purification, gained by the stripping away of worldly dross. *Brideshead Revisited* thus becomes not only Waugh's denunciation of modernity but also, and more generally, his adaptation of the ancient Christian theme of *contemptus mundi*, according to which the world is not something to be enjoyed but, at best, a place of sorrows and trials preparing one for a better existence.[17]

In these changes or developments of Sebastian, his alcoholism plays an important part. It is his chief trial or mode of suffering; paradoxically, it is the spiritual illness that, more than any other change he experiences, moves him toward spiritual wholeness or health. For this reason the alcoholism is neither a vice to be deplored nor a source of division—*spiritus contra spiritum*, as C. G. Jung once put the deleterious effect of alcoholic "spirits" in a letter to Bill Wilson, co-founder of Alcoholics Anonymous.[18] Rather, although alcoholism seems to have had some such effect on Sebastian until the time of his last departure from Brideshead, thereafter it helps to cure "this long disease, my Life."[19] Imaging the world as hospital, sick bay, or lazaretto supports the *contemptus mundi* theme; such images figure prominently in descriptions of Sebastian's later life. His friend Kurt, with an infected foot and "secondary syphilis" (p. 213), is akin to Lazarus, and because of his alcoholism Sebastian is in and out of hospitals or infirmaries.[20] When Charles visits him in Morocco, he is struck by his friend's emaciation: "drink, which made others fat and red, seemed to wither Sebastian" (p. 214). This is a sign, of course, that alcoholism is having a desirable effect, wasting the flesh and increasing Sebastian's spiritual purity. By reducing him to a condition of abject, childlike helplessness and dependence on God, a condition not natural for one of Sebastian's station, his alcoholism further contributes to this purity.

Cordelia's final account of Sebastian raises some problems not easy to ignore. Even while he was living with Kurt, Sebastian displayed an unusual goodness in his self-sacrificing ministrations to this lowly person. But it is a greater strain on credibility when Cordelia flatly claims that Sebastian is holy and that his suffering from alcoholism has been the chief agency of his holiness (pp. 306, 309). Although Cordelia is generally a reliable observer and judge, in this instance she perhaps leaves too much to be taken on faith by not establishing or showing any real links between agency and effect. One could contend, of course, that God's grace to Sebastian, taking the form of alcoholism,[21] is simply inaccessible to human understanding, and that therefore the apparent disparity between form and end only evidences the weakness of human perception. Most readers may find it difficult to accept this position. Moreover, if Cordelia is maintaining, as she seems to be, that Sebastian's alcoholism is his cross,[22] she (and

Waugh) also come perilously close to the boundaries of comic satire, beyond which Robert Burns's Holy Willie excuses his fornicating three times with "Leezie's lass" on the grounds that he was "fou" that day, or beyond which Ernest Pontifex, annoyed by the smug announcement of Pryer that he would accept martyrdom if it befell him, derisively recalls an Irishwoman who proclaimed herself "a martyr to the drink."[23] To be sure, Waugh invites no such comparisons with Sebastian, and they may be farfetched; but if the associations are even conceivable, they serve to illustrate the dubious adequacy of alcoholism as a vehicle for Sebastian's holiness.

Another aspect of Sebastian's last transformation is at least as difficult to credit. Although Cordelia does remark that he "looked terrible . . . rather bald with a straggling beard" (p. 306), both she and Charles, on his earlier visit, pay scant attention to the physical ravages of his alcoholism. But Cordelia (or rather Waugh) goes beyond this neglect to a sanitizing or bowdlerizing of Sebastian, a visual softening of his alcoholism that seems unwarranted no matter what degree of spiritual purity or holiness Sebastian has reached. The naturalistic or realistic representation of his alcoholism recedes too completely. The Sebastian who, during his last stay at Brideshead, embarrassed the company by his "clouded eye and groping movements . . . his thickened voice" (p. 167) is replaced by a Sebastian whose drinking bouts are now decently invisible and whose alcoholism is indistinguishable from his status among the North African monks as a "queer old character . . . pottering round with his broom and his bunch of keys" (pp. 308–9). Although he has lost the magic beauty of his youth (p. 31), Sebastian has been compensated by a charming quaintness. The picture has its appeal; but as a delineation of alcoholism, it is disturbingly incomplete.

A basic fault of *Brideshead Revisited* as an investigation of alcoholism is that the more Waugh focuses attention on Sebastian's holiness and special destiny, the less interest there is in his alcoholism. The subordination of alcoholism as a source of interest becomes progressively clearer because it begins to emerge, after Sebastian leaves Brideshead, as merely the means to his holiness and salvation.

An even more fundamental problem lies not in the handling of Sebastian's alcoholism but in the character himself. On the subject of Sebastian, Anthony Blanche is usually malicious; but in calling Sebastian "a little insipid" (p. 56), he states an important truth. Discounting Anthony's ill will, this means that Sebastian's goodness is so simple and artless that he is unable to sustain the full weight of the novel as a central character; after about its midpoint, he simply disappears, thereafter to be infrequently reported on.[24] Behind the diminishing interest in Sebastian's alcoholism lies the diminution of Sebastian's role. This difficulty with his major "good" characters might almost be said to have been habitual with Waugh. Tony Last in *A Handful of Dust* and Guy Crouchback in the *Sword of Honour* trilogy are largely passive or acted upon; the libertines or blasphemers—Basil Seal, Anthony Blanche, even the Randolph Churchill of the *Diaries*[25]—seem to corner most of the vitality. Waugh's apparent inability to combine energy with goodness suggests that, whether he made alcoholism a center of intrinsic interest or a means to an end, he could not have created a character such as the Consul in Malcolm Lowry's *Under the Volcano*: half-crazed by drink, hallucinating, torn and tormented by good and evil spirits, above all vividly dramatized. In contrast to the Consul's tumult and his final, precipitous fall into the hellish barranca, there is something too restrained or genteel about Sebastian's alcoholic suffering. But, at least until Waugh becomes preoccupied with more transcendent matters, he gives a detailed, complex, and at times subtle delineation of Sebastian's alcoholism, especially of its spiritual aspects.[26]

THREE

The Iceman Cometh and the Anatomy of Alcoholism

I t would be difficult to imagine a work of literature more thoroughly steeped in alcohol than Eugene O'Neill's drama *The Iceman Cometh*; virtually every character in the large cast is or appears to be a confirmed drunkard. The central character of the play, however—Theodore Hickman, known simply and affectionately as Hickey to his drinking companions at Harry Hope's skid-row saloon—throws his friends into confusion when he shows up sober instead of drunk for what has customarily been his binge in celebration of Harry's birthday. The fact that Hickey was a periodic drunk who never mixed alcohol with work and who went on a spree only twice a year would not have raised doubts about the reality of his alcoholism for O'Neill, who was himself a periodic alcoholic until, at age thirty-seven, he began an almost totally successful lifelong abstinence.[1] Although Hickey's alcoholism may be surpassed in dramatic interest by his underlying psychological problems revealed late in the play, for a large portion of the performance most viewers will be curious about the remarkable change in Hickey from inebriation to sobriety. He claims to have achieved much more than abstinence; in claiming also the attainment of an unshakable peace or serenity, he seems to be implying that he has effected in himself a drastic reformation of character. As even most laymen know today, Alcoholics Anonymous has been far more successful than any other regimen or method in effecting sobriety. If, as we shall see, Hickey tends to deviate widely from some of the most fundamental principles and practices of AA, the viewer aware of these will have good reasons to doubt his assertions of a happy, peaceful sobriety long before his terrible self-disclosures discredit them. Furthermore, if Hickey's means of reaching this sobriety is unsound, he can scarcely fulfill his enthusiastic mission of conveying it to his old drinking friends at Hope's tavern.[2] In short, throughout the play the principles of AA provide excellent tools for examining Hickey's salesmanship in order to determine the quality of his new product or "line," sobriety.

Hickey observes some principles and practices similar to those of AA. Just after he arrives at Harry's, he promises the men that he will not deliver any "temperance bunk," recognizing the futility or offensiveness of such an approach (p. 79). He stresses the importance of becoming honest with oneself, a major tenet of AA (p. 81). At first he also seems eager to share his "experience, strength, and hope," a phrase expressing a chief AA method for the establishment and maintenance of sobriety.[3] Although we find out late in the play that, as Larry had suspected, Hickey was withholding essential information about himself, much of the time he appears to be sympathetically sharing his experience with Harry's friends and noticing the similarities of their problems to his own: "I know exactly what you're up against, boys. I know how damned yellow a man can be when it comes to making himself face the truth. I've been through the mill. . . . I know you become such a coward you'll grab at any lousy excuse to get out of killing your pipe dreams" (p. 189). Like AA also, Hickey understands that his own alcoholic drinking and that of the others is only a symptom; once they eradicate the cause, which he assumes to be pipe dreams that torment them with guilt for not acting on them, the symptom should disappear (p. 81).[4] Even more impressive than his sharing and knowledge, by the time of his appearance in the play Hickey seems to have reached a major goal of AA, the acquisition of serenity and inner peace. He emphasizes this accomplishment most insistently (p. 79 et passim).[5]

Hickey's practices, ideas, and achievements, closely as some of them may seem to resemble some of AA's, are inauthentic. In fact, one enlightening way to characterize Hickey is to see his actions as a parody or travesty of genuine adherence to AA principles and procedures. For example, he doubtless succeeds, in a verbal sense, in avoiding "temperance bunk," but his efforts to reform the denizens of Hope's saloon by persuading them to surrender their pipe dreams are so zealously obsessive that Harry quite reasonably likens Hickey to "a bughouse preacher escaped from an asylum" (p. 244). This is one of the least of Hickey's failures. Not only is his sharing of "experience, strength, and hope" extremely incomplete until late in the play; it is prompted by reasons about which Hickey is apparently unconscious and which are much less praiseworthy than the motive of helping others to achieve sobriety. As his impatience with their intractability grows, his proselytizing fervor recedes and is diluted by cynicism. He refers to his efforts as "selling my line of salvation" and compares them to the times when he would trick some "dame, who was sicking the dog on me," into believing that "her house wouldn't be properly furnished unless she bought another wash boiler" (p. 147). There is something more reprehensible at work here than Harry's "bughouse preacher," for Hickey derives pleasure from the attempt to wield power over his former drinking companions. Instead of bidding them to turn their drinking problem over to God, as one AA principle would have them do,[6] Hickey plays God himself. Even as he reveals that his efforts to change them are a species of salesman's con, he expects them to entrust themselves to his care and guidance.

In general, then, Hickey makes a mockery of the AA program. He claims to have achieved a degree of mental and emotional tranquility that AA thinks possible only after action and much deliberation on twelve extremely demanding principles.[7] In fact, AA holds that work on most of these must be lifelong and that complete mastery is impossible, just as it holds that the serenity Hickey regards as permanent can be enjoyed only at intervals (*12 & 12*, p. 75). Progress, not perfection, is the modest but realistic hope that AA extends to those who follow its program (*AA*, p. 60). Hickey, in contrast, would have his friends believe that he has gained almost instant perfection. By persistently failing to explain how he has achieved his serene sobriety, Hickey implies that it took only will power to vanquish his pipe dreams. AA, though, contends that will power usually plays havoc with alcoholics and tries to supplant it with other sorts of strength. Hickey's exertion of will, then, is a striking instance of the "easier, softer way" or shortcut that AA specifically warns against as a snare for anyone seeking reliable sobriety (*AA*, p. 58). When Hickey attempts to impose his will on the others and to convince them that they must submit to his notions, he resembles the actor who wants to manage or direct everyone with whom he comes in contact on the stage of life; when they refuse to behave exactly as he wishes, the actor's subsequent conduct and emotions accurately mirror Hickey's: "He decides to exert himself more. . . . Still the play does not suit him. Admitting he may be somewhat at fault, he is sure that other people are more to blame. He becomes angry, indignant, self-pitying" (*AA*, p. 61).

Hickey's most fundamental problem is a lack of self-acceptance. In his important study of alcoholism, Vernon Johnson sees the biblical Prodigal Son as the paradigm or prototype of the alcoholic, especially in his intense feelings of self-abasement or self-loathing.[8] Johnson also notes that this is one of the most difficult but necessary hurdles the alcoholic must surmount in his pursuit of a lasting and contented sobriety. Hickey never surmounts it. Although he acknowledges his alcoholism and thus takes a step toward self-acceptance, further progress is halted by the obsessive cycle of guilt and self-hatred turned to murderous anger against his wife.

Because of his compulsiveness, Hickey is particularly unable to achieve honesty about himself. AA practically guarantees sobriety to anyone willing to work hard at its principles—except for those who are "constitutionally incapable of being honest with themselves" (*AA*, p. 58). Although "constitutionally" might pose questions of interpretation in some contexts, Hickey is so crippled psychologically that he falls in this group. His disability prevents him from practicing anything like the vitally important Steps 4 and 5 of AA: making a searching and fearless moral self-evaluation, and admitting the faults uncovered to God, oneself, and at least one other person. Although Hickey appears to work out both these steps by telling the story of his life to the habitués of Hope's barroom, in reality the results are only a grotesque travesty. The elaborate network of projection, denial, self-justification, and self-deception woven by most alcoholics and destroyed by Steps 4 and 5 of AA is, in Hickey's case, left largely intact. Though it is frayed around the edges by his reiterations of guilt and self-hatred, he quickly repairs its only major hole when he confesses the words of hatred he uttered over Evelyn, declaring that he must have been insane at that moment. Furthermore, even if Hickey's story exhibits some honesty, he tells it reluctantly and involuntarily, only when other methods of winning the habitués to his views have apparently failed. Being only grudgingly and peripherally honest, Hickey achieves none of the benefits usually derived from real work on Steps 4 and 5. Hickey's self-assessment is not fearless but full of fear, for he knows that it must lead to the disclosure of his murder of Evelyn. Instead of bringing relief from guilt, remorse, and similarly oppressive emotions, as the two steps are designed to do, Hickey's travesty of them revives and aggravates these feelings.

The most basic flaw of Hickey's Step 4 is that instead of increasing or deepening his honesty, it actually increases his dishonesty. As he reviews his marriage and his continued bouts of drinking and whoring, Hickey projects more and more of his self-hatred onto Evelyn, until finally he blames her for his behavior and even suspects her of deliberately augmenting it by her repeated forgiveness (p. 239). This massive displacement of responsibility exactly reverses the direction of an honest fourth step, which would be inward; its concentration on the self should overcome all resentments and, even in situations not altogether one's fault, should "disregard the other person involved entirely" (AA, p. 67). From his disingenuous fifth step, in addition, Hickey receives none of the advantages specified in AA literature: transcending alienation or isolation; achieving a sense of being forgiven and a concomitant ability to forgive; and gaining humility, defined as "a clear recognition of what and who we really are" (12 & 12, pp. 58–59).

Hickey fails to bring about any desirable change in himself; his one resounding, if short lived, success is in transmitting his kind of peace to his friends at Harry's. But this is scarcely the attractive peace he imagines it to be, "a healing tranquillity" and "a resting place" referred to in an AA description of the results of the fifth step (12 & 12, p. 63). Rather, judging from one of Hickey's descriptions quite early in the play, it sounds more like a permanent rest or the lethal peace he bestowed on Evelyn in his travesty of the "amends steps," eight and nine, of AA. (On pp. 226–27 he speaks of his murder as "the one possible way to make up" for all his wrongs to her.) Freed of their pipe dreams, Hickey assures the others at Hope's, "You can let go of yourself at last. Let yourself sink down to the bottom of the sea. Rest in peace. There's no farther you have to go." Alternatively but no less ominously, especially if we know the story of the morphine addiction of O'Neill's mother and her counterpart, Mary Tyrone in Long Day's Journey into Night, Hickey also compares the effect of this new peace to a powerful drug dosage, "like when you're sick and suffering like hell and the Doc gives you a shot in the arm, and the pain goes, and you drift off" (pp. 85–86). But most often his metaphors intimate death. When they kill tomorrow, Hickey informs his friends,

"You've finally got the game of life licked" (p. 225). Until his salesman's spell over them is broken by his pleas of insanity, his friends do suffer a kind of death; though desperately trying to get drunk in order to escape Hickey's goading, they find, as Harry repeatedly puts it, that the "booze" has lost its "kick" or "life" (pp. 202–3). The implication of the AA concept of peace or serenity is that of a pause before renewed effort and activity. The result of Hickey's peace is a deathlike trance, severing his friends from him and one another, whereas for those who work hard at practicing AA principles, the promised result is a vital brotherhood of love and caring (*AA*, pp. 152–53).

Perhaps the broadest promise in a group of statements sometimes collectively designated as the AA promises is that "our whole attitude and outlook upon life will change" (*AA*, p. 84) for the better. Hickey's most significant changes are disastrous: he moves from a viable though tormented way of living to a desperate and untenable solution to his problems, from accepting responsibility for his faults to heaping much of it on Evelyn, from human anguish or suffering to the calm of death. Whether by AA standards or by those of common-sense observation, one of Hickey's most appalling failures is his misjudgment in trying to force his ideas on people who are plainly unreceptive to change.[9] His persistence might seem completely incomprehensible were it not for the fact that much more is at stake than helping the others or impressing them with his new strength. Through their conversion he seeks vindication not only of the soundness of his ideas but also of his sanity, justification and even forgiveness for the murderous length to which he went to achieve peace.[10] Even so, it remains somewhat puzzling that Hickey could have fallen into such palpable error without assuming that he is more thoroughly insane or blind to reality than he appears to be; in detecting the faults or foibles of others, he proves time and again to be remarkably shrewd. Yet he misses the essential and unbridgeable difference between himself and the derelicts at Harry's. Whereas he is so intolerably tortured by the unrealizable pipe dream of sobriety that he must finally annihilate its source, the derelicts are content with themselves, their pipe dreams, and the alcohol that helps them to postpone attempts to fulfill these dreams and to anesthetize any sense of moral or social responsibility. Their dreams are so anachronistic that efforts to fulfill them would amount to insanity: although he has not left his saloon for twenty years, Harry thinks that hundreds of people in the neighborhood would still remember him affectionately; Jimmy Tomorrow, one of Hope's denizens, thinks he can retrieve from a laundry the clothes that he evidently left there years before, when he hit the skids (pp. 51–52). Men so addled cannot take kindly to any disruptive idea, such as Hickey's assertion that Harry really hated his deceased wife for making him "have ambition and go out and do things, when all you wanted was to get drunk in peace" (p. 195). This is doubtless true, and it has the intended effect of driving Harry to such fury that he leaves his saloon for that almost interminably delayed walk around his neighborhood. Hickey supposes that its abortive failure will have the further effect of exploding Harry's pipe dream and reconciling him to reality, whereas it brings him only an empty, ghostly peace, similar to the results of the other derelicts' attempts to act. But left to his pipe dream and alcohol, Harry, like the others, has no trouble avoiding change or transforming reality: his fading memories of his wife are for the most part comfortably sentimental.

Harry and his friends, then, feel nothing like the agonized guilt and self-loathing that Hickey expresses with increasing frequency and that have impelled him to act. This basic difference suggests that these characters are drunks rather than alcoholics. Although the irrational behavior of both types of drinkers will usually appear identical, Vernon Johnson observes that, beneath the surface, the alcoholic is deeply troubled by the growing discrepancy between his drunken conduct and the values or standards to which he still maintains an allegiance. Eventually, Johnson says, although the drinker's awareness may have been dimmed for many years by alcohol, a crisis or a series of crises in his life may restore his sense of this discrepancy and actuate a strong commitment to quit drinking. Johnson's most fascinating example is an alcoholic physician whose turning point and reformation came when his wife confronted him with the fact that a seriously ill patient died because he, the physician, was passed out at home. In contrast, Johnson characterizes drunks as psychopaths or "sociopaths [who] appear to lack the values or conscience essential to the conflict we observe in alcoholics. They *actually* feel no guilt or shame."[11]

If "psychopath" or "sociopath" seems rather harsh language for Harry and his friends, on reflection one begins to see its relevance.

The pipe dreams entertained by all the habitués of Harry's are an innocuous form of psychopathology, for, until compelled by Hickey, these characters have no intention of acting; nor do they feel much guilt or shame because of their failure. Because they comprise a small society that functions quite amiably until Hickey's intrusion, their sociopathy seems less evident. In a larger perspective, however, these are almost all either highly unstable or marginal people, disreputable if not positively hostile to or potentially destructive of society: two pimps, three prostitutes, a former circus con man (Mosher), a former New York policeman expelled from the force for graft (McGloin), the mentally unbalanced son of a corrupt father (Willie), a former ward heeler (Harry), an embezzling gambler and a coward on opposing sides in the Boer War (Lewis and Wetjoen), a former anarchist with an ill-concealed contempt for the masses (Hugo), and a former proprietor of a gambling house (Joe). The "former" attaching to most names indicates that they have abandoned even their shady occupations. They could scarcely suffer from the alcoholic's conflict between behavior and values, for gambling, collecting graft, and like pursuits cannot be said to display values in any generally accepted sense.

Perhaps one reason why they are satisfied to remain drunk is that they are just enough influenced by society to recognize that their old activities were corrupt or worthless and therefore warrant no struggle for recovery. For their own sake, moreover, and that of the society surrounding them, it is just as well that heavy use of alcohol combines with their pipe dreams to keep them in good humor by obscuring or hiding ugly truths. While temporarily deprived of intoxication and of the pipe dreams it nourishes, some of them nearly erupt in pathological violence. Rocky, reaching for a gun in a quarrel with Chuck, unites with him instead in turning against the "doity nigger," Joe. Joe, "snarling with rage" at this epithet, goes after them with a knife; bloodshed is averted only by the derisive laughter of Larry. A bit earlier, Wetjoen and Lewis have had a scuffle just offstage, which almost breaks out a second time (pp. 130, 167–68, 177). There are also near fights between Cora and Pearl and between Mosher and McGloin (pp. 100, 134).

If, then, by Vernon Johnson's distinction almost all of the characters in *The Iceman Cometh* are drunks, who are the alcoholics in the play? There can be only two, Hickey and Larry; but for different reasons this designation must be tentative for each.

Hickey's intense guilt and revulsion with himself plainly imply his awareness of failure to meet some standard. The source is Evelyn and their love. Attempting to overcome his fecklessness and to fulfill his love for Evelyn, he finally murders her because he realizes that he cannot purge his flaws. But in making the attempt he at least seems to demonstrate his alcoholism, not being able, like the drunkard Jimmy Tomorrow, to regard his love with indifference. Bleakly candid, Jimmy confesses that drunkenness always had such paramount importance for him that he now cannot even recall why he married (pp. 229–30). For Hickey, the alcoholic in conflict, whoring and sprees are followed by agonies of remorse at having betrayed his love.

The major question about Hickey is whether his self has sufficient identity or coherence to be described as alcoholic. According to AA, the primary step toward ending alcoholic drinking occurs when the drinker accepts that he is an alcoholic. Hickey's personality is so badly divided that this unitary designation may not be feasible.[12] In Freudian terms, Hickey seems to consist of an id locked in recurring tension or struggle with a superego, represented by Evelyn and her values, that is never satisfactorily assimilated or internalized; Hickey's ego is radically polarized by the warfare between these two forces. Freud has a description of conflict in some types of obsessional neurosis that fits quite exactly the psychological condition of Hickey: "the ego defends itself vainly, alike against the instigations of the murderous id and against the reproaches of the punishing conscience. It succeeds in holding in check at least the most brutal actions of both sides; the first outcome is interminable self-torment, and eventually there follows a systematic torturing of the object, in so far as it is within reach." If by "object" we may understand Evelyn, whose forgiveness Hickey comes to conceive of as punishment, we see how his torment becomes so excruciating that he seeks relief in causing Evelyn to suffer and ultimately ceases to restrain his "murderous id."[13]

The roots of Hickey's id are his strong and apparently innate attraction to the low life of the small town where he was born: to the beer drinking in its pool halls, to its whorehouse, and to the madame, Mollie Arlington, whose bantering cynicism, deriving from the view that the world consists of a multitude of fools waiting to be duped and sold a bill of goods, reflects and confirms Hickey's own (pp. 232–33). Hickey's account of his early life, however, poses a couple of puzzles: why he is not entirely at ease with his cynical outlook, and why he is attracted to Evelyn. To the extent that Evelyn represents Hickey's superego, she would seem to reinforce values that Hickey had already absorbed from one or both parents. But Hickey does not refer at all to his mother, and toward his preacher father he seems as harshly cynical as he is toward the rest of the world and, at times, toward himself, considering his father's talents to have been merely a variety of sales pitch.

Hickey, then, appears to be utterly devoid of principles or values when he meets Evelyn. Yet beyond his camaraderie with the town whores and the hangers-on at the pool halls (forerunners of the denizens of Harry Hope's saloon), we see, though without quite knowing why, that Hickey was not only dissatisfied with this life but even self-hating because of it. Hickey seized upon Evelyn to rescue him from the innate preferences for which he despises himself, perhaps because of unadmitted guilt engendered by his rejection of his father, and to supply a worthier motive in his life than triumphs over an endless stream of gullible sales prospects.

The marriage ultimately fails. Psychologically speaking, the major elements of Hickey's personality, the id and superego, failed to cohere in a single, relatively stable whole. With his urge to shed the fetters of responsibility through drinking and his tendency to see the world with the eyes of men like the onetime circus grifter Ed Mosher, Hickey has much in common with the sociopaths at Harry's. Unlike them, however, he has a powerful superego or conscience. If Harry's companions have occasional twinges of self-hate, they can dull or obliterate them by alcohol. Such a solution is only temporary for Hickey: driven by the opposed forces of his id and superego, his motives are further complicated by alternating and irreconcilable attitudes of love and hate, attraction and repulsion toward his superego. The tension from the polarity of these emotions is too great for Hickey to tolerate indefinitely; hatred finally gains the upper hand and leads him to kill the superego's source, Evelyn. Putting the matter another way, Hickey's self-hatred, growing like a malignancy from his years of failure to arrest it or remove its causes, at last becomes so unbearably painful that he must project it onto another person: his wife, who exacerbated his awareness of failure by repeatedly forgiving his faults.[14]

One can suppose that if Hickey's personality had been better integrated, he might finally have stopped his drinking by making a renewed and determined commitment to the responsibilities and values represented by his love for Evelyn and their marriage. As it is, however, one may regard Hickey as an anomaly, half a drunk and half an alcoholic. His id, with drunkenness as one of its gratifications, also uses this as a chief weapon in its intermittent but inveterate defiance of the superego, which might be thought of as the potentially redeemable alcoholic in Hickey and its chief support, Evelyn. The repeated enactments of defiance or rebellion carry Hickey away from, rather than toward, self-acceptance: given his native cynicism, they feed his contempt for the part of his self that possesses values, for time and again it demonstrates its ineffectuality in exerting control. When it and Evelyn are conquered by the id, one might imagine that Hickey could slide into the untroubled drinking of his friends at Harry's. But extinguishing a part of the self, or total repression, never succeeds; and so Hickey's superego, now twisted by hate, seems to resurface as an ostensible desire to save his friends from themselves, taking the form of his father's preaching that Hickey thought he had long ago rejected with contempt.[15] Because his id and superego had been nearly balanced in strength, and because the tension of this balance provided a functional dynamic that compensated in part for his lack of integration, Hickey's conquest really spells his defeat, the dissolution of a personality precariously held together only so long as its tensions were unresolved. The overthrow of Hickey's superego, and with it the alcoholic self, brings not the ascendancy of the drunken id but the end of a workable self. As Hickey's ideas of peace have insistently suggested, all of his words and actions in the play are merely the final twitches or spasms before a rigor mortis of self sets in.[16]

Larry Slade is an alcoholic who would rather be a drunk, released from his love for Parritt's mother and his residual loyalty to the "Movement" of which she was a leader, indifferent to all values or moral codes, convinced of the delusiveness of truth and of the desirability of pipe dreams. But he is unable to achieve this escape from values. Judging by the amount of liquor he consumes or its effect on him, Larry seems not much of a drunk or an alcoholic; although he is described early in the play as having a "half-drunken mockery in his eyes" (p. 9), he is the only character besides Hickey and Parritt whose faculties or moods never seem significantly altered by his drinking. His alcoholism is to be measured not by glasses or bottles drained, but by the degradation of his life in an attempt to break with the reality of old ties and values. His escape, like Hickey's, engenders substantial self-hatred, as evidenced when Larry refers to his cowardly clinging to life, to his "dirty, stinking bit of withered old flesh," "with a sneering, vindictive self-loathing" (p. 197). Both men are adept at clothing their self-hatred in cynicism, Larry articulately debunking ideals in general, Hickey manifesting contempt for the suckers who buy his sales pitch. As the play ends, both seem to be looking forward to death.

But such similarities should not be allowed to conceal the fundamental differences between Hickey and Larry. Despite his apparently genuine if rather shallow affection for Hope and his friends, for example, Hickey's cynicism and contempt are more pervasive than Larry's. Finally even Hickey's efforts to help the others evince his hatred, the quality of his peace being death: he hates them as he hates himself, for they are reminders of his condition when, as he says disgustedly, he used to return to Evelyn after a binge looking like "something they threw out of the D.T. ward in Bellevue along with the garbage" (p. 237). Larry's attitudes are primarily three: a sweeping cynicism or nihilism, pity or compassion for suffering, and anger with himself for this pity. Pity is probably the strongest of his feelings. It is not only that Larry is less tortured than Hickey and thus can refrain from involving others in his self-hatred or inner conflicts. Being inherently more compassionate, he would spare the others pointless suffering and protect their only happiness. All of the inhabitants of Harry's recognize Larry's benevolence, but Jimmy Tomorrow expresses it most concisely: "You pretend a bitter, cynic philosophy, but in your heart you are the kindest man among us" (p. 44).

Jimmy's version of Larry is, however, sentimentalized and only partly accurate. Larry's cynicism is more than a pose beneath which beats a heart of gold; his struggle between compassion and cynical indifference is real and dramatic. Parritt provides the most severe test of Larry's allegiances. Because the younger man is signally unappealing and possesses virtually no redeeming features, having evidently betrayed both the woman (his own mother) and the "Movement" Larry has loved, and being personally dishonest, wheedling, and cowardly, he seems designed to afford Larry every opportunity to practice dismissive callousness. Larry appears to succeed in maintaining this attitude until, with the departure of Hickey, Parritt at last prevails on Larry to mete out the death sentence he had been longing for. A few minutes later, Parritt commits suicide. Unlike the vacancy, the pure negation, of the peace that Hickey would impose on Hope's friends, Parritt's death is a redemption, the only way he can remove from himself an intolerable load of guilt and dishonor. Larry's sentence may be an example of what is sometimes referred to in AA circles as "tough love."

By enabling Parritt to take certain steps similar to AA principles in order to heal his psyche and find peace, it is as if Larry himself is practicing certain AA principles in an abbreviated fashion. As a result, he experiences important change. Committing suicide, Parritt in effect takes AA's Steps 8 and 9, making amends to the mother he has betrayed even though he cannot effect her release from prison. In his protracted and sporadic exchanges with Larry, tracing a faltering course (with Hickey's unwitting help) from dishonesty to truth, Parritt makes the kind of searching self-evaluation demanded by Steps 4 and 5 of AA. Larry also may be said to undertake a searching and honest self-evaluation, although without the subsequent happiness promised by AA.

To appreciate Larry's changes, one must glance at several of his attitudes in the early and middle sections of the play. In one of his first speeches, he ridicules truth as "irrelevant and immaterial" to life, stating his preference for "the lie of a pipe dream" (pp. 9–10). Though he denies it at this point, one of his own pipe dreams is that death is a comfortable sleep that he will welcome. Beleaguered by Parritt's importunities for help, Larry at about the midpoint of the play reaches his nadir of cynicism and self-deception: "Honor or dishonor, faith or treachery are nothing to me but the opposites of the same stupidity which is ruler and king of life, and in the end they rot into dust in the same grave. All things are the same meaningless joke to me" (p. 128). This nihilistic vision, meant to rebuff Parritt, also represents an extreme in Larry's refusal to examine himself as the source of such views.

Goaded by Hickey, Larry later achieves a disconcerting discovery about himself: rather than looking forward to death, he is actually afraid of it (pp. 196–97). When he sanctions Parritt's suicide, Larry takes another major step in his moral "inventory," to use AA's term, for he belies his professed indifference to values by acknowledging, however reluctantly, the truth of honor and moral responsibility.[17] In Parritt's death Larry finds a way to resolve some highly disturbing and seemingly irreconcilable feelings: to signify his lingering affection for Parritt's mother and the "Movement" and to take revenge on Parritt as the betrayer of both, yet to indicate his pity for Parritt by enabling him to find the only morally satisfying solution to his anguish. The temporary nature of this resolution for Larry must be emphasized, for he also realizes, to his dismay, that he is condemned to see "the two sides of everything." Just as he has seen Parritt with both love and hate, both as detested turncoat and suffering, pitiable human being, so he has viewed the "Movement" and Parritt's mother, swinging between sardonic cynicism and compassion or pity. The antinomies or dualities of his vision are ultimately irreconcilable. Yet Larry, who berates himself as a "weak fool" (p. 258) for being thus divided, is stronger than Hickey, who, unable to bear the tension of his love and hate for Evelyn, simplified his feelings to a murderous hatred.

Finally, as he nears completion of his inventory, Larry recognizes that fear or cowardice—"Life is too much for me!" (p. 258)—is his worst fault.[18] He must know that Parritt coerced him into an involvement in life that will not continue. Perhaps the shame of this realization transforms Larry's desire for death from a philosophical pose to a genuine longing. Though he seems unaware of it, there is one important sign of Larry's headway against fear. As the play ends, he is the only one not joining in the general intoxication. In reply to the query of a woman who once asked why men sometimes lower themselves to the level of beasts by drinking, Samuel Johnson is reported to have said that "he who makes a *beast* of himself, gets rid of the pain of being a *man*."[19] Larry, it seems, will no longer seek the refuge of drink to escape the pain of a self with irreconcilable dualities of vision.

Hickey and Larry are powerfully moving characters because O'Neill invested important elements of himself in both of them. If Hickey may represent something like the person that O'Neill feared he would become if he continued his periodic drunkenness, with his arrest of it there emerged an O'Neill more like Larry: bleakly unillusioned, wanting for years to die, yet renouncing alcohol as a relief from his awareness of the painful antinomies of self and existence.[20]

F O U R

Drinking and Society in the Fiction of John Cheever

John Cheever may be the American writer who shows the most thorough and diversified familiarity with drinking in modern American society.[1] At times the familiarity relaxes into comedy. As Cheever sketches the suburban milieu for his novel *Bullet Park*, he introduces the reader to the Wickwires, at first glance an unexceptionally attractive couple but for the arresting fact that "they were always falling downstairs, bumping into sharp-edged furniture and driving their cars into ditches." Their vulnerability to accident is sufficiently explained by an intimate look at the detritus of their Monday mornings. Mr. Wickwire, badly hung over, utters a

> cry of pain when he sees the empties on the shelf by the sink. They are ranged there like the gods in some pantheon of remorse. Their intent seems to be to force him to his knees and to wring from him some prayer. "Empties, oh empties, most merciful empties have mercy upon me for the sake of Jack Daniels and Seagram Distillers." Their immutable emptiness gives them a look that is cruel and censorious. Their labels—scotch, gin and bourbon—have the ferocity of Chinese demons, but he definitely has the feeling that if he tried to placate them with a genuflection they would be merciless. He drops them into a wastebasket, but this does not dispose of their force.[2]

It is doubtful that a reader can be disturbed by the drinking problem of a man who is so wry and witty about his condition. It is even more doubtful that one would prefer the condition of a doctor, portrayed later in the same novel, who has recently joined Alcoholics Anonymous. In a trenchant parody, Cheever reveals what appears to be first-hand knowledge of two of the least attractive features of some

AA parlance: its confessional banalities and the logorrhea of its evangelicalism (pp. 47–48). Not only the Wickwires' life but even a Rabelaisian abandon to drink would be more fun, at least if one may judge the latter spirit from a scene enacted in another novel by Moses Wapshot and Mrs. Wilston in a room at the Viaduct House, St. Botolphs's hotel. Both are far gone in drink. Moses, attempting to carry his rather too generously proportioned inamorata to bed, "weaved to the right, recouped his balance and weaved to the right again. Then he was going; he was going; he was gone. Thump. The whole Viaduct House reverberated to the crash and then there was an awful stillness. He lay athwart her, his cheek against the carpet. . . . She, still lying in a heap, was the first to speak. She spoke without anger or impatience. She smiled. 'Let's have another drink,' she said."[3]

Although Cheever is capable of using alcohol for nothing more significant than comic shock, as when a character urinates into a sherry decanter and the rector arrives "and sipped piss," or for spinning a kind of grotesque tall tale, as when a woman turns to drunken promiscuity and then commits suicide because her appliances repeatedly break down and she has difficulty getting them repaired,[4] he characteristically goes beyond these relatively easy achievements. Perhaps one reason for his parody of Alcoholics Anonymous in *Bullet Park* is his desire, conveyed in "A Miscellany of Characters That Will Not Appear," to avoid such clichés as "the alcoholic." The section of this story that deals with the stereotype is in fact an effective satire on it ("X" has a ridiculously exaggerated attack of the shakes, for example) and on its potential for sentimental exploitation. X, having been offered a fresh start in Cleveland, is returning home from a trip there. His family, meeting him at the station, is a model of propriety, support, and affection: "His pretty wife, his three children, and the two dogs have all come down to welcome Daddy." Daddy practically flows off the train. Cheever briskly aborts both the scene and the section at this point. It is perhaps not so much that Cheever objects to sentimentality (he himself is guilty of it on occasion—for instance, in the death of the boy in "An Educated American Woman") as that he objects to the simplicity that enables it. The drunk or alcoholic as such, stripped of every other trait, is neither interesting nor instructive in "the way we live."[5]

When Cheever resorts to stereotyped drinkers, it is usually for some extremely short vignette or some transitory effect. The bibulous Irish maid Nora Quinn, in "The Day the Pig Fell into the Well," briefly parallels the action of the title by tumbling down a flight of stairs (p. 226). But "The Sorrows of Gin," centering in part on another Irish servant, Rosemary, is complicated by irony and by shifting, largely unreliable perspectives on drinking. We see many of the events and persons through the eyes of a fourth-grade girl, Amy Lawton, who, after looking in on her parents' cocktail party near the beginning of the story, listens at length to their new cook, Rosemary. Unlike her fellow servant and sister, who was repeatedly dismissed from positions for drinking and who died in Bellevue Hospital, Rosemary implicitly eschews alcohol and professes to find her strength in the Bible. About the drinking of Amy's parents she is contradictory: after calling it "all sociable," she counsels Amy quite vehemently to empty her father's "gin bottle into the sink now and then—the filthy stuff!" (pp. 199, 201). One irony is that this seemingly respectable domestic, on her first day off, returns from New York totally intoxicated, her coat "spotted with mud and ripped in the back." When Mr. Lawton reprimands her for drinking in front of Amy, Rosemary cries, "I'm lonely. . . . I'm lonely, and I'm afraid, and it's all I've got" (p. 202). Evidently the Bible has deserted her. She is discharged at once, and as a result of this object lesson in the ravages of alcohol, Amy pours one of her father's gin bottles down the sink. This act leads the very next day to the discharge of a second newly hired cook, Amy's father angrily assuming that she has drunk the gin and meanwhile inveighing against various other servants who have consumed his liquor. Just as he reduces these people to stereotypes, so, in another irony, his daughter reduces him to the level of Rosemary and pours out still more of his gin. This loss produces a third perspective on the father's drinking, one that seems to bear some resemblance to Amy's and Rosemary's. Having discovered another empty bottle, Mr. Lawton accuses the babysitter, Mrs. Henlein, a member of the suburb's decayed gentility. Her reaction is not only to denounce him as drunk but also to telephone the police with the same disclosure, vociferously urging them to arrest him (p. 207).

Partly because of the unreliable perspectives, the realities of the Lawtons' drinking are not easy to determine. If the advice of Rosemary and the hysteria of Mrs. Henlein are obviously based on exaggeration, there appears to be an element of truth in their—and

Amy's—view of the parents. But even Amy's view is not consistent: when not aroused by fears traceable to Rosemary, she seems able to achieve a degree of objectivity. Although Amy detects several changes that alcohol works in her father, most notably a happier mood, she firmly denies to herself any similarity between him and the drunks she has heard about, people who hang on lampposts or fall down. But then she recalls occasions when her father missed a doorway by a foot and once when a cocktail guest, Mrs. Farquarson, missed a chair she went to sit in. Amy concludes that the main difference between clownish drunks and her parents and their friends is that "they were never indecorous" (p. 205). When the other guests and Amy's parents pretend that Mrs. Farquarson did not miss her chair, they imply, for the reader if not for Amy, that such excess is not approved. As if to dispel any lingering possibility that Rosemary or Mrs. Henlein may be right about the Lawtons' drinking, Amy's father, in the final section of the story, awakes "cheered by the swelling light in the sky . . . refreshed by his sleep" and hoping to find some way to teach his daughter, who had tried to run away, "that home sweet home was the best place of all" (pp. 208–9). On these notes, vaguely suggesting that the Lawtons have no serious drinking problem—but perhaps also hinting at paternal repentance and reform—the story closes.

As my concluding remarks on "The Sorrows of Gin" may indicate, Cheever's primary interest in drinking is societal: not so much in enlarging our understanding of alcoholism or in exploring its influence on individuals as in seeing its manifold effects, potential or actual, in marriages, families, or society. This focus is not surprising; it would be hard to think of a modern American writer more concerned with society and less concerned with the introspections of the romantic ego.[6] In a number of Cheever's stories, drinking may be seen in one of three ways, though sometimes in a variety of combinations and permutations: (1) when practiced outside a recognized social form or to excess, drinking usually signals some kind of societal trouble; (2) drinking is occasionally used as a token or an affirmation of a social or familial bond; (3) occasionally, abstemiousness or abstinence is viewed just as dimly as excess, and for much the same reasons—its actual or potential harm either to the abstinent person or to his society. As illustrations of one or more of these approaches to drinking, three stories—"Reunion," "Goodbye, My Brother," and "The Swimmer"—seem the most remarkable for their intensity, their skill, or their complexity. Even more notable, perhaps, because of its transcendence of these approaches and their limitations, is "The Scarlet Moving Van." Finally, in three of Cheever's later stories we shall consider the evidence that Cheever becomes skeptical of society as a satisfactory norm by which to measure and criticize deviation. Instead, these stories suggest, it may be that society is deviant and that heavy drinking, drug abuse, or other forms of behavior traditionally reprehended as deviant are potentially redemptive.

Of the three views of drinking enumerated above, the first is the most common in Cheever's stories. Even extremely brief examples may be memorable and poignant. As the lonely narrator of "The Angel of the Bridge" gazes from his Los Angeles hotel window in the early morning hours, at the entrance of a restaurant across the street there emerges "a drunken woman in a sable cape being led out to a car. She twice nearly fell" (p. 494). Like the images of Blake's "London," this little scene seems only the visible tip of some larger derangement. For what other reason would a woman of means whose companion or husband shows her "solicitude" drink herself into this condition? No explicit answer is provided, but that her condition is either a symptom or a representative cause of social malaise is suggested by another brief scene immediately following, in which the occupants of two cars stopped for a traffic light get out, assault one another brutally, then drive off (p. 494). Both scenes indicate, whether as cause or effect, a rupture or absence of the social bond. Though escorted, the woman is so isolated by her condition that seeing her can only deepen the narrator's sense of loneliness.

Infidelity, adultery, seduction, or promiscuity is often seen by Cheever as either abetted by or associated with drinking. In "The Five-Forty-Eight," Blake, a married man who is one of the most repugnant characters in Cheever's fiction, makes his move to seduce a newly hired secretary—an accomplishment that proves easy because he takes unconscionable advantage of her gratitude for his hiring her when other prospective employers, learning of her history of mental troubles, would not—by proposing a drink after they have both worked late one night. In "Brimmer," the title character, whose name of course denotes drinking, is portrayed as a master seducer, satyrlike even in appearance, whose natural ally is drink; he is sometimes glassy-eyed and "almost always had a glass in his hand" (p. 386). Although Brimmer arouses a little sympathy when he is later reported to be dying, for the most part the narrator regards his behavior with distaste as a potential source of "carnal anarchy," especially when Brimmer shows no hesitation about seducing a woman he knows to be married (p. 388). Georgie, the mostly docile and inarticulate husband of "An Educated American Woman," is finally made so unhappy by an increasing awareness of his empty marriage that his wife is awakened one night when he falls, noisily and drunkenly, in their bathroom (p. 530). Shortly thereafter, more from loneliness than from sexual ardor, Georgie has an affair; as is usual with adultery in Cheever, it is facilitated by drinking (p. 531). Mrs. Flannagan, the adulteress of "The Brigadier and the Golf Widow," enters an affair with Mr. Pastern for another reason; as he learns to his dismay, it is not love but a key to his bomb shelter that she is after (p. 504). Again, drinking seems an essential component in initiating the adultery (pp. 500–501). In "Artemis, the Honest Well Digger," the title character, a canny rustic, discovers that the lust and drinking that excite him in the woman he loves, Maria Petroni, are united with flagrant promiscuity. When she declines his proposal of marriage and he asks whether she wants a younger man, she replies, "Yes, darling, but not one. I want seven, one right after the other. . . . I've done it. This was before I met you. I asked seven of the best-looking men around to come for dinner. . . . I cooked veal scaloppine. There was a lot to drink and then we all got undressed. . . . When they were finished, I didn't feel dirty or depraved or shameful. I didn't feel anything bad at all." Although Artemis continues to see Maria for a while longer, that account "was about it" for their relationship (pp. 652–53).

It is, however, "Reunion"—a story of only two and a half pages, the shortest of the sixty-one in Cheever's collected stories—that has the greatest power as a depiction of the devastating effect of excessive drinking on human relations. There are several reasons for this power. One, no doubt, lies precisely in the extreme brevity and concentration; these contrast with a tendency in quite a few of Cheever's stories toward diffuse and multiple effects, authorial or essayistic reflection.[7] "Reunion" is perhaps the most fully dramatized of Cheever's stories. Except for the opening paragraph, which supplies information about the circumstances of the meeting of father and son, nearly everything is carried on by speech or action. Another source of its power may be that the situation it deals with—a boy's profound embarrassment by an inebriated father—draws on some indelibly mortifying experience of Cheever's own boyhood or youth. Judging from the surprising number of times that Cheever has incorporated versions of this experience in other works, though usually in just a few sentences or in short scenes, clearly he is fascinated with it almost to the point of obsession.[8] If these other stories afford only peripheral treatments of this experience, "Reunion," by giving it exclusive attention, also maximizes its force.

A further aspect of the story's artistry is Cheever's tact, what he leaves unsaid. The son, who is also the narrator, at no point refers directly to his discomfort or embarrassment; although our only evidence is his growing insistence that he must leave his father to catch a train, the tacit quality of his feelings renders them all the more affecting. For the most part the narrator-son is only an unobtrusive recorder and the focus is on the behavior of the father. Here too Cheever chooses to underplay: though vivid and loud, the father is by no means grossly obvious about his intoxication;[9] we know that he has been drinking (or that he is a habitual drinker) when he meets his son for lunch only by the observation that the father's smell "was a rich compound of whiskey, after-shave lotion, shoe polish, woolens, and the rankness of a mature male" (p. 518). We know that he is drunk only from one ludicrous slip as he orders drinks ("two Bibson Geefeaters") and from his anger with a waiter for smiling (p. 519). Probably the father's behavior is only a heightening or extension of his natural personality. For the son, however, this heightening is intolerable. Although he has been living with his divorced mother and has not seen his father for three years, he "was terribly happy to see him again" and to meet him for lunch in New York; he even wants a photograph to commemorate the occasion (p. 518). But when, at the end of the story, he says that he never saw his father again after this meeting, it is also clear that he never made another attempt. In a mere hour and a half, then, a father's intoxicated behavior ends his relationship with an affectionate son.

The father seems just as eager to demonstrate his love for his son as the son is to have it, but his expression of that love is abysmally misconceived. In slightly different circumstances, his rudeness to waiters in ordering drinks might display a refreshing audacity. The climax of the restaurant scene in the film Five Easy Pieces, in which

Jack Nicholson sweeps everything off the table and then leaves, evokes gasps of admiration from the audience. Nicholson's rudeness, however, is retaliatory; the waitress fully deserves it. The father's insolence, in contrast, is unprovoked, and, where Nicholson acts deliberately, the father appears simply compulsive. In this characteristic also lies a basic difference between the father and Gee-Gee, the hard drinker of "The Scarlet Moving Van." Not only are his insults less trivial; for the most part Gee-Gee seems to know what he is doing and to be calculatedly indifferent to the consequences. The father is not indifferent to the impression he is making on his son. After they are turned away from four restaurants, either by direct invitation to leave or by refusal of service, the father says to the boy, "I'm sorry, sonny. . . . I'm terribly sorry" (p. 520), though whether he refers to his behavior or their failure to have lunch, or both, is impossible to know. Yet the father then proceeds to treat a news vendor with exactly the abusiveness that he has inflicted on a series of waiters: "Kind sir, will you be good enough to favor me with one of your God-damned, no-good, ten-cent afternoon papers?" (p. 520). The most striking irony of the story is that a man enslaved to drunken compulsiveness seeks to impress his son with his mastery over people. Perhaps not by chance, he resembles the drinker, in one of the most searching parables from the so-called Big Book of Alcoholics Anonymous, who plays at being a kind of cosmic stage manager, with other people merely so many puppets to be manipulated in order to display his power (*AA*, pp. 60–61). We can respond with a sense of liberation to Gee-Gee's insults in part because his primary audience is one of adults and equals capable of shrugging him off like the waiters of "Reunion." But the primary if silent auditor of that story is the son; and if his father is as indifferent to the humanity of waiters as Gee-Gee is to that of his fellow suburbanites, we may surmise that, in driving his son away, the father has sentenced himself to a desolating and permanent loneliness.

"Reunion" focuses on the shock of embarrassment, only hinting at a pathos to follow. "The Seaside Houses," though more diffuse and less effective than "Reunion," develops its latent pathos. The narrator, knowing at first only the name, Greenwood, of the owners of a house he is renting for the summer, is saddened and disturbed by his discovery of several empty whiskey bottles around the house and grounds. Cheever, an alcoholic, must have been drawing from fears about his own drinking; his daughter has recorded that "long before I was even aware that he was alcoholic, there were bottles hidden all over the house, and even outside in the privet hedge and the garden shed."[10] The narrator learns from a neighbor that, although the Greenwoods had built a curved staircase for their daughter's wedding, she "was married in the Municipal Building eight months pregnant by a garage mechanic" (p. 487). Then, going to New York on business, the narrator by chance sees Mr. Greenwood in a bar, recognizing him from his photograph: "you could see by the way his hands shook that [his] flush was alcoholic" (p. 487). Cheever captures pathos partly by emphasizing the isolation of such men— Greenwood is one of a "legion" of "prosperous and well-dressed hangers-on who, in spite of the atmosphere of a fraternity" in the bar, "would not think of speaking to one another" (pp. 487–88)— and partly by not characterizing Greenwood extensively. But in his only words, Greenwood exhibits his close kinship to the father of "Reunion": "'Stupid,' he said to the bartender. 'Oh, stupid. Do you think you could find the time to sweeten my drink?'" (p. 488). And in the manner of his daughter's marriage and the words (probably hers) that the narrator has found scrawled on a baseboard of the rented house—"My father is a rat. I repeat. My father is a rat" (p. 484)—"The Seaside Houses" may be regarded as a companion to "Reunion," enlarging on the loneliness and pain stemming from filial affections destroyed by a father's drinking.

Excessive drinking, then, can lead to grievous ruptures of the bonds of domestic affection. But two of Cheever's stories indicate the desirability of moderate or social drinking, in particular as a ritual that affirms or strengthens domestic ties and affections. During summers in the Adirondacks over a period of many years, the Nudd family of "The Day the Pig Fell into the Well," whose primary means of maintaining closeness is its ritual retellings of the story of the unfortunate pig and other events of that day, gathers each evening for drinks. When Russell Young, a local boy once almost a part of the family, is reinstated in its good graces, he is included in this drinking. Joan, who at age forty is the Nudds' problem child, has a temper tantrum at one point but is calmed by a drink and a game of checkers with her father (pp. 233–34). So drinking has the effect of a ceremony by which the Nudds quietly reassure one another of their acceptance and affection.

Similarly, and even more prominently, the ritual of family drinking has beneficent significance in "Goodbye, My Brother." This is also one of a couple of Cheever stories in which the contrast or conflict between social drinking and apparent or actual abstemiousness is especially important.

Through images, allusive hints, and some well-chosen names, "Goodbye, My Brother" suggests that the tension within the Pommeroy family reflects a larger cultural struggle between freedom and Puritanism. As implied by the names of the narrator's sister and wife, Diana and Helen, most of the family has gained emancipation; and although he reverts to a moment of savagery in smiting his brother Lawrence (an act obviously meant to recall the story of Cain and Abel), the narrator binds Lawrence's wound. The spirit of beauty and liberation is triumphant as the story ends with Helen and Diana emerging naked from the sea after Lawrence has left the family's summer home in Massachusetts. Lawrence is associated with Puritan asceticism; he alone preserves the attitude of his ancestors that "all earthly beauty is lustful and corrupt" (p. 6).

Lawrence's abstemiousness is a major sign of this spirit. He evidently has a long-standing hostility to drinking; he has avoided neighbors for this reason, and he once moved out on a college roommate with whom "he had been very good friends" because "the man drank too much" (pp. 18–19). Reuniting with his family for the first time in four years, he accepts a proffered drink only with indifference and reluctance, thereby indicating his attitude toward the rest of his family, for whom predinner drinks on the evening of his arrival are a rite of inclusion. Ironically, although the family has drunk too much while waiting for Lawrence to appear, it is he who speaks with the effrontery of one with inhibitions lowered by alcohol. Inquiring about a man who comes for his divorced sister Diana after dinner, he asks, "Is that the one she's sleeping with now?" (p. 6). When his mother opens a favorite subject, improvements on their summer home, he asserts that "this house will be in the sea in five years" (p. 7). Though she has had too much to drink, she is at worst indulging in a harmless fantasy, whereas Lawrence is egregiously severe in speaking what he conceives to be the truth. The contrast is not in favor of sobriety.

The story is not simplistically black and white. We see enough of the mother to agree in part with Lawrence's judgment that she is rather frivolous and domineering (p. 7); and when she becomes definitely drunk late in the evening of his arrival, she shows that she can be cruel as well. Her inebriation on this occasion, however, is a half-conscious contrivance to protect herself against Lawrence's harshness, as is her apparently intentional exclusion of him from an invitation the next day to "have Martinis on the beach" (p. 9). Because the narrator is careful to state that his mother "doesn't get drunk often," Lawrence's charge that she is alcoholic is palpably false (pp. 7, 19). Normally, the family's drinking is moderate; like its shared swimming, tennis, picnics, and backgammon, it is both symbol of and aid to its loyalty and warmth. If Lawrence remains outside this circle, it is by his own choice.

The chief spiritual heir of a forebear "who was eulogized by Cotton Mather for his untiring abjuration of the Devil" (p. 6), Lawrence himself and his narrow abstemiousness are seen as devils that the family must abjure or exorcise in favor of light, beauty, and such innocent, alcohol-inspired fun as diving for balloons off the dock after the boat-club party (pp. 16–17). At one point the narrator notices that "the wild grapes that grow profusely all over the island made the land wind smell of wine" (p. 17). This touch, appropriate for a family that fosters its solidarity by drinking, is also a fitting portent of the scattering and banishment of puritanical sobriety to the hinterlands, to places such as Kansas, Cleveland, and Albany, where Lawrence has lived.

More complex and problematic than "Goodbye, My Brother," "The Swimmer" also employs a contrast between apparent abstemiousness and drinking. The meanings or values of the two sides of this contrast are in some ways difficult to ascertain, and a reader's responses may undergo major adjustments as the story progresses. At first the protagonist, Ned or Neddy Merrill, seems largely admirable, like a Ulysses seeking to free himself from the impurities and beguilements of his Circean suburban environment. Its most marked impurity appears to be its dissoluteness. In the opening paragraph, the setting a pleasant summer Sunday afternoon, we hear a litany of complaints about having drunk too much the night before. So although the diminutive, "Neddy," raises some doubts about Merrill's maturity and therefore about his credibility as a hero in the customary sense, we probably approve of his decision to leave the poolside company in which he finds himself as the story opens—a company already drinking again—and to "swim" the eight miles to his home via a series of pools. He fancies that there may be an almost legendary quality about this adventure. If, like his name, this notion may make him seem slightly absurd, the aspiration and energy required for his undertaking at least appear preferable to the torpor and overindulgence of his friends. He is, it seems, becoming a quasi-allegorical figure suddenly set apart from the rest of his society by a destiny or quest, even if this quest is puzzlingly unlike the quests of traditional heroes. Gradually, however, and finally in ways that drastically change these initial impressions of Merrill, we may reach three conclusions: that the difference between him and his society is not nearly as great as he may want to think; that his quest does not represent a clearly preferable alternative; and that the quest itself is seriously compromised by Merrill's confusion about or ignorance of its aims or purposes.

Water, the medium of Merrill's quest, has a number of established associations and symbolic meanings. In addition to its salubrious contrast with the alcohol being consumed by the others, Neddy's repeated immersions in the swimming pools may resemble baptisms;[11] his apparent unconsciousness of any desire to wash away his sins does not necessarily make this meaning illegitimate. Another association, lying closer to Merrill's awareness, seems more plausible in the context of this story: that of water as a preserver or restorer of youth. Merrill is a little like a caricature of the faddish jogger who seems to hope that his exertions will endow him not only with eternal youth but also with a kind of corporeal immortality. A third association of water in the story is with the protection and comfort of the womb; swimming in his first pool of the afternoon, Neddy thinks that "to be embraced and sustained by the light green water was less a pleasure . . . than the resumption of a natural condition, and he would have liked to swim without trunks" (p. 604). This association is an extension of the second one carried to its extreme; to avoid aging, Neddy would apparently go all the way back to a fetal state.

Either of the last two interpretations of water helps to make clear the aptness of the retribution that Neddy experiences for his unworthy, immature longings. In place of youth and its summery weather, in the course of a single afternoon he finds the season becoming autumnal and himself aging. To put the matter another way, Neddy is punished for making a travesty quest. By trying to move away from, rather than toward, the maturity and enlightenment that are the usual goals of a quest, he debases or trivializes it. Perhaps more accurately, Merrill does achieve a type of maturity—but it is a part of his punishment. Instead of culminating in enlightenment, its fruit is the incomprehensibility of Neddy's finding, at the end of his swim, that his house is abandoned and derelict, and evidently has been for some while. By an enormous acceleration, time has taken an apposite if harsh revenge on Neddy for hoping to exempt himself from its vicissitudes and in fact to reverse its flow.

A couple of scenes are especially helpful for seeing not only how Neddy's swim differs from a true quest but also how fundamentally similar he is to the rest of his society. Despite the growing chill of the afternoon, the gathering bleakness of autumn, and Neddy's progressive exhaustion and aging, his pilgrimage is altogether too easy. Unlike the genuine spiritual wayfarer, Neddy ventures into no unknown realms, seeks no real perils or tribulations. The hollowness of his journey is most sharply exposed in scenes reminiscent of but contrasting with the Vanity Fair episode of *Pilgrim's Progress*. Christian and Faithful courageously and unhesitantly reject the snares of Vanity Fair; for this reason and their ability to make converts, they are first smeared with dirt and displayed in a cage, then beaten and put in irons; Faithful is finally burned at the stake.[12] By contrast, during his brief stops at parties of the Grahams and the Bunkers, Neddy is the epitome of temporizing politeness. Although he continues on his swim, he views the practices of these Vanity Fairs not with the aversion of Christian and Faithful but as "hospitable customs and traditions . . . to be handled with diplomacy." He feels "a passing affection . . . a tenderness" for the Bunkers' party, kisses several women, and shakes hands with an equal number of men (pp. 604–5). Compared to Faithful and Christian, Neddy is practically indistinguishable from the others at the two parties. Unlike Bunyan's figures, who firmly proclaim their destination to be "the Heavenly *Jerusalem*,"[13] Neddy just sneaks off from the gatherings—in part, no doubt, because he could not formulate his purposes even to himself.

The thoroughly compromised quality of his quest is also suggested by his drinking. At the outset of his sojourn, in his apparent concern with demonstrating or recapturing a youthful vigor or purity, Neddy seems to reject the dissipation of his drinking friends, but the story as a whole indicates that drinking is no less important to him than to the rest. Although he may only be holding a glass of gin beside the Westerhazys' pool as the story opens, and although he perhaps deliberately refrains from drinking at either the Grahams' or the Bunkers', by the time he reaches the Levys', at nearly the mid-point in his journey, he has had four or five drinks (p. 605). Later in the afternoon his desire or need for a drink increases (p. 609); he has one more before his swim is finished, and he tries to get at least three. A pedantically exact count is unnecessary for showing that Neddy's drinking is probably no more moderate than that of his society.[14] There are even a couple of hints (though one is highly ambiguous) that his behavior has violated limits observed by this society. He has had not just a casual suburban flirtation but a mistress, at whose house he pauses in the course of his swim. At another house he overhears the hostess talking about a man who "showed up drunk one Sunday and asked us to loan him five thousand dollars" (p. 611), though she may not be referring to Neddy.

Before the end of the story, Neddy himself seems to regret having left the company of his drinking friends (pp. 607, 612). Whatever their excesses, this is his milieu. Vaguely seeking to transcend it, he has won for his efforts not only a reminder (possibly two) of his past turpitude but the most radical kind of displacement. Moreover, a second look at the opening paragraph may lead to a suspicion that Neddy's quest never had adequate warrant. Cheever's tone, the best indication of his attitude toward the excessive drinkers of suburban society, is one of at least half-amused tolerance, and the refrain of "I *drank* too much last night" (p. 603) conveys a sense of commonality or community that, though far from ideal, is better than the apparently irremediable dislocation of Merrill. As the story ends, he seems to be a kind of aged but infantile Adam, shivering, tearful, and mostly naked, expelled by his own folly from the only Eden he will ever know and with no other world before him.[15]

Gee-Gee, the hard drinker of "The Scarlet Moving Van," achieves a transcendence of society that contrasts completely with Neddy's final misery. In this story, perhaps for the first time, Cheever questions whether society (or its smaller units, couples or the family) offers a valid norm by which to determine or implicitly censure deviations such as heavy drinking. But Gee-Gee's transcendence is difficult to characterize and is made more elusive by the fact that Gee-Gee's wife, his only friend, and Gee-Gee himself evaluate him in ways that are inadequate or unreliable.

Peaches's view of her drunken husband is the most obviously simplistic and unrealistic; she just wants him to return to being the All-American football player, "fine and strong and generous," that he was in college (p. 361). Fortunately, he is a good deal more interesting than this. But Gee-Gee, too, lacks proper appreciation of his present self. When he manifests any self-awareness, he seems to believe that his role is something like the one Robert C. Elliott has ascribed to the archetypal satirist: that of telling his society such dangerous or mortifying truths that he is often turned into a scapegoat and banished.[16] Although Gee-Gee is driven to move frequently because of his affronts to society and the resulting ostracism (the title of the story may also suggest a branding or stigmatizing like Hawthorne's scarlet letter), Gee-Gee's criticisms of society are extremely rudimentary even for an archetypal satirist. They consist mainly of his repeated declaration "I have to teach them" (pp. 360, 362, 363), together with accusations of stuffiness and such outrageous actions as stripping to his undershorts at parties and setting fires in a hostess's wastebaskets (p. 362). These words and deeds scarcely justify any attention to Gee-Gee as a satirist or critic of society.

Charlie Folkestone, the friend and neighbor at whose house Gee-Gee becomes uproariously drunk on his first night in town, is equally unsuccessful at making a satisfactory appraisal of him. Evidently believing in Gee-Gee's self-professed role of teacher, Charlie at one point attempts to define it: "Gee-Gee was an advocate for the lame, the diseased, the poor, for those who through no fault of their own live out their lives in misery and pain. To the happy and the wellborn and the rich he had this to say—that for all their affection, their comforts, and their privileges, they would not be spared the pangs of anger and lust and the agonies of death" (p. 363). In a way somewhat similar to Gee-Gee's own error of self-judgment, these reflections give him a didactic weight and a moral authority for which there is not nearly enough supporting evidence. How Gee-Gee could be thought to offer any lessons to the wealthy is a mystery that Charlie fails to clarify, and, as a representative of the poor or wretched, Gee-Gee is certainly an odd choice. Though without a visible source of income, he is scarcely one of the poor: his frequent moves must cost a good deal of money and seem always to be from one upper-middle-class suburb to another, and one Christmas he is able to send his wife and children to the Bahamas (p. 364). If Charlie's reference is not to material want but to loneliness or isolation, a poverty of soul or spirit, Gee-Gee appears to be in circumstances that make this poverty inevitable when Charlie goes to see him one Christmas in another suburb. Gee-Gee is alone; having broken his hip, which is in a huge cast, he can move about only with the aid of a crutch and a child's wagon. His home is in a new subdivision, with most of the surrounding houses still unoccupied and looking, to Charlie, raw and ugly. Oppressed by a sense of dreariness and desolation, Charlie tries to convince himself that these must be Gee-Gee's feelings. In fact, however, Gee-Gee insists that he does not mind being alone, and his heartiness confirms his assertion (pp. 364–65). To be sure, after returning home Charlie receives a telephone call from a frightened Gee-Gee, who has fallen out of his wagon and beseeches his friend to return. Although Charlie fails to go, we learn at the end of the story that Gee-Gee next called the fire department, one member of which drank "a quart of bourbon every day" with Gee-Gee until Peaches and the children came back from Nassau (p. 369).

Gee-Gee, then, simply refuses to be victimized by the conventional horrors or disasters of the alcoholic. If he suffers some misfortunes, he recovers with amazing speed and resilience. Nowhere is Charlie quite so wrong as when he associates Gee-Gee with death or dying. He is correct, however, in attributing to Gee-Gee "some tremendous validity" (p. 363) even if he never comes close to defining it. One clue may lie in Gee-Gee's name, which, as his wife explains, is a contraction of "Greek God," a designation given him by admirers in college (p. 361). Later in the story, when Charlie visits him, he notices Gee-Gee fumbling with some matches and observes to himself that "he might easily burn to death"; a moment later he thinks that "there might be some drunken cunning in his clumsiness, his playing with fire" (p. 365). If the last phrase sounds a little like a reference to Prometheus, Gee-Gee's liver is being consumed neither by vultures nor by liquor. But we are probably not supposed to identify him with a specific god; it is more illuminating simply to see him as an undifferentiated life force or spirit, presided over, as he says, by a guardian angel (p. 365) that Cheever characterizes as "boozy" and "disheveled" (p. 369). We may be further enlightened by remembering that an old name for alcohol is "spirits." Because of his indomitability, his sheer power of survival, Captain Grimes of Evelyn Waugh's *Decline and Fall*, who is also something of a drinker, seems remarkably similar to Gee-Gee even though more fully developed as a novelistic character.[17] If Gee-Gee has a function as social critic, it is conveyed by his spirit rather than by his trivial words or actions. Perhaps Cheever and Waugh suggest that in the almost preternatural vitality of Gee-Gee and Grimes—or in the creative imagination needed to invent them—lies the best hope of surmounting the deadness of society.[18] But the fate of Charlie, who by the end of the story has apparently begun to experience all the alcoholic suffering and degradation that Gee-Gee avoids, may represent Cheever's warning that Gee-Gee's transcendence of society will not always succeed.

In three later works, including the novel *Falconer*, Cheever further utilizes characters whose excesses or aberrations are better than a society that either fails to function as a positive standard or is corrupt. As "The Fourth Alarm" begins, the anonymous narrator sits alone drinking gin at ten o'clock on a Sunday morning. Although he is not yet intoxicated, his isolation seems ripe for excess, and the unnaturalness of the hour and the day for drinking (why is he not in church, or at least innocently playing golf?) may seem to promise the portrait of a man justly expelled from society. But perhaps the chief surprise, in a story of surprises that Cheever handles with unusual adroitness, is that his drinking, even if it should become excessive, seems entirely justifiable as a defense against pain. His wife has virtually abandoned him and their children in order to play a leading part in a nude Broadway show that features simulated copulation and audience participation. The success of the show suggests its eager approval by the rest of the narrator's society. He attends and undresses, as bidden, in an attempt to understand his wife; but when his bourgeois instincts prompt him to carry his valuables on stage, the entire cast jeers him (pp. 648–49). Although a solitary drinker, the narrator is the only embodiment in the story of the old social decencies and proprieties. His abstemious wife, who now and then will drink a polite glass of Dubonnet (p. 646), represents the madness of sexual freedom, far more corrupting to society than any conceivable alcoholic excess.

One of the several unconnected stories in Cheever's "The Leaves, the Lion-Fish and the Bear" focuses on a one-night homosexual relationship, with excessive drinking a facilitating agent. Though the story is unconvincing as a look at homosexuality or its causes, the moral implication perhaps fares better. In a society of solitary travel and strange motels (two components in the setting) a homosexual encounter may be a defensible protection and warmth against otherwise overpowering loneliness. The two men, Stark and Estabrook, are conventional enough that they must get drunk before the encounter in order to lower their inhibitions; but their experience has redeeming social value, for when Estabrook returns home, he is said to find his wife lovelier than ever.[19]

Cheever seems to show some nervousness or uncertainty in his handling of the subject matter of this story. He is a little too insistent on the innocence of Stark and Estabrook. Because Cheever remained uneasy and circumspect about his own homosexuality, which he allowed himself to face and act on only late in his life, he must have had grave misgivings about treating the subject at all in his fiction.[20] *Falconer*, however, is more assured; it is also Cheever's most extended representation of the positive value of alcohol, drugs, and other excesses. Farragut, characterized by his wife as suffering from "clinical alcoholism," is also and more prominently a drug addict; he is in prison for having murdered his brother "while under the influence of dangerous drugs."[21] But in Farragut's several mental returns to the slaying, a reader finds mitigating, perhaps wholly extenuating circumstances, including the brother's odiousness. In this he resembles Lawrence of "Goodbye, My Brother," but, unlike the narrator-brother of that story, who after striking Lawrence a potentially lethal blow saves him from the ocean's undertow and binds his head, Farragut manifests not the slightest compunction about his deed. The novel presents no reasons to condemn his attitude; on the contrary, though Farragut sometimes seems ambitious of little more than shock (as when, in a flashback to his professorial days, he recalls how he and his department head "would shoot up before the big lecture," or when he imagines a priest placing an amphetamine on a communicant's tongue and saying "Take this in memory of me and be grateful"), there is little material in the book to dispute Farragut's claim that "drugs belonged to all exalted experience" (pp. 44, 46). Instead, just as in the South Pacific battles of World War II in which Farragut served, so now in the usually less violent but more corrosive conflicts between prisoners and guards, drugs or alcohol seems almost a sane, civilizing force. The alternatives are the sadism of some of the guards or the futile rioting of some prisoners, behavior that simply imitates the barbarity or senselessness of most of the world outside the prison walls, as illustrated by Farragut's wife and brother.

Apart from Farragut, the only heroes of *Falconer* are Jody (his homosexual lover, whose escape foreshadows the ingenuity of Farragut's own) and the first person Farragut meets after escaping. This unnamed stranger, impoverished (though he denies it), crude of speech, physically unattractive, and smelling of whiskey, has just been evicted from his lodging, probably for drunkenness, and is on his way to stay temporarily with a sister whom he hates.[22] Nevertheless, this misfit is Cheever's version of the good Samaritan, paying Farragut's bus fare, inviting him to share his new quarters, even giving Farragut a coat (one of four, he says—but perhaps, like most modern Samaritans, he is embarrassed about his own goodness and therefore minimizes it). When Farragut leaves the bus before he does, the stranger extends his blessing: "Well, that's all right." It is no wonder that at this point, as the novel ends, the thought running through Farragut's mind is "Rejoice . . . rejoice" (pp. 223–26). By the time he wrote *Falconer*, Cheever was a recovering alcoholic and a successful member of AA; so Farragut's benediction at the end of the novel is most of all Cheever's self-forgiveness. But these two characters—the drunken outcast from society and Farragut, murderer, fugitive from justice, and drug and alcohol addict—seem strange occasions for rejoicing when one remembers Cheever's earlier fiction. Although, as Glen M. Johnson points out, Farragut breaks his drug addiction while in prison,[23] he is the hero of *Falconer* even while still an addict. This fact sets him sharply apart from the prosperous New Yorkers or suburbanites for whom heavy drinking was a regrettable departure from desirable social norms in much of Cheever's earlier work.

F I V E

Allbee's Drinking
Bellow's *The Victim*

Like most writers, Saul Bellow tends to be fascinated with and to work variations on certain recurring patterns, relationships, and character types. Von Humboldt in *Humboldt's Gift* is a greatly expanded and complicated version of Kirby Allbee in *The Victim*, with even more of Allbee's eloquence and of his significant, spectacular failure. Charlie Citrine, in his responses to Humboldt, is a more intelligent and sympathetic version of Leventhal in *The Victim*. There are, to be sure, more differences than similarities between Allbee and Humboldt; yet something of Allbee's natural appeal and attractiveness emerges, enhanced, from such descriptions of Humboldt as "that grand erratic handsome person with his wide blond face, that charming fluent deeply worried man." Humboldt actually experiences the fate—death in a flophouse—that Leventhal only imagines for Allbee.[1]

Even though *Humboldt's Gift* seems to be better liked by critics and readers than *The Victim*, Bellow's earlier novel deserves attention as a rich commentary on drinking, the attitudes toward it and reasons for it. Of the two main characters, Asa Leventhal furnishes many of the attitudes and reactions; but Kirby Allbee, a supposed problem drinker, has a good deal to say on the subject himself. The richness comes in part from the fact that Leventhal has not one but several attitudes, which collectively undergo a real though not total change. Allbee, moreover, suddenly and (it seems) easily quits drinking, thus adding to doubts about the reality of his problem and raising questions about the adequacy of some common views of alcoholism. But the -*ism* and the clash of culturally conditioned attitudes toward drinking are not of paramount interest to Bellow. What absorbs him are the half-hidden roots or sources of Allbee's excessive drinking,

Leventhal's terror-stricken reactions to it as an emblem of irredeem-able failure, and Leventhal's means of vanquishing this fear.

To Allbee, who has lost everything and hit bottom, Leventhal re-sponds in some ways that are quite predictable and stereotyped. The stereotyping is partly an unconscious defense against Allbee's accusa-tion that, years before, Leventhal was responsible for Allbee's losing a good position by being deliberately offensive in a job interview that Allbee had arranged for Leventhal with Allbee's boss. But Leventhal would probably resort to most of the stereotyping in any case; it is an easy way to limit Allbee's humanness, to "package" him (a metaphor used by Schlossberg, an elderly Jew who supplies several thematic terms and concepts in the novel) and thereby to control or circum-scribe Leventhal's own feelings about him. Stereotyping is especially tempting when Leventhal's antipathy, fear, or anger is strong. At one point, when Allbee accuses Leventhal of having ruined him and even clutches his shirtfront, Leventhal shouts, "You're a crazy stumble-bum. . . . The booze is eating your brain up." Reflecting on this inci-dent afterward, Leventhal decides that Allbee is "too degenerate a drunk to hide his feelings."[2] Attributing to Allbee an insanity caused by alcohol, Leventhal repeatedly assumes that his overriding, uncon-trollable desire is to drink (e.g., pp. 145, 201, 204, 209), although Allbee is definitely drunk at only one of their frequent encounters. Even after their relationship has been complicated, deepened, and ended, Leventhal maintains a belief in the inevitability of Allbee's al-coholic fate: "By now he was in an institution, perhaps, in some hos-pital, or even already lying in Potter's Field" (p. 287). In the final chapter, Allbee belies his doom and briefly encounters Leventhal at a Broadway theater; one of Leventhal's few observations to his former acquaintance is that he still drinks (p. 292). Leventhal persists in viewing this fact as the key to Allbee.

If Leventhal continues to treat Allbee as less than human by pack-aging him as an incorrigible drunk, Allbee has his own ideas about stereotyped Jewish attitudes toward alcohol and more than once de-livers these opinions to a skeptical or hostile Leventhal. The stereo-types used by both men perhaps tell us more about the user than about the intended object; Allbee's, for instance, reveal an unmistak-able tinge of anti-Semitism but also some rather unexpected knowl-edge of an alien culture. There is one important difference between the stereotypes held by the two. Allbee, though he several times be-

Allbee's Drinking: Bellow's *The Victim*

wails his inability to gain control of himself, must finally be taken at his word when he asserts that he is not really an uncontrollable alcoholic (p. 204), for he not only stops drinking (p. 224) but just as suddenly appears to halt the deterioration of his life. In contrast, the general or stereotyped attitudes toward drinking that Allbee ascribes to Jews are of some value in illuminating Leventhal's particular attitudes.

Jewish culture and history have tended to make Jews more consistent in their disapproval of excessive drinking than most other ethnic groups. Allbee cites an Old Testament story to demonstrate this disapproval: "When Noah lies drunk—you remember that story?—his gentile-minded sons have a laugh at the old man, but his Jewish son is horrified. There's truth in that story. It's a true story" (p. 76). Leventhal reacts with enough animosity to suggest that Allbee has struck a nerve. Earlier, Allbee had evinced a knowledge of Jewish attitudes much more unusual for a Gentile by quoting to Leventhal the refrain from a Yiddish song: "You Jews have funny ideas about drinking. Especially the one that all Gentiles are born drunkards. You have a song about it—'Drunk he is, drink he must, because he is a Goy . . . *Schicker*'" (p. 34). Leventhal reacts "contemptuously," but this does not necessarily mean that he is unfamiliar with the song or innocent of the attitudes implied by it.[3] In fact, he makes a remark just a few moments later that seems to validate Allbee's charge; Leventhal automatically assumes that Allbee was fired from his job because of his drinking (p. 35). To be sure, even this early in the novel and at the very outset of his relationship with Allbee, Leventhal has compelling reasons for his hostility and fear, reasons that have nothing to do with his being Jewish. But stereotyped thinking about Gentile drunkenness does influence his attitudes toward Allbee.

Leventhal finds himself taking a conservative position, against Jewish "assimilation," during a discussion of Disraeli with several other Jews in a Fourteenth Street cafeteria (Ch. 10). Leventhal's only friend, Harkavy, is appalled by Leventhal's position, so one might expect Harkavy to manifest a less rigorously condemnatory attitude toward drinking when his friend gets drunk. Although the needling jocularity he directs at Leventhal (pp. 249–51, 259) is different from Leventhal's sometimes vehement disgust with Allbee, Harkavy's attitude toward drunkenness seems basically no less disapproving than Leventhal's. Both Harkavy and Leventhal appear to assume a great disparity between the drunken and sober sides of the same person, and an almost complete incapacity of the person who has imbibed to conduct or heed rational discourse. Thus Harkavy wishes to discontinue a serious discussion with Leventhal until his friend's "head is clearer" (p. 251); Leventhal thinks that Allbee's supposed drunkenness at a party years before is an adequate reason to ignore the views he expressed then (p. 34), and he later is surprised that Allbee displays the same pleasure in philosophical speculation when sober as he does when drunk (p. 227). While these attitudes are by no means uniquely Jewish, they do sharply separate Leventhal and Harkavy, who are quite different from each other in several respects, from Allbee.

Allbee accuses Leventhal of having one other stereotyped Jewish attitude when he asserts that Leventhal has to blame him for his drinking:

> "You won't assume that it isn't entirely my fault . . . . It doesn't enter your mind, does it—that a man might not be able to help being hammered down? What do you say? Maybe he can't help himself? No, if a man is down, a man like me, it's his fault. If he suffers, he's being punished. There's no evil in life itself. And do you know what? It's a Jewish point of view. You'll find it all over the Bible. God doesn't make mistakes. He's the department of weights and measures. If you're okay, he's okay, too. That's what Job's friends come and say to him. But I'll tell you something. We do get it in the neck for nothing and suffer for nothing, and there's no denying that evil is as real as sunshine. Take it from me, I know what I'm talking about. To you the whole thing is that I must deserve what I get. That leaves your hands clean and it's unnecessary for you to bother yourself." [p. 146]

Admittedly this is scarcely impartial: it is calculated at once to make Leventhal feel guilty and to exonerate Allbee from any blame for his own fall by depicting him as the victim of some inexplicable evil. Nevertheless, Leventhal's near speechlessness may seem to validate Allbee's claims, as do two other characteristics of Leventhal's behavior. First, he is tenaciously reluctant to "bother" with Allbee even after acknowledging responsibility for his losing his job. Second, he manifests a recurring compulsion to blame Allbee, as in the conversation of Chapter 18 with Phoebe Williston, although in this instance

Leventhal is also motivated in part by a desire to exculpate himself and in part by annoyance at Phoebe's apparent determination to preserve unchanged her memory of a younger, more charming Allbee. To the Jew who, however faintly or unconsciously, regards his people as God's chosen, drunkenness may seem both a chief symptom of and a just punishment for the moral degeneracy of the profane Gentile.[4] Leventhal evidently possesses at least a vestige of such thinking.

Allbee, however, is not simply a profane Gentile. He is (so Leventhal thinks) a skid-row bum, the lowest of the low. Although the slums of the destitute can usually be avoided and the dangerously insane are commonly kept out of sight in institutions, skid rows often impinge on the central business districts of cities; their denizens are therefore perhaps the last conspicuous and inescapable emblems of stark failure—a reminder uniquely unwelcome in a society obsessed with success. Allbee, the embodiment of this failure, is an especially intense source of fear for Leventhal. If Allbee were merely a derelict seeking a handout—that is, if he could be wholly contained in this "package"—he would be easy to satisfy and dismiss; what troubles Leventhal is his inability to understand why Allbee, instead of panhandling, seems to be holding him responsible for all the injustices of society (pp. 79–80). Leventhal, moreover, is unusually sensitive or vulnerable to such issues, for he is aware that his own modest prosperity, instead of being a vindication of the just workings of the social and economic order, is largely or wholly a matter of luck. Although he is ready enough to admit his luck to his wife, he is reticent or actually objects on the several occasions when Allbee stresses the importance of luck in determining success. Evidently Leventhal fears that, if he conceded any truth to Allbee's contentions, a simple turn of the wheel of fortune could bring him to Allbee's position of utter failure.

Heightening this fear and making it seem more than an abstract possibility is the fact that Leventhal was formerly in an economic condition uncomfortably close to Allbee's. After the death of his early benefactor, the elder Harkavy, Leventhal found himself "beginning to drift" and "living in a dirty hall bedroom on the East Side, starved and thin." Later, "for about a year, he clerked in a hotel for transients on lower Broadway" (p. 14), a job that brought him into close proximity, both geographically and materially, to the Bowery and that doubtless accounts for the extraordinarily detailed and exact images with which he is able to summon up the life he imagines Allbee has been leading:

> men . . . sleeping off their whisky . . . lying in the doorways or on the cellar hatches, dead to the cold or the racket or the straight blaze of the sun in their faces. . . . living in a moldy hotel somewhere, hanging out in bars, sleeping whole days, picked up off the streets by the paddywagon or the ambulance. . . . men wearily sitting on mission benches waiting for their coffee in a smeared and bleary winter sun . . . flophouse sheets and filthy pillows; hideous cardboard cubicles painted to resemble wood, even the tungsten in the bulb like little burning worms that seemed to eat up rather than give light. Better to be in the dark. [pp. 28, 38, 69] [5]

When Leventhal envisions Allbee's place of burial, it is Potter's Field (p. 287), not the generic cemetery for the destitute but a specific location on Hart's Island in New York City, [6] a place that would be known only to someone with an exceptionally thorough and intimate knowledge of the New York derelict.

Because Leventhal clerked in a hotel for transients, his dread is derived from firsthand observation. The strength of this fear can scarcely be exaggerated; the only other fear that may equal it is his terror of seemingly uncontrolled emotion, such as he thinks more than once that his sister-in-law displays. This fear stems from an imagined resemblance between Elena and his mother, who was hospitalized for insanity, though Leventhal does not know the exact nature or duration of her illness. His fear of the life Allbee represents also involves his "deepest feelings." He was "frequently mindful" of how close he had come to the irremediable failure of "the lost, the outcast, the overcome, the effaced, the ruined" (p. 20)—the luxuriance of synonyms here, rare for the taciturn Leventhal, drives home the strength of his fear like the thudding of blows. When Allbee appears, Leventhal seems almost to sense that, by suffering his presence, he will be infected with the contagion of Allbee's failure.

Although Leventhal is terrified by the resemblance between Allbee's present condition and the images from his year as a clerk in a hotel for transients, his fear does not reach its peak until he perceives a difference beyond or beneath this resemblance. The perception occurs in a scene of unusual interest because Allbee, ordinarily loquacious, needs few words to convince Leventhal of an error and because Leventhal is surprisingly open to correction. After Leventhal asserts that he too has been "down and out," Allbee responds with little more than "a tolerant smile" and "a gesture of passing the comparison away." The denial immediately triggers in Leventhal's mind a train of "the most horrible images" of derelicts and their haunts (p. 69), followed by Leventhal's admission, to himself, that Allbee was right. The horror, though brief, is intense, because it signifies Leventhal's realization that his former degradation was not closely similar to Allbee's, that still deeper abysses may yawn for him if he lets Allbee into his life. The difference beneath the similarity seems to involve Leventhal's recognition that, even if he has experienced a material poverty close to Allbee's, the great horror Allbee represents is not economic but metaphysical or spiritual, the inner defeat or despair of which poverty and alcoholic drinking are only manifestations.[7]

Leventhal grasps this source of his fear only dimly at best, and there seem to be important reasons behind Allbee's drinking that are so strange or alien to Leventhal, so far removed from his stereotyped ideas about alcohol or alcoholism, that they completely elude his comprehension.

One of these reasons is revealed by Allbee, shortly after he accuses Leventhal of just this ignorance, in the course of a stunningly harsh attack on Jews. Because of its apparent anti-Semitism—more apparent, however, than real—that attack can easily distract attention from the cogency of the revelation: "You people take care of yourselves before everything. You keep your spirit under lock and key. That's the way you're brought up. You make it your business assistant, and it's safe and tame and never leads you toward anything risky. Nothing dangerous and nothing glorious. Nothing ever tempts you to dissolve yourself. What for? What's in it? No percentage" (p. 146). Leventhal seems to miss the irrelevance of his reply that millions of Jews have been killed (p. 147), an apparent reference not only to Hitler's exterminations but also to innumerable pogroms. Allbee is referring not to collective suffering inflicted by persecution but to a deliberate, individually willed courting or risking of dissolution. Alcohol is, for Allbee, a chief means to this end; if at times he is out of control and behaves like Leventhal's stereotype of the drunk, it is far more important to see that Allbee *lets* himself behave in this way because he wishes to flirt with his own destruction.

There are some obvious reasons for this wish: his loss of job and wife, followed by his destitution and near despair. Other reasons may not be readily apparent because they seem largely independent of All-bee's misfortunes. When Leventhal awakens one morning to observe a scene in which a husband is attempting to assault a wife who has evidently been out drinking and fornicating all night with a couple of soldiers now standing nearby, he reflects that the scene, like Allbee, represents those "strange things, savage things" (p. 94) that constantly threaten him. A bit later, somewhat more calm, he concludes that the woman was simply trying to be herself "to the limit. . . . in this case, a whore" (pp. 98–99). But, since both are alien to Leventhal, the woman is probably no more simply a whore than Allbee is simply an alcoholic. It is likely that, for both, alcohol is a species of courage or virtue, a means of exploring limits and establishing a self-definition.

For Allbee, this quest requires having the courage to let go and to fail, completely and resoundingly enough that recovery becomes problematical. He is a quixotic figure with no appropriate outlets for his antiquated, chivalric idea of honor; instead of signalizing his valor by helping the distressed, he can do so only by becoming distressed himself, through a spectacular failure abetted by alcohol. That such a failure could be a deliberate, courageous choice is well beyond the comprehension of Leventhal, who more than once tells Allbee that he would have done anything, taken any kind of job, to avoid that extremity. In a general way, Leventhal is able to appreciate the need for taking risks in life; in one long, ruminative passage (pp. 98–99) he puts these risks in the metaphorical terms of flashing a mirror and running with an egg in a spoon. But he fails to see that Allbee's failure, the result of his risk-taking, is admirable or even necessary.

Although Allbee is no more a practicing Christian than Leventhal is a practicing Jew, Allbee had, as Williston once informed Leventhal, "ministers in his family." If these are also for Allbee, according to Williston, "influences to throw off" (p. 42), certain Christian values seem a deeply ingrained part of Allbee's code of conduct or honor, and alcohol plays a role in his attempt to fulfill these values.

Occasionally Allbee refers to his deceased wife, Flora, with seeming lack of emotion, as when he remarks of her, to Leventhal, "Dead is dead" (p. 74). But here he is trying to justify his failure to attend her funeral; as he comes to know Leventhal better and to reveal more of himself, it is clear that Flora, who died more than four years before the time of the story, remains a source and object of some of Allbee's strongest feelings. Specifically, he seeks to expiate his wrongs against her, a cleansing process that he begins while drunk by confessing his blame to Leventhal (p. 196) and that he completes by spending the last of her insurance money on liquor. "The money had to go the way the rest did. It would have been cheap and dishonest to use the last dime differently from the first. . . . I wasn't going to use a single cent of it to advance myself with. . . . I didn't become a success at her expense. I didn't become what I wasn't before she died" (pp. 201–2). Leventhal is, to say the least, skeptical of Allbee's sincerity in both of these instances; but even if some rationalization is involved in explaining the use of Flora's money, there is no good reason to doubt that Allbee is honest or even that his logic, though eccentric, makes sense to him as a way of relieving his guilt. He was a heavy drinker before his separation from Flora; his drinking was partly responsible for the separation; it is therefore consistent with his sense of sin as well as his notion of honor that he should drink still more heavily to atone for his wrongs to her. His ability to do so with her insurance money makes his atonement even more exquisitely just.[8]

Allbee also becomes aware of his more general wrongs and, on the one occasion when he is definitely drunk, seems to use alcohol for three different but related ends: to overcome inhibitions that might have kept him from grappling with a difficult subject; to effect a cleansing of his soul; and to achieve spiritual truth or insight, much as some Indian tribes have used peyote and other drugs.[9] The wrongs that concern Allbee in this scene are his wrongs against society; they are rooted in his sense of alienation or dislocation, which in turn engenders hostility—to Jews in general, whom he at one point characterizes as so many Calibans (pp. 144–45), and to Leventhal in particular. No doubt one reason why Allbee chooses to pursue Leventhal is so that he can test the validity of these feelings of hostility. But the problem is larger than antipathy to Leventhal or the Jews; in a crowded world, in which every man has a right to exist and an equal right to a limited or dwindling supply of material goods, it is hard to feel anything except fear or hostility toward everyone else. Allbee, having gained awareness of the power of such feelings, is also aware of a moral obligation to struggle against them and to replace them with nobler ones, feelings of tolerance or brotherhood (pp. 193–94).

Allbee speaks in a somewhat exasperated tone of the need of understanding his neighbor. He may realize that, in order for him to carry this spiritual quest to successful completion, nothing less is required than repentance or rebirth, a subject on which he discourses at some length in Chapter 19. But while alcohol has no place in effecting this radical metamorphosis, it has evidently been a necessary agent in bringing Allbee to see its desirability. As he observes, most people will not accept or want sweeping change in their lives without first experiencing terrible pain (p. 227)—which for him has meant heavy drinking and hitting bottom.[10]

Leventhal understands almost nothing of these reasons behind Allbee's drinking. Indeed, at a conscious level he understands very little about the sources of his own fears, hostilities, and feelings of alienation, and therefore he takes very little action to combat or overcome them. Nevertheless, gradually and unconsciously he makes headway against them. This entails more than toleration or sympathy; it requires entering into a feared role or even a feared identity.[11] To a great extent Leventhal must *become* what he fears; that is, he must risk entering into Allbee's identity, seeing things as he does, and allowing himself to be invaded or "penetrated" by Allbee just as he is by the crowd in the park (pp. 183–84), that sea of alien humanity, similar to the faces in the epigraph to the novel from De Quincey's *Pains of Opium*, of which Allbee is the individual representative.

In spite of their very different backgrounds and cultures, Leventhal and Allbee have some surprising similarities of character and experience. Although Leventhal is seldom consciously aware of these, they are important in suggesting that a basis exists for the entry and penetration that Leventhal must experience in order to surmount his fears. Some of his modes of thinking or behavior seem to exhibit the loss of control supposedly typical of the alcoholic.

Leventhal assumes loss of control to be a definitive trait of Allbee because of his alcoholic drinking; yet Leventhal, for all his impassivity, exposes this same quality at some crucial and potentially disastrous points in his life. He pushed his future wife down in a restaurant booth on learning that she had continued to see another man; his act ended their relationship for two years (p. 16). Several times Leventhal meditates violence against Allbee and more than once perpetrates it; when he slams Allbee into a wall of his apartment hallway (p. 78), his loss of control could well have produced more trouble than Allbee ever manages to contrive for him. Moreover, during his periods of job seeking after he rashly left the civil service, the sober Leventhal nevertheless manifested several of Allbee's traits: "he became peculiarly aggressive. . . . the provocations and near-quarrels continued. . . . he was despondent and became quarrelsome once again, difficult, touchy, exaggerating, illogical, overly familiar" (pp. 19, 41). To a great extent these feelings and actions could be attributed to a single cause: resentment, the number one enemy of alcoholics unless brought under control, according to Bill Wilson, cofounder of Alcoholics Anonymous (*AA*, pp. 64, 66). Leventhal has no trouble perceiving this quality in Allbee, whom he imagines to be "haunted in his mind by wrongs or faults of his own which he turned into wrongs against himself" (p. 38); but he lacks the sympathy to see the connection between this self and his former self.

The major result of Leventhal's cumulative frustrations and resentments was his conduct during the job interview with Rudiger. Here Leventhal had two experiences common to alcoholic drinkers: a partial blackout or memory blank, and a loss of control so complete that it involved a total change of personality—"like a seizure or possession" (p. 44) or, one might say, intoxication.[12] Perhaps the most shocking evidence of Leventhal's failures of rational or emotional control is to be found in several of his judgments of his brother and his family. At one point he thinks of Allbee as "an idiot" (p. 41) for supposing that he could have so exaggerated a minor anti-Semitic embarrassment caused by Allbee that he would seek revenge for it through his interview with Allbee's employer. If Allbee deserves this label, however, what is one to think of Leventhal, who at various points in the novel blames his brother for being a neglectful father, is convinced of the insanity of his sister-in-law (p. 182), and refers to her mother as "the old devil" (p. 240)? Leventhal is completely wrong in each of these judgments, as he later realizes.

With falterings, regressions, and a resistance that never disappears for long or for good, Leventhal comes to accept and, at fleeting intervals, even to feel close to Allbee. He becomes a provider, a good Samaritan, and even a confessor. In order more thoroughly to overcome his fears of Allbee, however, and to allay the horror of his own extinction or annihilation by being dragged down to Allbee's level, Leventhal must undergo experiences of near-union or identification with Allbee. By losing our lives we find them, according to the Christian paradox. Leventhal must incorporate a version of this paradox in his own life by risking its loss in union with Allbee, the homeless drifter and apparent alcoholic failure. It matters little that Leventhal is almost entirely unconscious of this process or its significance; the important thing is that he emerges not only largely free of his old fears but, for the first time, whole.

The elements in the process are by no means consistently subtle or solemn; some casual, almost humorous touches (though Leventhal, predictably, is not amused) suggest his readiness or involvement. Leventhal almost has hallucinations in which mice dart across his apartment (pp. 25, 77); ironically, Allbee, who has presumably been drinking heavily for years before reentering Leventhal's life, is clearheaded most of the time and has apparently never had hallucinations.[13] The morning after his first encounter with Allbee, Leventhal is not feeling well: "His legs were tired, his head ached, and his eyes—he examined them in the long mirror in the pillar before the coffeeshop—were bloodshot; he looked drawn" (p. 37). These symptoms of a hangover (a cashier in a cafeteria later asks Leventhal whether he has one) somehow seem more than accidentally assigned to Leventhal; and the weary legs, as if he had been one of the homeless derelicts walking the Bowery, foreshadow a restlessness or rootlessness that becomes increasingly marked in Leventhal's life.

One important and fundamental experience of union with Allbee occurs at a moment of extreme fear, aroused by a sequence of images of derelicts and their habitations. It culminates in an uncompleted and unanswered question: "And if it were *his* flesh on those [flophouse] sheets, *his* lips drinking that coffee, *his* back and thighs in that winter sun, *his* eyes looking at the boards of the floor . . . ?" (pp. 69–70). Unwittingly, Leventhal is already beginning to overcome his dread of a fall to Allbee's level by the intensity of his imaginative, almost sympathetic identification with him.

The union with Allbee comes closest to completeness in Chapter 21. Oddly enough, Allbee is not present in this chapter except marginally, asleep, at its outset; most of it involves a birthday party for Harkavy's niece. In Chapter 13 Leventhal had permitted a homeless Allbee to share his apartment, into which he has introduced the squalor of a Bowery cubicle. Now, from a desire to avoid his guest, Leventhal himself becomes a homeless wanderer for a day. In the afternoon he spends a few hours in the library—the New York Public, well known as a shelter for drifters and one to which Allbee has resorted (p. 145).[14] After arriving at the party and listening to Harkavy's mother comment on a predicted scientific conquest of death, Leventhal seems to reject this idea as ridiculous (p. 248), perhaps under the influence of one of Allbee's more strikingly unusual opinions: "And as for eternal life, I'm not letting you in on any secret when I say most people count on dying" (p. 194). But it is the condition Leventhal is in when he responds to her idea that is most interesting. The man who sternly disapproves of intoxication, whose attitudes toward it are primarily fear or disgust, who so far as we know has never been drunk—this man is now getting drunk himself.[15] In this condition, his grin (p. 248) seems a direct legacy of Allbee's most characteristic expression. Just as Allbee's grin or smile often indicates or implies an assumed superiority of insight, so Leventhal now grins at the absurdity of Mrs. Harkavy. Leventhal at this moment reaches his closest resemblance to Allbee and, consequently, his greatest estrangement from his own self.

The alienation from or loss of self also marks the beginning of its recovery; or perhaps one should say *discovery*, for Leventhal has hitherto been too insecure and anxious to know himself. The recovery or discovery is symbolically furthered by rites of purgation (rather like a gigantic metaphysical bowel movement) and ablution in Chapter 22,[16] though the actual expulsion of Allbee from his apartment comes in the following chapter. The most salient evidence that Leventhal has overcome the central fear of his life—fear of being plunged to the degradation and failure symbolized by skid row—comes in the following passage:

> Both of them, Allbee and the woman [whom Leventhal has also expelled from his apartment], moved or swam toward him out of a depth of life in which he himself would be lost, choked, ended. There lay horror, evil, all that he had kept himself from. In the days when he was clerking in the hotel on the East Side, he had been as near to it as he could ever bear to be. He had seen it face on then. And since, he had learned more about it out of the corner of his eye. Why not say heart, rather than eye? His heart was what caught it, with awful pain and dread, in heavy blows. Then, since the fear and pain were so great, what drew him on? [p. 277]

At a glance, this passage seems quite similar to if less vivid than an earlier one (pp. 69–70), in which a series of "the most horrible images" of skid-row life is presented. But the difference in Leventhal's responses, though relative, is fundamental. In the first passage his horror is unmitigated; in the second, Leventhal is able to be somewhat more detached or analytical. Thanks to his close involvement with Allbee, he now possesses a clearer definition of self; he knows his limits. He now answers the question left unanswered in the earlier passage: What would be his fate if he were in Allbee's position on skid row? The answer is that he could not stand it; it would kill him. Even this simple perception would not be possible if Leventhal were still as overwhelmed with terror as he had been. The question with which the later passage ends seems curious, for no apparent or explicit answer is provided. But it surely lies in the cumulative experiences of Leventhal. "What drew him on," unconsciously, was the need to enter Allbee's identity with sufficient intimacy or intensity that he could surmount his fears of it. Only in this way can he refute what is perhaps Allbee's most damning accusation against him, that he timorously keeps his soul "under lock and key" (p. 146). Nor does Leventhal suffer any longer from guilt about his modest prosperity (p. 285); though he does not fully understand how, he has earned that prosperity by risking loss of success, and even self, in entering Allbee's self.

The major irony of *The Victim* is that Leventhal—rigid, impassive, stubbornly reluctant to change throughout most of the novel—grows more than Allbee, who at one point discourses eloquently on the importance of repentance and spiritual rebirth.[17] Though initially impressed by Allbee's look of well being at their last encounter, Leventhal quickly perceives something wrong. Allbee has not "become a new man" (p. 228)—certainly not the kind implied by his talk of repentance or by Phoebe Williston when she refers to the young Allbee as "very promising" (p. 214). In particular, Leventhal notices a "decay" (p. 292) in Allbee's appearance; his resumption of drinking seems to be one sign of this decay. Paradoxically, Allbee's failure, while he was drinking heavily and living at the Bowery level, in several respects ennobled him; his worldly success at the end of the novel is more truly a decline or fall. Whereas he now drinks for reasons of social conformity, as he admits to Leventhal, he once used, or was used by, alcohol for more compelling and honest reasons: to fulfill a sense of honor, to help him experience failure and to risk destruction, to facilitate the expiation or purgation of wrongs against his wife and society.

The Victim is concerned at several levels with drinking. On the surface it presents an interesting clash of culturally stereotyped attitudes about alcohol and drunkenness. These, however, soon appear inadequate to account either for Allbee's drinking or for Leventhal's reactions to it. The problem or concept of alcoholism seems at most only a starting point for a deeper exploration: Allbee comes to be seen in his full humanity, and Leventhal to a great extent overcomes his stereotyped attitudes toward alcoholic drinking, and his fears of the failure it emblematizes, by entering the being of the fallen derelict.

SIX

The Winding Road
to Pat Hobby
Fitzgerald Confronts Alcoholism

F. Scott Fitzgerald was an alcoholic. Sheilah Graham, who knew him intimately during the last three and a half years of his life and who writes more fully about his drinking than any other biographer, comments on Fitzgerald's change from Jekyll to Hyde when he was drinking, a personality transformation that is one definitive mark of the alcoholic.[1] One example of this change is especially striking: sober, Fitzgerald was almost puritanical about language; drunk, however, he once told a film critic that Graham was a "cunt." There is abundant testimony, some of it from Fitzgerald himself, that his problems with alcohol began early: he once told Graham that he was suspended from Princeton's Cottage Club "for making a drunken fool of himself,"[2] and from Robert Benchley she heard how an intoxicated Fitzgerald, while living in France, once wantonly kicked an old vendor's tray of sweetmeats out of her hands. Graham affords further evidence (though she seems not always aware of its significance) that Fitzgerald manifested traits typically or frequently found in alcoholics: he often had blackouts, rarely remembering what he had done on a binge; he deceived himself, thinking that he could stay sober by drinking beer; when drunk, he apparently sometimes sought low company. (Graham once found him in the process of giving two tramps his money and best clothing.)[3]

Fitzgerald's alcoholism is too well known to require further recitation or proof. What is much less well known—and, in my opinion, much more interesting and deserving of study—is how Fitzgerald's experience of alcoholism or his attitudes toward it appear in or shape his work.[4] I believe such a study can trace an intelligible pattern that, though complicated and sometimes speculative, can do much to re-

veal and account for the peculiarities and difficulties of much of
Fitzgerald's writing.

Fitzgerald's second novel, *The Beautiful and Damned* (1922), is
such a powerfully authentic portrayal of alcoholic decline and fall
that perhaps it could only have been written by an author rapidly
becoming alcoholic himself.[5] The portrait of the alcoholic Anthony
Patch is sometimes weakened, in part no doubt by Fitzgerald's need
to shift the focus from Anthony to his wife and back, in part because
of his inexperience as a novelist. The onset of Anthony's alcoholism
seems rather sudden, insufficiently prepared for or supported by earlier scenes; and Fitzgerald fails to establish firm or convincing connections between some of Anthony's other qualities—his indolence
and self-indulgent aestheticism, for example—and his alcoholism,
though in fairness it should be admitted that even expert students of
alcoholism have had trouble establishing this kind of relationship.
Occasionally, too, Fitzgerald fails to realize the full potential of an
alcoholic scene: one, which involves the sinister Joe Hull and the hallucinatory picture of a room full of drunken houseguests "staggering
in grotesque fourth-dimensional gyrations through intersecting
planes of hazy blue,"[6] ends at a railway station with a friend of Anthony's, Maury Noble, delivering a comic monologue.

The strengths of Fitzgerald's portrayal of Patch's deterioration,
however, far outweigh any weaknesses. In the novel's first detailed
depiction of the intoxicated hero, Fitzgerald unerringly reveals three
of the most common and disturbing characteristics of the alcoholic:
his tendency to self-deception about his condition, his violence, and
his change of personality. Gloria, Anthony's wife, who wants to leave
a party, rightly accuses her husband of being drunk. Anthony not
only denies it; although he is naturally dependent and gentle, he also
conceives a sudden desire to dominate Gloria and, to keep her from
leaving without him, grips her arm hard (pp. 197–98). From their
first, relatively brief appearance, Anthony's personality changes and
his violence become uglier as his alcoholism deepens, finally resulting in the Jew-baiting of a character named Bloeckman (p. 437) and
in his increasingly frequent flashes of hatred for his wife (p. 389).
The mutual self-deception or rationalization of Anthony and Gloria
also increases as Anthony's drinking grows worse. Having lost most of
their old friends, they prefer to think this the result of their reduced

income, rather than ascribing it to its more probable cause. In his downward spiral toward poverty, Anthony makes one of his infrequent attempts to work, instead of waiting to inherit his grandfather's fortune. In so doing, he illustrates an observation of Alcoholics Anonymous that alcoholics display a "positive genius" for getting drunk at the most inopportune times (*AA*, p. 21). Selling something called "Heart Talks," Anthony first plies them to bartenders along Lexington Avenue, then, totally inebriated, to the customers of a delicatessen, from which he is of course ejected (pp. 385–87). Even this early in his writing and drinking career, Fitzgerald was capable of extraordinarily subtle perceptions about the alcoholic. Late in the novel, Muriel, an old friend of the Patches, turns up and witnesses the couple quarreling, after which Anthony stalks out of the apartment. Gloria remarks, "He's just drunk." When Muriel expresses incredulity—"Drunk? Why, he's perfectly sober"—Gloria interrupts: "Oh, no, he doesn't show it any more unless he can hardly stand up, and he talks all right until he gets excited. He talks much better than he does when he's sober. But he's been sitting here all day drinking" (p. 411).

If we set aside the excessively melodramatic, contrived ending of *The Beautiful and Damned*—an old lover of Anthony's suddenly reappears; he may (or may not) murder her; against all probability he wins the lawsuit for his grandfather's fortune; he goes insane—the more appropriate ending is an extended drunk scene, the most powerful in the novel, culminating in and completing Anthony's fall. Now in the advanced stages of alcoholism, Anthony has ceased to have other interests; his whole existence centers around obtaining drink. Having discovered that his bank account has been closed because of overdrafts, he sets out to pawn his watch, stopping on the way to drink up a little remaining pocket money at a speakeasy in the raffish company he has already begun to keep. Drunk, broke, and finding the pawnshops closed, he tries to take advantage of a chance encounter with his old friend Maury, who snubs him. At this point he thinks of getting money from Bloeckman, whom he had previously regarded only with resentment and jealousy because of his supposed attentions to Gloria. Nevertheless, after considerable effort and confusion, he locates Bloeckman at a nightclub. The Jewish insult previously mentioned then occurs. Retaliating, Bloeckman smashes Anthony several times in the face. A seedy but friendly passerby takes Anthony home, but becomes infuriated when Anthony cannot produce the taxi fare; cheered on by the driver, he beats Anthony as severely as Bloeckman had. Regaining consciousness on his apartment steps, Anthony hears "a distinct and peculiar murmur" coming from his own mouth: "the unmistakable sound of ironic laughter. And on his torn and bleeding lips it was like a pitiful retching of the soul" (pp. 424–41). The irony perhaps unnoticed by Anthony is that, though suitable to his former self, the young man of carefully cultivated taste and sensibility, such laughter is shockingly grotesque from the gutter bum he has almost become. This metamorphosis may point also to the irony of the chapter title, "No Matter!" Emphasizing the dizzying completeness of his fall, the title reminds us that there is nothing of the former Anthony left, "no matter," only the ghost of his manner disappearing on the night.

One might contend that the utter degradation of this ending would be more fitting for a naturalist such as Dreiser, and that perhaps Fitzgerald realized its inappropriateness for him. But an appreciation of the effectiveness of his portrayal of alcoholism depends not on a particular ending or scene, but on two other qualities not yet mentioned and on our perceiving differences between *The Beautiful and Damned* and two later novels. In contrast to *Tender Is the Night*, Fitzgerald's second novel has that large accumulation of specific detail on alcoholism without which Dick Diver's addiction seems more asserted than demonstrated. And in contrast to his next novel, *The Great Gatsby*, Fitzgerald views the drinking of Anthony Patch with critical detachment rather than through a haze of enchantment. In short, it is surprising that Fitzgerald, inexperienced as a novelist and, one might say, as an alcoholic, never again wrote at length of drinking with as much trenchant honesty as in *The Beautiful and Damned*.

It would, of course, be inadequate to dismiss Fitzgerald's treatment of drinking in *The Great Gatsby* with a phrase about enchantment, but there he presents heavy drinking in very different ways. Martin Roth has examined some of these ways.[7] Of particular interest is the tendency of the drinking to be curiously invisible to the narrator despite its pervasiveness. The novel is almost drenched in alcohol, but, for all Nick's fascination with this drinking, he characteristically neglects to make connections or see consequences. For example, he does not perceive that Tom's heavy drinking probably fostered his racism and violence. As an extreme example of this detachment of drink from source or agency, Roth notes a scene in which a tray of cocktails appears as if from nowhere, floating in through the twilight.[8] *The Great Gatsby*, in fact, establishes some of Fitzgerald's most recurrent modes or patterns of treating drinking in the rest of his work. These include a tendency toward dissociation or detachment and an inability or refusal to see connections between cause and effect, to trace consequences and reach conclusions where alcohol is concerned. They also include several forms of what might variously be called denial or evasion, including a preference for oblique glances at rather than sustained examination of drinking, and a tendency toward softening by sublimating or romanticizing the effects of drink. (Roth cites the example of Nick, who, having had "two finger-bowls of champagne," finds the scene before him "changed . . . into something significant, elemental, and profound.")[9]

The differences between treatments of drinking in *The Beautiful and Damned* and *The Great Gatsby* may of course be attributed to a conscious desire on Fitzgerald's part to avoid repeating himself. The truth, however, is probably more complicated. A further attempt to explain the difference between *The Beautiful and Damned* and most of Fitzgerald's other treatments of drinking may have to take into account the rapid worsening of Fitzgerald's own drinking in the early 1920s and his development of certain attitudes toward drinking that commonly accompany this kind of change. More specifically, perhaps only before the development of Fitzgerald's own alcoholism was complete—that is, in *The Beautiful and Damned*—was he willing and able to examine drinking with something close to unflinching honesty.

Although Fitzgerald's drinking was evidently abnormal from the start, more than one critic or observer has noted that, by about the time of *The Great Gatsby*, his drinking had become unmistakably alcoholic.[10] One of the most significant changes in Fitzgerald, both as a person and as a writer, was a change that befalls virtually every alcoholic: a powerful, often unconquerable urge to deny his alcoholism. Indeed, alcoholism is sometimes referred to as a disease of denial, both because the alcoholic finds it extremely painful to admit this illness even to himself and because admission would logically lead to an effort to stop drinking, a step that he is often unwilling or unable to take.[11] Two striking examples of the strength of Fitzgerald's denial of his alcoholism are mentioned by Sheilah Graham. Right after the drunken fiasco of March 1939, when Fitzgerald went to Dartmouth to work on the film script of *Winter Carnival*, Graham arranged for him to talk to a psychiatrist about his drinking. Even apart from Budd Schulberg's memorializing the bender in his novel *The Disenchanted*, it was in fact one of Fitzgerald's worst. Combined with the flu and exposure to the New Hampshire winter, it could easily have killed him; by causing him to be fired from the job by Walter Wanger, it deprived him of money that he desperately needed. If Fitzgerald was ever going to be receptive to help, this would have been the time. Instead, entering the room near the end of the session, Graham found Fitzgerald psychoanalyzing the psychoanalyst. In the second example from the same period, following what she terms another "bad drinking period," he rejected Graham's suggestion that he join Alcoholics Anonymous, which was then a fledgling organization. Though he probably knew very little, if anything, about AA, he dismissed it with confident contempt as being of use only for weaklings—implying, of course, that he was strong enough to stop drinking any time he chose to.[12] It would be a mistake to think that Fitzgerald denied a drinking problem only late in his life: in another plausible (if overdramatized) example from the '20s, Hemingway shows that Fitzgerald's tendency toward denial was already in place.[13]

Premature death was the worst result of Fitzgerald's alcoholic irrationality and self-deception. (Although a heart attack was the immediate cause, many doctors now recognize that alcoholic drinking can be a major cause of heart trouble as well as of a host of other afflictions.[14]) But what happens to the work of a writer as autobiographical as Fitzgerald when he refuses to accept the reality of his alcoholism? He must thereby violate the principle of not lying to himself, a principle that he thought important enough to record with underscoring in his notebooks.[15] After the early 1920s, Fitzgerald apparently found it too painful to write a full and honest portrait of a heavy or alcoholic drinker; except for two or three of the shortest portraits, there are always signs of evasion, of a desire to mitigate the harsh ugliness of alcoholism. In short, Fitzgerald's denial of his own alcoholism had a consequence disastrous for any writer: it compromised his integrity.

Like most alcoholics, Fitzgerald may have swung between two extremes: brief periods of admitting his problem (at least to himself) followed by more characteristic and protracted periods of denial. Fitzgerald's changeableness on this subject can be traced in his correspondence. In a letter to Hemingway of 9 September 1929, for instance, he virtually though facetiously confesses to alcoholic behavior during a period of hard work when he refers to his "usual nervous depressions and such drinking manners as the lowest bistro (bistrot?) boy would scorn. My latest tendency is to collapse about 11:00 and, with the tears flowing from my eyes or the gin rising to their level and leaking over, tell interested friends or acquaintances that I haven't a friend in the world and likewise care for nobody, generally including Zelda." Yet in a letter written to Maxwell Perkins on 19 January 1933, by which time Fitzgerald's drinking was almost certainly worse, he is clearly pleased at the prospect of disproving Hemingway's opinion of his alcoholism. "Am going on the water-wagon from the first of February to the first of April but don't tell Ernest because he has long convinced himself that I am an incurable alcoholic due to the fact that we almost always meet on parties. I am *his* alcoholic just like Ring [Lardner] is mine and do not want to disillusion him, tho even *Post* stories must be done in a state of sobriety." In replying to a letter from Harold Ober expressing concern about his drinking, Fitzgerald (8 December 1934) writes a series of rationalizations that deny any real alcoholic problem. Matthew Bruccoli, moreover, correctly describes as "minimizing his dependence on alcohol" a letter Fitzgerald wrote to Zelda's psychiatrist, Dr. Forel, in 1930.[16] When addressing only himself, however, Fitzgerald could sometimes be more honest. In a chart of how or where he spent each quarter of each year from fall 1931 through summer 1938, Fitzgerald's entries for the spring and summer of 1934 and for the spring of 1936 are laconically the same: "Drunk."[17]

Let us turn again to his writings and begin to test these generalizations. Even though Dick Diver, like Anthony Patch, is an alcoholic and Fitzgerald was a much more experienced writer by the time of *Tender Is the Night* (1934), his depiction of alcoholism in the later novel is much weaker. Fitzgerald had once entitled his later novel *The Drunkard's Holiday*; his change may reflect a desire to soften the impact of alcoholism. One oddity of the novel is that Fitzgerald divides the alcoholism between the hero, Diver, and Abe North, with most of the stereotypically crude or obnoxious traits of the alcoholic going to North. This division exempts Diver from any strongly objectionable behavior; in spite of his alcoholism, he remains an attractive though somewhat puzzling and lifeless figure. His appeal stays intact partly because his alcoholism becomes clear only when the novel is nearly two-thirds finished, erupting in a scene of violence in which Diver strikes a policeman and lands in jail. Diver's previous drinking had demonstrated no tendency toward violence; indeed, his major problem had seemed to be an excess of control or propriety. Moreover, Diver's alcoholism surfaces so long after any characteristics that it might help explain that it is never properly attached to them. A similar though less pronounced failure of connection can be found in *The Beautiful and Damned*, as can two other faults of *Tender Is the Night*: the belatedness with which Anthony's alcoholism is revealed, and the abruptness with which it becomes important in the novel. But the early novel is an incomparably more convincing delineation of alcoholism, because we see Anthony's intoxication and his resulting changes of character in repeated and abundant detail. In contrast, even after Diver's arrest for drunkenness, Fitzgerald's representation of him as an alcoholic simply fails to develop. For example, Diver's discharge from his position in a psychiatric clinic on the grounds of alcoholism seems almost trumped up, because there is no depiction of his supposed misconduct at the clinic.

The flaws in Fitzgerald's portrayal of Diver are in fact so radical that they should be ascribed to Fitzgerald's probably inconsistent and conflicting attitudes toward his own alcoholism. There seems no other way to explain the major, almost incomprehensible anomaly of Diver—his alcoholism should be highly important, yet it seems not at all important—than to suppose that his creator was going through the most extreme tergiversations regarding his own addiction during the novel's long gestation. If such confusion could not have been easy for Fitzgerald to live with, it was even more of an obstacle to his presentation of Diver as a believable character. Readers and critics have experienced difficulties in trying to make sense of Diver or to understand the place of alcoholism in his character.[18] Their attempts have generally failed because Fitzgerald was apparently able to go no further than to assign alcoholism to Diver. To give a full, convincing picture of Diver's alcoholism might have been as intolerably painful to Fitzgerald as fully accepting his own.

These attempts to elucidate the problems of *Tender Is the Night* may seem a little easier to credit if they are supplemented by a brief look at two of Fitzgerald's short stories, both written while he was at work on the novel. Like *Tender Is the Night*, "One Trip Abroad"

(1930) is a story in which alcoholism assumes great importance, yet it lacks concrete illustrations of the drinking problem of the hero, Nelson Kelly. The strangeness of the story lies not so much in this dearth of evidence as in the suddenness with which the drinking problem achieves importance. This results in what appears to be a serious inconsistency, almost a contradiction: after explicitly being told that Kelly "was not a drunk, he did nothing conspicuous or sodden," at the climax the reader finds a terror-stricken Kelly staring with recognition at another character, his double, with "the kind of face that needs half a dozen drinks really to open the eyes and stiffen the mouth up to normal."[19] Because the double seems to require several stiff drinks in the morning, he would certainly qualify as a sodden drunk. One might interpret the second passage referred to as representing Kelly's moment of honesty and truth, his admission of alcoholism, sudden because of his previous denial. Because this rather long story pays scant attention to Kelly's drinking, there is little support for this interpretation. Another is just as likely: Fitzgerald was vacillating, unwilling to decide (as he may have been in his own life and in *Tender Is the Night*) whether drinking was a trivial pastime or a terrifying problem.

Another story written while Fitzgerald was working on *Tender Is the Night* is "Family in the Wind" (1932), whose hero, Forrest Janney, is, like Dick Diver, an alcoholic doctor. His alcoholism notwithstanding, Janney is a revered figure in a small Southern town; he performs admirably in helping those injured by a tornado, and at the end he is about to become a volunteer father to a girl orphaned by the storm.[20] Kenneth Eble evaluates the story aptly: "it is marred by the author's excessive sympathy for the alcoholic central character and by elaborations of plot which evade a simpler, more painful, examination of that character" (p. 44). If anything, this assessment is too mild—the story is insufferably false and sentimental. As an alcoholic anxious to deny his alcoholism, or at the least to deceive himself about its importance, Fitzgerald was capable of writing a story in which the alcoholism of a central character was only a minor blemish, no more important than mention of his favorite brand of toothpaste. This belief, of course, also helps to explain why Dick Diver is essentially and incredibly untouched by his alcoholism. Sheilah Graham was much more realistic in noting the Jekyll-to-Hyde metamorphosis of the alcoholic—any alcoholic, not just Fitzgerald. Alcoholism is not a small, incidental bit of character; it is a total illness. The longer it lasts, the more it submerges and eventually extinguishes all virtues or strengths of character. This is a truth that Fitzgerald, after *The Beautiful and Damned*, was never able to see for long or for good.

Some of Fitzgerald's later fiction continues to afford precious glimpses of these and other truths about alcoholism. However precarious his hold on it may have become, Fitzgerald never totally deserted an honest and realistic view of alcoholism. Two of his shortest stories about alcoholism, freed of the exigencies of romantic padding for a popular readership, achieve an impressive power; and two of his longer stories deserve respect, though one is somewhat vitiated by evasion.

"The Lost Decade"[21] is more of a sketch than a story. The piece seems to have been written for the sake of the shock administered when Trimble, who has been absent from America for a decade, is being shown the sights of New York, including a building erected in 1928. Trimble responds, "Yes—I designed it. But I was taken drunk that year—every-which-way drunk. So I never saw it before now." Trimble's guide neatly conveys the reader's reaction: "'Jesus,' he said to himself. 'Drunk for ten years.'" The architect's unexpected, matter-of-fact hyperbole is highly effective: had Fitzgerald written this way more often, his fictional treatments of drinking and alcoholism might carry a greater impact. The hyperbole is acceptable, even honest, because it has a basis in the reality of alcoholic blackouts. And it is not so extreme as it might appear: though one could wish for more exact dates, the jazz clarinetist Pee Wee Russell once told Whitney Balliett that, after nearly ten years of a diet consisting mostly of whiskey and "brandy milkshakes," there was a period of a year or more during which he remembered nothing: "Everything . . . is a blank, except what people have told me since."[22]

Another *Esquire* story, "An Alcoholic Case," is less effective. The trouble lies not in the length, which is not much greater, but in Fitzgerald's decision to focus on the reactions of the alcoholic's nurse, a character of minimal intelligence and no intrinsic interest. There is even a bafflingly extraneous dialogue between the nurse and her supervisor, a Mrs. Hixson. Nevertheless, the story offers genuine rewards as a discerning study of alcoholic psychology. When the nurse, deciding to remain with her alcoholic "case," returns from her agency to his hotel room, she discovers that although he is pale and feverish, he is dressed "in dinner clothes" to go out. He casually asks her to help him find his studs and even invites her to accompany him. The dinner clothes are evidently a gesture of imaginative self-deception, for all the alcoholic really wants is more drink. This scene is powerful mainly as a disturbingly authentic revelation of the irrationality of the alcoholic.[23] Another authentic touch follows almost at once, in a sudden and characteristically alcoholic mood change: the nurse's case abruptly loses his desire to go out and lets her start to undress him. Unfortunately, this penetrating scene is marred by some ensuing fustian about the alcoholic's "Will To Die" (Fitzgerald's capitals, apparently) and about "death" lurking in the corner of the bathroom, where the alcoholic had earlier smashed a bottle of gin. That alcoholics have such a will is beyond question; Fitzgerald's melodramatic language, however, is unworthy of the vividly rendered scene preceding it.

Of Fitzgerald's longer stories dealing with alcoholism, "A New Leaf"[24] is perhaps the most honest and convincing. As in "An Alcoholic Case," the alcoholic of this story, Dick Ragland, is seen through the eyes of a woman, Julia. Because she is intelligent and because an intimate relationship develops between her and Dick, the focus on her is less irritating than the focus on the nurse in "An Alcoholic Case." In fact, the story of Julia's responses to Dick sheds light on Fitzgerald and his alcoholism. Though revolted by Dick's extreme drunkenness when he arrives to take her out to lunch, Julia remains immensely susceptible to his charm and good looks when he is sober; she has fallen instantly in love with the sober Dick and later agrees to marry him if he can maintain that condition for a year. (Her reactions seem prophetic of Sheilah Graham's attitudes —though she was repeatedly and deeply offended by Fitzgerald's drunken behavior, she always returned to him and would probably have married him had it not been for Zelda.) Julia's reactions also anticipate and resemble the story told by Tony Buttitta, in *After the Good Gay Times*, of how Fitzgerald was hotly and tenaciously pursued by two attractive women when he was living in Asheville, North Carolina, in the summer of 1935, even though this was one of the worst periods of his drinking. But even by 1931, Fitzgerald seems to have known that his attractiveness to women was not effaced by his drunkenness. Quite possibly this knowledge enabled him to maintain his drinking and the self-deception connected with it.

"A New Leaf" illustrates another quality of Fitzgerald's that was related to his alcoholism and may have abetted it, namely, his expectation of being nursed or mothered in his alcoholism, a characteristic to which Kenneth Eble calls attention (pp. 46–47) and a desire which Julia satisfies in "A New Leaf." Although there seems to be no biographical evidence to confirm the existence of this desire as early as 1931, Sheilah Graham noticed that Fitzgerald "craved infinite succor from the world, especially from the women he loved."[25] Although she claims she never nursed him after a spree, she seems not to have realized that her willingness to return to him repeatedly, a willingness of which Fitzgerald took full advantage, constituted a kind of nursing, enabling him to continue alcoholic drinking and to ameliorate or avoid some of its worst consequences. As John Henry Raleigh suggests, Fitzgerald's expectation of nursing might even have been typical of the Irishman or Irish-American of a few generations ago. Raleigh instances the drunkard Jamie's mothering by Josie Hogan in O'Neill's *A Moon for the Misbegotten*, an instinct that may seem misdirected to later twentieth-century audiences cut off from the Irish heritage.[26]

One other view of the alcoholic Ragland seems to have had a sound and authentic biographical basis. Disgusted by his drunken appearance—"face . . . dead white. . . . the fixed eyes, the drooping mouth . . . the chin wabbling like a made-over chin in which the paraffin had run"—Julia nevertheless finds on next meeting him that Ragland has completely regained the handsomeness with which she fell in love, "a fine figure . . . in coloring both tan and blond, with a peculiar luminosity to his face" (pp. 300, 303–4). Even during the worst of his drinking it evidently required only a few days without alcohol to work a comparably remarkable metamorphosis on Fitzgerald himself. After one such brief spell of abstinence, Buttitta describes Fitzgerald, previously seen to be pale, sweating, and shaking, as "once more the college athlete or stage juvenile. There was about him the quality of a phoenix rising from its ashes."[27]

In addition to the authenticity derived from the reader's knowledge of the alcoholic Fitzgerald behind Ragland, "A New Leaf" is authentic in its presentation of truths common to all alcoholics. There is the Jekyll-and-Hyde contrast between Ragland's sober self (handsome, courteous, charming, appealingly vulnerable) and his drunken alter ego (scandalous, sneering, contemptible). Even if Ragland's suicide while drinking has no literal parallel in Fitzgerald's death, at some level Fitzgerald must have known that alcoholic drinking is a type of suicide.

"Babylon Revisited"[28] seems conscientiously to strive toward an honest treatment of and a critically objective attitude toward alcoholism. It is one of Fitzgerald's most praised and celebrated stories, but it seems less successful than "A New Leaf" as a study of an alcoholic. The alcoholism of Charlie Wales, the hero, is dormant; because his drunkenness is past, the reader is spared its sordid details. To be sure, the retrospective view of Charlie's alcoholism largely justifies these omissions, but one may wonder whether Fitzgerald is too easy on him when he recalls his wife's death in such a way that "wild anger" (p. 223) at his wife's flirting rather than his own drunkenness seems to have been Charlie's reason for locking her out one night, in an action that led to her death, according to Charlie's sister-in-law.

Despite his last name, Charlie has a handsome "Irish mobility" of feature (p. 212) and bears other resemblances to Fitzgerald. To his credit, Charlie accepts much responsibility for the drunkenness and drunken deeds of his past; he also has a powerful if low-keyed horror of its emptiness and waste. But Fitzgerald also exposes the incompleteness of Charlie's otherwise commendable change. Charlie maintains a link with his past by continuing to have one drink a day for a reason that sounds suspiciously like alcoholic self-deception or rationalization: "so that the idea of alcohol won't get too big in my imagination" (p. 219). By leaving his address for Duncan Schaeffer at the Ritz bar (p. 210), he enables the dissipated past to reenter his present and thus to end, at least for the time being, his chances of regaining custody of his daughter, the only goal that really matters to him any longer.

There are other possible flaws in the story and in his hero of which Fitzgerald himself may not have been entirely cognizant, perhaps because he failed to accept fully the consequences of his own alcoholism. The reader is evidently intended to agree that he has suffered sufficiently for his past and that his sobriety entitles him to have his daughter back. It is a touching desire, made even more appealing by the attitude of his daughter's guardian, his sister-in-law Marion, who is represented as being excessively suspicious and perhaps vindictive in her reluctance to surrender her ward to Charlie. Because Fitzgerald has unwittingly or deliberately blurred the part that Charlie's drinking may have played in his wife's death, the reader's sympathies in this tense conflict may all go to Charlie. On reflection, however, the sufficiency of Charlie's atonement for his drinking may seem both problematic and dubiously relevant. It is not hard to imagine how a different writer could have portrayed Marion's attitude toward Charlie as estimably prudent in light of the ravages of Charlie's alcoholic behavior, which she correctly sees as lying at no great distance in the past and which for her resumes importance in the present when Charlie's drunken friends Duncan and Lorraine intrude into her apartment in search of him. As the story ends, Charlie feels keenly that the continuing separation from his daughter is unnecessary and unjust. The reader may be more aware of Charlie's limitations, however, especially the limits of his change and his acceptance of responsibility, than is either Charlie or the author. More specifically, a reader who understands the alcoholic's evasions and self-deceptions may discover in Charlie at the end of the story a rather unpleasant and unwarranted tinge of self-pity, perhaps deriving from the fact that, although he now accepts much of the responsibility for his past, he is still trying to displace some of the blame onto other persons or causes, such as Marion, the general debauchery of the era recently ended, or sheer bad luck.

That Fitzgerald continued to equivocate about his alcoholism during the decade of his worst drinking and the period of his most frequent fictional attention to the problem is demonstrated in his autobiographical essay, "The Crack-Up."[29] Although Hemingway criticized it for its excessive candor, "The Crack-Up" would have been both more candid and more informative had Fitzgerald been more probing about the part alcohol played in his collapse. As the essay stands, there is scarcely a hint of this; instead, the work's most memorable passages are its rueful or humorous conceits ("and cracked like an old plate," p. 72), which seem to spring from an Olympian analytical detachment rather than from the agonies of alcoholism. In fact, Fitzgerald explicitly rejects alcoholism as an explanation of his crack-up on the grounds that when it occurred he had "not tasted so much as a glass of beer for six months" (p. 71). A periodic alcoholic or binge drinker like Fitzgerald can go without a drink for much longer than six months. Independent accounts, however, give the lie to Fitzgerald's claim to have been without beer for six months; during the period of his crack-up, his consumption of beer was so gargantuan (estimated by a friend to have reached a high of thirty-seven bottles in one day) that it led directly to his hospitalization in September 1935.[30] Even more unsettling (because it smacks a bit of perverse snobbery) is Fitzgerald's implicit rejection of the possibility of alcoholism because it is too simple a phenomenon to account for *his* difficulties and symptoms. He contrasts his own case with that of William Seabrook, whose "unsympathetic book" about his own alcoholism has a "movie ending" (p. 71).[31] Some students of alcoholism might suspect that Fitzgerald would not have read this book had he not been much more disturbed by the possibility of his alcoholism than he admits in "The Crack-Up." With progress in the understanding of alcoholism has come the view of it as a threefold illness—physical, mental, and spiritual (*AA*, p. 219). This concept might have seemed sufficiently complex even to Fitzgerald; indeed, in describing his crack-up, he also appears to suggest something like this tripartite effect, even though he rejects alcoholism as its source. Compounding an irony lost on him, Fitzgerald notices in his crack-up another major symptom of alcoholism—the unmanageability of his life, by which many members of Alcoholics Anonymous mean particularly the unmanageability of emotional life—when he observes that "in a single morning I would go through the emotions ascribable to Wellington at Waterloo" (p. 71). Even if Fitzgerald had not had a drink for six months, an AA member might say that he was on a "dry drunk," an emotional bender to which even sober alcoholics are susceptible and which closely resembles a "wet" drunk in its lack of emotional control (*12 & 12*, pp. 92–93). Furthermore, in referring to his loss of a capacity for loving or liking people, Fitzgerald unwittingly reveals a leading manifestation—isolation and emptiness—of alcoholism as a spiritual illness. (I have previously discussed its symptoms in Chapter 2 with reference to Sebastian Flyte of *Brideshead Revisited*.) As he develops the portrait of a devitalized self in "The Crack-Up," Fitzgerald assumes a striking resemblance to Dick Diver, whose alcoholism is at least admitted. But with Diver as much as with Fitzgerald, there is a dissociation of cause from symptoms, a failure to make clear connections. Because "The Crack-Up" shows that this was not an aesthetic or structural but a personal failure, stemming from Fitzgerald's apparent inability to face and accept his alcoholism, one should not be surprised at the wrongness of Fitzgerald's remedy. He will, he says, continue to be a writer but "cease any attempts to be a person" (p. 82). Indeed, the total unworkability of any such solution might seem ludicrous, were it not for one's awareness of the anguish of alcoholic confusion and self-deception that probably underlay it.

The excellence of some of Fitzgerald's stories about alcoholism in the 1930s suggests that he must have had periods when he was able to be honest and therefore shrewdly perceptive about his own. But as "The Crack-Up" indicates, Fitzgerald also clung to the denial more typical of the alcoholic, and this may help to explain why he continued to write weak (that is, evasive and dishonest) stories about alcoholics.

Perhaps the poor quality of "Her Last Case"[32] has nothing to do with Fitzgerald's denial and everything to do with its being a pot-boiler, written in haste for money. Whatever the reasons, Fitzgerald contrives every imaginable way to soften, tone down, or turn aside from his ostensible central subject, the drinking problem of Ben Dragonet. Far more than in "An Alcoholic Case" or "A New Leaf," adopting the viewpoint of a woman and tracing her reactions to the alcoholic seem to thwart serious attention to alcoholism. Other developments also remove Dragonet and the reader from his drinking problem. Dragonet's ancient and honorable Virginia lineage is emphasized, the implication apparently being that such a gentleman could not possibly be a drunken stumblebum. Dragonet obviously holds this belief about himself; and since the local doctor and (very soon after her arrival at Dragonet's house) the nurse share it, the possibility that he might be practicing alcoholic self-deception is quickly dismissed. A realistic sort evidently unimpressed by Dragonet's genealogy, the Baltimore doctor who dispatches Bette to Dragonet regards him as alcoholic, instructing the nurse to taper off her patient's liquor if he is drinking and to substitute paraldehyde. (This used to be thought a good means of weaning an alcoholic.) There is no reason to suppose that Bette is prepared to heed these directions, for she begins falling in love with Dragonet almost on sight and just as hastily concludes, with a consummately unprofessional indifference to any consideration of evidence, that such a nobly romantic figure as Dragonet "was not drunk. He was not the kind who would ever be drunk" (p. 578). Unfortunately for the credibility of the story, the reader is meant to accept this conclusion. The rest of the story, full of unlikely twists of plot and appearances of other characters, deserves to be dismissed as quickly as Fitzgerald dismisses Dragonet's drinking. His last (and virtually only) attempt to account for it comes with the appearance of Dragonet's wife, whom his housekeeper terms a "devil" and "vampire" and whose previous appearance, she says, launched Dragonet on a six-month drinking bout (pp. 584–85). Because the wife bears some resemblance to Zelda, one can speculate that the housekeeper's comments reflect Fitzgerald's covert blame of Zelda for his drinking. If so, then the housekeeper's rationalization of her master's drinking becomes not just absurd but reprehensible. In any event, the nurse's decision to stay on and act as a mother to Dragonet's daughter may well reflect Fitzgerald's own desire to be mothered.

Although "Crazy Sunday,"[33] like "Babylon Revisited," is one of Fitzgerald's celebrated stories, it is his least satisfactory in its handling of drinking. Kenneth Eble summarizes the reality out of which the story grew. In Hollywood as a writer for MGM, Fitzgerald attended a party given by Irving Thalberg and Norma Shearer. According to a "fellow writer . . . who accompanied him to the party, Fitzgerald got drunk, insulted Robert Montgomery, and insisted on singing a banal song about a dog. The song embarrassed everyone, though Norma Shearer sent Fitzgerald a telegram the next day: 'I THOUGHT YOU WERE ONE OF THE MOST AGREEABLE PERSONS AT OUR TEA,' which Fitzgerald used almost word for word in the story. At the end of the week he was fired" (pp. 44–45). Fitzgerald's dismissal must have been a blow; and if he had been able to be honest, the drunkenness that evidently caused it would have been even more painful, for it would have provided virtually irrefutable evidence of his alcoholism.[34] But Fitzgerald was unable to face this. Practically the only actuality that is not omitted from the story or changed almost beyond recognition is Miss Shearer's telegram, which (for all Fitzgerald knew) was prompted by pity for a famous writer who had become a drunk. But Fitzgerald believed what he wanted to believe—above all, that he had not made a drunken fool of himself. So his story revises reality to soften or escape otherwise unbearable pain. One can question this hypothesis, of course, and argue that in altering real events Fitzgerald was only exercising artistic license. But when all these changes soften or evade the realities behind them and result, besides, in some palpable weaknesses and improbabilities, the alcoholic denial and self-deception that evidently prompted them instead suggest thralldom to an underlying guilt.

From Eble's summary of the story, one might suppose that the party and the drunk scene were at its center. These, however, take up not quite five pages of the eighteen. This brevity may itself have been one means of softening painful reality, but it is certainly not the only means. Fitzgerald passes so lightly over the drunkenness of his central character, Joel Coles, that one is scarcely sure that he gets drunk and may almost fail to notice it. Although Joel reflects the morning after the party that Miles Calman, the movie director and host, may now regard him as a rummy, only once in the narration of the party is the word "drunk" attached to Joel: as he leaves, he bows "rather drunkenly" (p. 236) to Stella, Miles's wife. Furthermore, if one wants to know how much Joel has had to drink, Fitzgerald mentions only two cocktails; although more may be vaguely hinted at, this is hardly enough to cause drunkenness.[35] On balance, the evidence fails to demonstrate Joel's drunkenness. He seems to be in complete possession of his faculties, for instance, when he senses that the little monologue he performs for the entertainment of the Calmans' guests is being greeted coolly; a drunk would have been largely oblivious to its reception. More than "drunkenness" or any variant thereof, "exhibitionism" (pp. 234, 236) is the prominent explanation of Joel's behavior; he uses it himself in writing a note of apology to Miles, diverting attention from the probable cause to its symptom. So even though Eble is correct in stating that "Crazy Sunday" "betrays" the "guilt" (p. 45) that Fitzgerald felt because of the actual incidents behind it, the extremely strange way in which this guilty conscience manifests itself in the story is even more significant. It takes the form, mainly, of Fitzgerald's effort to muffle or erase any evidence that might account for his guilt.

It is as if the guilt of his own alcoholism and his anxiousness to deny it were so overpowering that, using Coles and a story as surrogates, Fitzgerald was driven to extenuate or deny all of Coles's defects, whether or not they have any connection with his drinking. Without some such hypothesis it seems impossible to account for gross weaknesses in the story—flaws that Fitzgerald as a craftsman could surely have seen and corrected, had he been free of extreme guilt and anxiety.

The almost spotless purity with which Coles is supposed to emerge from the story is a measure of the depth of Fitzgerald's guilt over his disastrous drunkenness at Thalberg's party and the power of his desire to expunge all traces of that guilt. Coles's monologue is made to seem the product not of intoxication or even of "exhibitionism," but of an innocent desire to shine and to give pleasure: "It was his only parlor trick, it had amused several parties and it might please Stella Walker" (p. 234). The Calman guests are chilly toward the monologue, but a couple of extenuating circumstances are offered: Coles's performance follows that of a professional radio entertainer, and now the guests are eager to leave. In case these reasons fail to convince, Fitzgerald adds a third, transforming Coles into a kind of heroic underdog whose monologue has stirred "the resentment of the professional toward the amateur, of the community toward the stranger" (pp. 235–36). Fitzgerald also discredits the loud "Boos" of one of the Calman guests at Coles's performance. This boor, Coles's friend Nat Keogh tells him later, is a "ham" who deserved the kick in "his tail" administered by a Joe Squires "while he was bowing to the crowd" at Grauman's (p. 237). Again, it must be stressed that the urgent need to purify Coles in every way possible cannot be located in the story. Fitzgerald's deep but unadmitted shame and guilt about his drunkenness at the Thalberg party are its most likely source.

Indirectly or directly, these extenuations also constitute Fitzgerald's attempt to cope with the most glaring weaknesses of the story. He replaces drunkenness by anti-Semitism, a substitution that was evidently as close as he could come to depicting the horror of his drunkenness. Because many readers will trace not even a subliminal connection between Coles's apparent anti-Semitism and his or Fitzgerald's drunkenness, they will probably be at a loss to understand why Fitzgerald uses anti-Semitism in the first place, and at even more of a loss to know why he then goes to such tortuous lengths to minimize or nullify it. Coles's monologue seems distinctly anti-Semitic; it involves ridiculing the vulgarity of a Jewish movie producer named Silverstein, right down to mimicry of his accent ("sex appil," p. 235). Because a number of the Calmans' guests, if not the Calmans themselves, are Jewish, Fitzgerald never shows how this monologue can be reconciled with Coles's "happy and friendly" feelings "toward all the people" at the party only a few minutes before his monologue. And because his drinking, which might account for an irrational mood shift, is minimized almost to invisibility, the reader is left with no motive for Coles's tasteless performance. Nor are these the worst difficulties resulting from Fitzgerald's substitution of ridicule of

Jews for drunkenness. If not for themselves, then certainly for their guests, the Calmans could only have disliked Coles's performance in any credible story. Not so in "Crazy Sunday"—Stella is so delighted with it that she sends Joel a complimentary telegram the next day, invites him to a party at her sister's the following weekend (p. 237), and later almost becomes his lover; Miles Calman, even though suspecting a romantic interest between Joel and his wife, befriends and confides in him. Instead of being punished for his monologue, then, Coles is rewarded beyond one's wildest imagining. In this respect the story is more profoundly "crazy" than Fitzgerald may have suspected; indeed, it makes no sense unless we read it as a kind of total wish fulfillment, the forgiveness extended by the Calmans to Joel being Fitzgerald's fantasy of the forgiveness that he was unable to give himself for the drunkenness that he was unable to face, either in reality or in the story.

"Crazy Sunday" seems to be Fitzgerald's most desperate and least satisfying attempt to distance himself from his alcoholic reality. *The Pat Hobby Stories*, though regarded by their author as hack work, are an example of more artfully achieved distancing or sublimation. Coming at the end of his writing career, these stories about a Hollywood has-been and movie writer who now cadges film-studio piecework to survive have special interest as a sort of last testament about Fitzgerald's drinking. But what sort of testament?

We know from Arnold Gingrich, the original publisher of these stories in *Esquire*, that Fitzgerald thought of them as comedy and that "much of what he felt about Hollywood and about himself permeated" them.[36] But we should distinguish Fitzgerald's comedy both from the heroic comedy of the Consul in *Under the Volcano* and from the life-giving comic drunkenness of Jim Dixon in Amis's *Lucky Jim*. Hobby is a descendant of a broad comic type known as the *alazon*, perhaps more directly from one of several subtypes such as the *miles gloriosus* (braggart warrior).[37] Although not literally a soldier, Hobby wages a continual warfare to survive in the hostile environment of Hollywood; one of his chief weapons is boasting—sometimes clever, sometimes audacious, always so persistent that it may induce the movie bigshots who employ Hobby to suspend their disbelief in his slender talents. Because Fitzgerald (like Eugene O'Neill) was an Irish-American, Hobby seems a sort of comic inversion of O'Neill's doomed brother, James, or a variation on the proverbial yet actual bachelor uncle who used to be found in "any large Irish family." A charming wastrel who lives by his wits and "can never hold a job," he is devoted "to liquor and women, although the liquor is usually more important to him."[38] Whether treated with satiric exasperation, tragic gloom, or levity, such characters also tend to share a fundamental innocence; in Hobby it is a raffish appeal that some women notice despite his obvious material failure and that briefly softens the hearts of some flinty movie executives. Though he may possess several facets, Hobby remains almost a caricature; in one story a character refers to Pat as "Mike" (p. 33), suggesting his likeness to one of the two stock figures in the old Pat-and-Mike vaudeville sketches. The typing is one way Fitzgerald keeps Hobby within comic bounds.

Hobby is in some respects closely related to Fitzgerald, particularly as he half-reveals and half-conceals Fitzgerald's attitudes toward his own drinking. Through the Hobby stories Fitzgerald may have been seeking relief from his discomfort with Hollywood. Because his drinking was no less a problem then than at other times, these stories became a means of dealing with this problem; because Fitzgerald continued to deny it, in the stories he reduced it to comedy. Such a transformation of his drinking problem may have had a special psychological urgency for Fitzgerald, for his recent binge at the Dartmouth Winter Carnival, at which he was supposed to be working on a film (p. xxii), surely posed a strong threat to continued denial.

Though Hobby is treated mostly with an amused or affectionate contempt by the magnates for whom he works (as Fitzgerald must frequently have felt he was treated), he shows a Falstaffian resilience and, for every humiliation suffered, scores a compensatory victory of survival. Hobby's drinking, though clearly a habit and potentially a source of trouble, is another circumstance over which he repeatedly triumphs by holding it in check. His overindulgence is handled so briefly or obliquely in three stories as to be scarcely noticeable; in one he is given a sobriety test, apparently passes, and is released from jail. More characteristic of Fitzgerald's treatment of Hobby's drinking is a reference to "a soft purr of whiskey on his breath," suggesting that liquor to Pat is just a mellow, tame pussycat.[39] The half-pint of gin he carries is, together with the women he ogles or the racehorses he bets on, rather like one of the formulaic epithets in Homer—Achilles of the swift knees: Hobby of the half-pint bottle. It is a stage property that he pulls on to revive flagging spirits or for assistance through crises. Hobby may therefore represent a highly desirable fantasy for Fitzgerald, the fantasy of the bumbling and scorned yet nevertheless canny survivor who drinks mostly in the controlled way that Fitzgerald would have liked to.

The final tale of the series, "Pat Hobby's College Days," contains a parallel to an actual incident recorded by Sheilah Graham,[40] even to the detail that a secretary (not Hobby or Fitzgerald) is supposed to remove a large collection of his empty whiskey bottles and dump them, as though the writer or his stand-in were too ashamed to do his own dirty work. Although the story is hopelessly improbable at the level of realism, as a glimpse of Fitzgerald's psyche it makes excellent sense, having the stark vividness of a dream—which it might well have been. Hobby's bookie suggests that he approach a man named Doolan, the athletic superintendent of the University of the Western Coast, to get an idea for a movie about the university, an idea which he might then sell to a producer. Pat meets Doolan, who arranges almost instantaneously for Pat to present an idea for a movie to a faculty committee. As he waits to enter the committee room, Pat drinks a "long, gagging draught" (p. 154) from his ever-ready bottle. If the idea of a college movie and Pat's anxiety about it suggest Fitzgerald's Dartmouth assignment and his fear of failure,[41] the next scene suggests a much more powerful feeling: Fitzgerald's guilt about his inebriation. (The guilt probably had a more immediate source than the debacle at Dartmouth: according to Sheilah Graham, Fitzgerald wrote "Pat Hobby's College Days" "during a drinking period."[42]) Right in the middle of Pat's presentation to the committee, his secretary is ushered into the room with "a big clinking pillow cover" (p. 157). Unable to dump his whiskey bottles, she has unaccountably returned them to him here—unaccountably, that is, unless we recognize that the bottles symbolize the alcoholic guilt that Fitzgerald had been unable to purge. It is as if the Dartmouth disaster, or perhaps even the whole of Fitzgerald's drinking career, had suddenly caught up with him, with the incriminating evidence literally dumped at his feet. The guilt and remorse of Fitzgerald's alcoholic reality, however, finally do not shatter the carefully established and maintained comic pattern of Hobby's life in the other stories. Instead, the last story simply leaves an impression of irreconcilable incongruity with the rest of the portrait of Hobby, much as, in *Tender Is the Night*, Diver's alcoholism seemed more a puzzling appendage than a basic part of him.

It is somehow appropriate to close this chapter with the phantasmal clanking of Hobby's—or is it Fitzgerald's?—empty whiskey bottles. From early in his career to its end, Fitzgerald never neglected the subject of drinking for long; indeed, he was understandably haunted by it. Especially when able to look honestly at his own drinking, he was able to write of the price paid for alcoholism as incisively as anyone in our literature. Even in his apparently more characteristic periods of denial, times when he tended to soften or romanticize drinking in his fiction, his work almost always seems at least unwittingly honest. Some of the evasions and equivocations seem implausible, but they testify to the sorrows and pains of alcoholism perhaps better than Fitzgerald could have known.

SEVEN

John Berryman and Drinking
From Jest to Sober Earnest

n the course of reviewing two biographies of Tennessee Williams, Gore Vidal reserves his most trenchant manner for a digression, a satiric portrait of that fashionable stereotype, the *poète maudit*:

> High school valetudinarian. Columbia. The master's degree, written with heart's blood (on Rimbaud *in translation*). The awakening at Bread Loaf; and the stormy marriage to Linda. Precocious—and prescient—meteoric success of "On First Looking Into Delmore Schwartz's Medicine Cabinet" (*Prairie Schooner*, 1961). The drinking. The children. The pills. Pulitzer lost; Pulitzer regained. Seminal meeting with Roethke at the University of Iowa in an all-night diner. What conversation! Oh, they were titans then. But—born with one skin too few. All nerves; jangled sensibility. Lithium's failure is Lethe's opportunity. Genius-magma too radioactive for leaden human brain to hold. Oh! mounting horror as, one by one, the finest minds of a generation snuff themselves out in ovens, plastic bags, the odd river. Death and then—triumphant transfiguration as A Cautionary Tale.[1]

Although doubtless a mosaic drawing from more than one writer, the sketch at several points seems indebted to the life and career of John Berryman: his graduation from Columbia, his closeness to Delmore Schwartz, his Pulitzer prize, his marked tendency to lament the passing of the "finest minds" of his poetic generation (he composed an entire sequence of *Dream Songs*, his best-known work, to commemorate Schwartz), his committing suicide by jumping from a bridge onto a bank of the Mississippi River—and, of course, Berryman's notorious drinking.

Vidal's scorn for an outworn fashion, a stereotype that has lost its power either to shock or to inspire sympathy, may indicate a growing impatience with the *poète maudit*. Pearl Bell commends William Barrett's *The Truants* for rejecting this cliché and for refusing to attribute the doom of such poets as Plath, Schwartz, or Berryman to "'those abstract specters, Society or Poetry.'"[2] But it may be premature to suppose that the concept of the *poète maudit* has been entirely discredited; in other recent criticism it appears to be alive and well. In virtually the only previous attempt to explore the relationship between Berryman's alcoholism and his poetry, for example, Lewis Hyde instances the life and fate of Hart Crane as helpfully parallel to Berryman's. After remarking that Crane's father owned a candy business, Hyde says that Crane spent "one horrible hot summer" in Washington, D.C., "trying to sell the family sweets," concluding therefrom that "all that was offered to Crane was this thing that kills poets." Out of context, this passage might be thought to suggest that someone had slipped poison into the batch of candy that Crane sampled as he made his sweaty rounds. But in fairness to Hyde's argument, though with dubious benefit to his logic, one must restore the passage to its context and see that he is after much bigger game: a poet's selling candy is only one result of the "mechanical & monetary power" so dominant in our century as to be "lethal to poetry"; "it is not an exaggeration," Hyde declares, to hold that such "forces divided [Crane] from his own life energies and contributed to his alcoholism and his death."[3] One trouble with this line of thought is that there are exceptions—a Wallace Stevens living to a ripe and productive old age in the insurance business. And Hyde's logic fails in another way: if a mechanical or monetary society causes alcoholism, the poet with the best chance of escaping its lethal influence should be one who, like Berryman, spent most of his life teaching in universities (although some veteran professors might plead that their years of effort with recalcitrant and uncomprehending students literally drove them to drink). In any event, critics such as Hyde seem only to be varying an old fallacy well described by R. S. Crane, that of seeing authors or their views as merely products of "their 'age' or . . . the social or cultural 'conditions' amid which they flourished." Instead of being the fated spokesman of his culture, Hyde would see the poet as its fated victim, with alcoholism as a means to this end.[4]

Behind and nurturing this fallacy is an inadequate attention to the writer's actual work. Although Hyde announces elaborate plans to examine Berryman's *Dream Songs* as the locus of a "war between alcohol and Berryman's creative powers" (p. 9), his analyses of individual poems are not nearly numerous or detailed enough (nor, to be frank, sound enough) to carry out such an ambitious plan. Moreover, although Hyde's idea of a "war" within Berryman is useful up to a point, the metaphor largely ignores both the variety of Berryman's responses to alcohol and the complex tensions stemming from these.

Perhaps a more useful metaphor than Hyde's is James Dickey's, that Berryman was almost constantly at play. For Dickey this quality is contemptible; indeed, he expresses a sweeping and harsh contempt for Berryman as a "timid little academic who stays drunk all the time."[5] But the notion of Berryman's playing, for Dickey a self-conscious, artificial posturing, yields two other, more revealing senses. One of them conveys the duplicity or self-deception of the poet as alcoholic, finding ways to disguise his problem from himself. There are poems in which Berryman is almost certainly engaged in such play, a characteristic that resembles a recurring feature in the work of Fitzgerald, although the resemblance is limited because Berryman ultimately passed beyond self-deception. In another sense, Berryman played with his attitudes toward drinking by provisionally testing their validity or aptness for him. This sense would indicate a deliberate struggle to overcome conflict or perplexity[6] and would thus belie Hyde's opinion that Berryman was largely ignorant of the struggle, an unwitting victim of his own alcoholism. Even in a single poem, Berryman could be both honest and evasive about his drinking, both blind and perceptive.

For these reasons, Hyde's metaphor of a war within Berryman is finally inadequate, as is his conclusion that the war was "lost" before the *Dream Songs* ended. On the contrary, a major phase of this war continued in the three subsequent volumes —*Love & Fame* (1970), *Delusions, Etc.* (1972), and *Henry's Fate & Other Poems* (1977), the last a posthumous work collected by John Haffenden from over a thousand unpublished Berryman poems, many of them written after the *Dream Songs*. Hyde devotes just one paragraph to these later poems. Because Berryman's poetic output may have increased after the *Dream Songs* and certainly did not diminish, the *Songs* represent only a battle, rather than the entire war—especially when we find that the later poems introduce some distinctly new ways of seeing alcohol. If Berryman finally lost a war with alcohol, it was a much more problematic and absorbing struggle than Hyde indicates, a struggle whose complexity can only be appreciated inductively, by sacrificing the grand scope of metaphor to a sustained, detailed look at the poems themselves.

Although a character named Henry appears in many of the *Dream Songs*, we should not be misled by Berryman's declaration, in the note prefacing the volume, that Henry is "not the poet, not me."[7] To be sure, no character can ever satisfactorily represent a human being in all his living wholeness; but if Henry embodies only certain pieces or aspects of Berryman, these will bring us close to Berryman's actual reactions to his drinking.[8] Berryman's poems are, indeed, arguably a better vehicle for understanding his alcoholism than is his one novel, *Recovery*. This may seem a strange assertion, for *Recovery* addresses Berryman's alcoholism with an irreproachable honesty, in a more explicit and sustained way than the poems do; and Alan Severance, M.D., the hero of the novel, certainly bears as close a relationship to Berryman as does the Henry of the *Dream Songs*. But as a history of Berryman's drinking and his reactions to it, *Recovery* has the serious limitation, in spite of flashbacks, of covering an extremely short period, whereas his poems are the minutely detailed, sometimes almost diaristic record of years of his life. And whereas the novel necessarily concerns itself with plot, characterization, and setting, Berryman's verse admirably displays "the freedom of the poet" (to use the title of his collected essays) to bare his soul.

Eileen Simpson, Berryman's first wife, believes that his alcoholic drinking began at the time of his adulterous affair with "Lise" at Princeton in 1947.[9] Berryman wrote 115 sonnets about this affair; some of them establish a connection between heavy drinking and adultery or sex that persisted until late in his life. Evidently Berryman valued drinking for the liberation it provided from mundane responsibilities, the "audacities" (Sonnet 33) it enabled, and the sensual excitement it added. Sonnet 37 ends with a picture of Lise "tilting a frozen Daiquiri / Blonde, barefoot, beautiful, / flat on the bare floor rivetted to Bach." But, particularly as the affair wore on, alcohol could not shield Berryman from a strong sense of guilt, which manifests itself in Sonnet 93 as a desire "Sometime to dine with" Lise, "sometime to go / Sober to bed, a proper citizen."[10] Such reflections do not prevent him from associating drink with sex in the *Dream Songs*. Several of these, however, complicate a relationship that seems quite simple in the sonnets. Number 350, like many of the later *Dream Songs* written while Berryman was in Dublin, jokes rather grimly about various ways to end his adulteries, including cutting off his telephone service, hastening his senility, and "stroke four, put him on the wagon, Death, / no drinks: that ought to cure him."[11] Although the next Song, 351, concludes with a kind of broadly comic gesture—"Somewhere, everywhere / a girl is taking her clothes off"—the body of the song complicates without abandoning the dark jocularity of 350 by adding notes of pity and self-disgust as well as by hinting at the death of lust:

> Animal Henry sat reading the *Times Literary Supplement*
> with a large Jameson & a worse hangover.
> Who will his demon lover
> today become, he queried.
>
> .   .   .   .
>
> On all fours he danced about his cage, poor Henry
> for whom, my love, too much was never enough.

By far the most interesting poem having to do with sex and drinking is Dream Song 311. Its mixed tone perhaps reflects Berryman's inner confusion about how to regard his drinking:

> Hunger was constitutional with him,
> women, cigarettes, liquor, need need need
> until he went to pieces.
> The pieces sat up & wrote. They did not heed
> their piecedom but kept very quietly on
> among the chaos.

The tone here seems an incongruous combination of unsentimental, almost surreal pathos on one hand and boastfulness on the other, as though Berryman were saying: Look what I can do, even in my fragmented state. If it can be differentiated from tone, the substance of Berryman's attitude toward his appetites is equally difficult to determine. Although Berryman may be rationalizing when he says that his hunger for liquor is "constitutional," he may instead be honestly admitting the power or depth of his craving. On the whole, however, boastfulness seems to predominate: Berryman's appetites reflect a zest for life so strong that it keeps him going even in his piecedom and may recall such literary giants as Walt Whitman or Samuel Johnson, of whom Boswell wrote that "though he could be rigidly *abstemious*, [he] was not a *temperate* man either in eating or drinking."[12] This hint of heroism seems to be reinforced by the restoration of Berryman's wholeness as sexual magnetism in the final stanza: Henry is preparing to welcome a former mistress who he thought was three thousand miles away, a pleasure no ordinary man would likely experience. The poem, then, despite a briefly unsettling look at the results of Berryman's appetites, finally denies that these pose a problem; the imminent arrival of his onetime lover not only is flattering, but also enables Henry (and the reader) to transcend his fragmentation. This impression of Henry's wholeness would have been less secure had Berryman not omitted from the poem the actuality on which it is based: his ex-lover came for a drink, accompanied by her husband.[13]

These few poems contain the elements of most of Berryman's attitudes toward his drinking or his ways of dealing with it in the *Dream Songs*: escape, evasion, or denial, often using the technique of jocularity or facetiousness; but also honesty, which tends to increase in the later poems. These elements mingle in such a variety of ways that it is difficult to trace a line of development in Berryman's views of drinking.

Of a Berryman hospitalized for alcoholism in the spring of 1970, John Haffenden writes: "He joked with his misery."[14] In reality, as Haffenden's article elsewhere indicates and as a number of Berryman's later poems reveal, he was doing a great deal more than this about the misery of his alcoholism, which by 1970 had reached an acute stage. But, as some early *Dream Songs* show, joking in one form or another was one of Berryman's most characteristic reactions to his alcoholism. Often it is a defense mechanism, a means of minimizing or denying a problem. Dream Songs 54, 57, and 76 seem interrelated. The first finds the poet in a hospital. Although no explicit reason is given for his being there, alcoholism is at least a strong possibility:

> I have been operating from *nothing*,
> like a dog after its tail
> more slowly, losing altitude.[15]

This cogently expresses the emptiness, the exhaustion of inner resources often experienced by alcoholics at a crisis in their illness.
Song 57, then, may be seen as developing an attitude in response to
the condition of the poet: "something can (has) been said for sobriety / but very little." The attitude implies lack of acceptance of
sobriety; its mode is that of a witty, artfully clumsy epigram, as
though the issue of drinking versus sobriety mattered only as a
source of *bon mots*. Although this song says nothing further about
drinking, the subject has a more central place in Song 76. Humor,
though of a different type, is again present, as is an unwillingness to
accept sobriety. The poem, "Henry's Confession" (one of the relatively few Dream Songs with a title), begins:

> Nothin very bad happen to me lately.
> How you explain that?—I explain that, Mr Bones,
> terms o' your bafflin odd sobriety.
> Sober as man can get, no girls, no telephones,
> what could happen bad to Mr Bones?

The black dialect of Henry and his unnamed interlocutor, who figures in a number of Dream Songs and addresses his friend as Mr.
Bones, renders these lines humorous, perhaps suggesting that sobriety is so intrinsically dull that it needs the comic liveliness of a
blackface vaudeville routine. But in these lines and in the rest of the
poem there is also an argument seriously undermining sobriety. Not
only is sobriety unnatural ("bafflin odd") for Henry, it is sad—a
"handkerchief sandwich," as Henry puts it. If "nothin very bad happen" in sobriety, neither does anything exciting. It is in fact a common reaction of the newly sober alcoholic to find life rather flat and
dull. But the prospects of sobriety for Henry are much worse than
temporary sadness or boredom: "*If* life is a handkerchief sandwich,"
he says, he will "join" his father, a suicide. References to the suicide
of Berryman's father form one of the major motifs of the *Dream Songs*;
without doubting the impact of this disaster on Berryman or the
genuineness of his grieving for it, one might still conjecture that, in
Dream Song 76, it constituted a rationalization for his drinking. In
the last stanza the interlocutor tries to cheer Henry with a little song
and dance; but because Henry's sobriety is so sad and insipid that it
leads to thoughts of suicide, it scarcely seems a tenable condition.

In a number of other songs Berryman's treatment of drinking is also primarily facetious:

> Why drink so, two days running?
> two months, O seasons, years, two decades running?
> I answer (smiles) my question on the cuff:
> Man, I been thirsty. [Song 96]

This is a good example of what Lewis Hyde means by "the booze talking." Even though the rest of the poem makes clear that the poet is in a hospital, the breezy slang of his answer to the questions suggests his defiance, his denial of the seriousness of any problem. The opening lines of Song 225 use a reductive humor, converting a potentially serious question into an absurd logical conundrum:

> Madness & booze, madness & booze.
> Which'll can tell who preceded whose?
> What chicken walked out on what egg?

Most of the rest of this poem is unusually obscure, even for Berryman; but somehow, at the end, he manages to return to alcohol from a different angle: "Up Scotland! who only drunky sexy Burns / producing, which returns." Even if Berryman did not really believe the Burns myth implied by his two adjectives, the affirmation of the importance of drink for a major poet provides brief justification for his own drinking.[16]

The final example of Berryman's use of comedy to avoid a serious look at an alcoholic problem is Song 232, which is complex enough to warrant quoting in full:

> They work not well on all but they did for him.
> He wolfed friend breakfast, bolted lunch, & pigged
> dinner.
> Beastly yet, meat at midnight, juice he swigged,
> juices, avocado lemon'd, artichoke hearts,
> anything inner,
>
> except the sauce. Stand Henry off the sauce.
> He scrub himself, have nine   more matchless cigarettes,
> waiting upon the Lord.
> Pascal drop in, they placing cagey bets,

it's midnight! Being ample in their skins
they hang around bored.

Negroes, ignite! you have nothing to use but your brains,
which let bust out.—What was that again, Mr Bones?
De body have abuse
but is de one, too.—One-two, the old thrones
topple, dead sober. The decanter, pal!
Pascal, we free & loose.

In the opening stanza the poet seems to be following a regimen designed to supplant his craving for alcohol but plainly is not enjoying it ("pigged," "beastly"). The sudden appearance of Pascal, his wager, and midnight, the hour for death and for terminating a Faustian contract, complicates the poem. But something is strange; instead of the anticipated tension at the expiration of the contract, there is the boredom of sobriety. Stanza three explodes with a parody of the call to liberation in the Communist Manifesto. Applied to the present situation, it means that even though "de body have abuse" from alcohol, it is still number one, and its demands for free action should be met. The Faustian bargain may have been that the poet give up the "sauce," Pascal's wager that God would help him do it. But a revolution then occurs—"the old thrones / topple, dead sober"—suggesting that traditional powers or restraints die or can be vanquished *because* they are sober. The poet, released from his contract, immediately summons a "decanter, pal!" And Pascal is invited to forget his wager and join in allegiance to the true god, alcohol, in whom "we free & loose." Perhaps it is unfair to claim that in this poem Berryman was simply rationalizing his drinking problem; it may be an alcoholic's strikingly honest admission that the god he truly worships is alcohol. It is a remarkably unified and challenging poem, but it hardly represents Berryman's final word on or attitude toward drinking.

Even though he uses humor as a defense mechanism, a means of minimizing or denying a problem, Berryman also uses it occasionally for a wryly honest comment on his drinking.

Books drugs razor whisky shirts
Henry lies ready for his Eastern tour,
swollen ankles, one hand,

> air reservations, friends at the end of the hurts,
> a winter mind resigned: literature
> must spread, you understand. . . . [Song 169]

The incongruity of the items in the first line prepares us for the perception of a more important incongruity. Even if we feel some admiration for the pluck of this poet, who is setting out on a tour despite his battered condition, our primary question is likely to be: What can a man dependent on drugs and whiskey, one arm in a sling (stanza 2) perhaps because of a drunken fall, contribute to the spread of literature? Berryman of course facilitates our discovery of this question. Dream Song 250 begins:

> sád sights. A crumpled, empty cigarette pack.
> O empty bottle. Hey: an empty girl.
> Fill 'er up, pal.

The coarse levity of the third line exposes the equally coarse outlook of the addicted person: in his craving, both men and women (the connection between alcohol and sex briefly reappears) seem only physical receptacles waiting to be filled.

With and without humor, an awareness of unpleasant truths about his drinking is one of Berryman's most prominent characteristics in the *Dream Songs*. Although it is sometimes alloyed or compromised by other views in the same poem, its recurrence invalidates Hyde's view of Berryman as a helpless, unwitting victim of his alcoholism. Song 182, for example, describes Henry's habit of staying late at parties, "a bitter-ender." "Somebody called his wild wit" at such gatherings "riverine," an adjective perhaps implying an omnivorous, Whitmanesque appetite for life. But "bitter-ender" is Henry's (or Berryman's) self-appraisal, not an external judgment; being thus more reliable, it neutralizes the possible compliment of "riverine." Song 210 is full of images of emptiness, cold, and (most of all) flight. The poet's doctors send him to Atlantic City in the winter; while there he has "one drink" in a huge bar with one other man "a football field away," but in the last three lines of the poem he travels in quick succession home, abroad, "& then slunk back to his north." Read with some knowledge both of Alcoholics Anonymous and of Berryman's drinking, the poem becomes distinctly more ominous. In the context of the bleak imagery, the poet could scarcely have been so completely self-deceived as to think that his experiment with what AA calls "controlled" drinking could be successfully maintained. His restless, almost frantic movement is a good example of what AA refers to as the "geographical cure," an alcoholic's doomed attempt to stop drinking by changing location. Because his odd claim that his doctors sent him to Atlantic City "for privacy" is followed immediately by Berryman's account of his one drink in the nearly deserted bar, the claim seems meant to be seen through: the doctors have probably sought to remove him from the environment supposedly responsible for his excessive drinking. Song 210 is in fact altogether strange: the poet seems to make some attempt to deceive himself and his reader about his reason for going to Atlantic City, his success there, and his solution of his problem; at the same time, however, a combination of inauspicious imagery and a little analysis easily penetrates this rather flimsy guise and bares more probable truths. The poet is deceived yet, below the surface, not deceived.

Even a single line about drinking can afford glimpses sometimes more revealing than extended treatments. In Song 211 (which, unlike some adjacent Dream Songs, seems unconnected with 210), the poet reports that he is drinking ouzo, a Greek liqueur: "Ouzo was peaceful in the fearful nights." We know from other poems and from Haffenden's biography that Berryman suffered greatly from insomnia, which may be all that he means here by "fearful nights." But if we ask what caused the insomnia, we should know that, according to AA, fear is the alcoholic's most fundamental emotional problem, often wielding dreadful power as a pervasive "sense of impending calamity" without identifiable or definable source. Moreover, E. M. Jellinek suggests, as does the line from Song 211, that drinking is the alcoholic's only way to curb these fears and achieve peace, even though, as the line does not suggest, drinking to a great extent causes them.[17]

In general, the later Dream Songs, many written while Berryman was in Ireland on a Guggenheim Fellowship in 1966–67, show that his honesty about his drinking continued and perhaps increased. There are exceptions, one of them occurring in Song 323, an extended comparison of Henry and Winston Churchill in which Berryman notes that "they both drank, heavily." To the poet's advantage, this blurs a real and important difference between heavy and alcoholic drinking.[18] In Song 256, however, Henry, "possessed of many pills / & gin & whiskey," manages to achieve only five minutes of "tranquillity." Neither Berryman nor his reader needs to be familiar with the AA idea of serenity to realize that there is something wrong with such an ephemeral peace and the means of reaching it (*12 & 12*, pp. 63, 107–8). Song 275, apparently written shortly before Berryman's departure for Ireland, looks forward to it and its "cold fogs" as a kind of geographical cure; the rest of the poem is foreboding and honest enough to make one wonder whether Berryman himself believed in this cure. The central incident recounted is the poet's throwing two chairs to the floor while teaching. It is clear even to him that his justification of this action as "good" for the students is a rationalization; the real reason is his tense nerves, begging for "A little more whiskey please. / A little more whiskey please." This repetition, suggesting the strength of the craving and the probability that only a great deal of whiskey will suffice, also suggests how unlikely it is that a change of location will help. Berryman may want to believe it will, but the honesty of his poem undercuts him. Similarly, in Song 292, Berryman (by now in Ireland) tends to recoil from an uncompromising look at his alcoholic condition, though this time the tendency is early rather than late in the poem, and its form is humor (a punning on *pub* and *pub-erty*) rather than imagined flight. Again, however, honesty leaves the stronger impression:

> Henry, who was always a crash programme,
> smiled, and the smile was worse than the rictus of the victim,
> "Another drop" said Mick.

Berryman, Mick, and the reader are well aware that "another drop" is ironic understatement. More than one of Berryman's Irish poems trenchantly notes the differences between the young man full of hope and life who visited there at twenty-one and the "wreck" who has returned (Song 283), and there is little doubt about the chief cause of this difference. Song 300 redeploys the difference by a partly implicit pun on "spirits": when he was young, the poet recovered them "at once" and naturally soon after arriving in Ireland; now, drinking bottled spirits, he is slower to recover from the unsettling effects of arrival.

The last three Dream Songs to be considered display such painful honesty that they seem to portend some major changes in Berryman's drinking or his attitudes toward it—changes amply illustrated in the poetry following the *Dream Songs*. In Song 365, Henry "woke half-sane / & screamed for stronger drinks. Open the main!" This image has lost all trace of an appealingly gargantuan or Whitmanesque zest for life; it conveys raw, naked need. Song 310 concludes:

> He was *all* regret, swallowing his own vomit,
> disappointing people, letting everyone down
> in the forests of the soul.

Because drinking is nowhere mentioned in the poem and because a possible reason for the self-disgust is given in the opening line, "His gift receded. He could write no more," the image of swallowing vomit may be only an unusually vivid metaphor for this disgust. But the overpowering regret or remorse, another leading characteristic of alcoholics, coupled with the fact that drunks are more likely than other people to have the experience of swallowing or choking on their own vomit, may suggest that Berryman's alcoholism, rather than a writer's block, lies at the root of the poem.[19] Dream Song 356 seems to present a poet almost at the end of his tether or, in AA parlance, about to hit bottom:

> With fried excitement he looked across at life
> wondering if he could bear it more,
> wondering,
> in the middle of a short war with his wife,
> deep in the middle, in short, of a war,
> he couldn't say whether to sing
>
> further or seal his lonely   throat, give himself up.
> Tomorrow is his birthday, makes you think.
> The London *TLS*
> are mounting só much of him he could scream.
> There was a time he marched from dream to dream
> but he seems to be out of ink,
>
> he seems to be out of everything again
> save whiskey & cigarettes, both bad for him.
> He clapped both hands to both ears
> and resigned from the ranks of giving men.

In a minute now he'll wake, distinct & grim.
I'm not, he cried, what I appears.

The contrast between this poem and Song 169 is worth observing. In the earlier poem the incongruous spectacle of the poet setting out to spread literary light with drugs, drink, "swollen ankles," and one arm in a sling is at least partly a source of amusement. But in Song 356 the discrepancy between appearance and reality conveyed most explicitly by the final line, between the flattering attention of the *TLS* and the poet's abject dependence on "whiskey & cigarettes," is a source of something close to despair: "he could scream." As he says, he seems to be out of all resources and desires except his addictions.

Before turning to Berryman's later poems, we must consider a possible connection between drinking, suffering, and poetic inspiration that some commentators claim to see in Berryman's life and work. William Heyen, basing his opinion on personal acquaintance and an interview, says, "I suspect that Berryman . . . felt . . . that intense suffering led to the greatest poetry." Haffenden is less tentative about making such a connection: "Until April 1970, Berryman took alcohol for the blood of his life, the force behind his poetic powers." Because *The Maze*, by Eileen Simpson, is a novel, one should not simply equate its leading male character, the hard-drinking poet Benjamin Bold, with Berryman; nevertheless, a remark about Bold by his wife illuminates the connection between suffering and art: "Benjamin courts, even collaborates with disaster. He has a very limited tolerance for happiness. I sometimes think that if he felt he wasn't paying a high enough price for his gift he would get panicky, afraid that his talent might dry up."[20] That this connection may exist for other drinking writers and that they may fear a loss of inspiration in sobriety are asserted in an interview with Jill Robinson, author of *Perdido* and *Bed / Time / Story*: "The fear a writer has about being sober is, 'My God I'm going to lose that stuff. I'm going to lose the nightmares and those dreams and all of that sensitivity, that dark attitude.'"[21] For any alcoholic, the adoption of sobriety is fearful: it removes all his old props, requiring a radical alteration of thinking and outlook. But because of the connection between drinking, suffering, and inspiration, for an alcoholic artist this change may be doubly difficult. Berryman wrote his major poem, the *Dream Songs*, during the period of his worst alcoholic drinking, and this same period saw

John Berryman and Drinking

the arrival of his fame as a poet. Because fame and his status among contemporary poets had an extraordinary importance to Berryman, and because fear, certainly including fear of poetic failure, was of no less importance, it must have occurred to him that the removal of alcohol from his life might cause a disastrous drying up of the source of his distinctive inspiration.

Despite the plausibility of this connection, very little in Berryman's work substantiates or illustrates it. In Dream Song 157, one of the several elegies on Delmore Schwartz, Berryman writes that "every first-rate soul" will make "sacrifices" for fame and glory, an idea that he could certainly have applied to himself as well; but the poem does not suggest that drinking, or the suffering it can cause, may be one of these sacrifices. Song 250 seems to posit a connection between alcohol and "the valid & a mad; yeah, mad, and so / the valid, man." But the connection is so tenuous and brief that the example is of little value. *Recovery* seems to be the only place where Berryman makes a clear connection between drink, suffering, and inspiration: "Severance was a conscientious man. He had really thought, off and on for twenty years, that it was his duty to drink, namely, to sacrifice himself. He saw the products as worth it. Maybe they were—if there had been any connexion."[22] Were it not for the fiction that Severance is a doctor, "poems" could well have been substituted for "products." But it is definitely worth noting that Severance, undergoing therapy for his alcoholism, now doubts the existence of any connection between his alcoholic suffering or sacrifice and its "products." And Berryman in Song 356 goes beyond doubt: "whiskey & cigarettes," he intimates, instead of furnishing inspiration, are the powers that have totally desolated him, depriving him of his ability to write ("he seems to be out of ink") and to march "from dream to dream."

For whatever reasons or from whatever fears, a number of poems after the *Dream Songs* show that Berryman was ready for change and working to effect it. This does not mean that his struggle with alcoholism, his confusions and evasions, had ended. Because his progress was fitful, some of the same attitudes and elements observed in the *Dream Songs* reappear. Much more important, however, we shall also observe that the struggle largely shifts to a different plane, which can best be called the spiritual. Between the *Dream Songs* and the writing of many of the later poems, Berryman underwent what AA, by which he was strongly influenced,[23] would call a spiritual experience. This experience did not permanently dispel Berryman's fears, which is to say that it did not wholly or permanently change him. But from it, from Alcoholics Anonymous, and from his struggles for sobriety Berryman seems quite suddenly to have derived a new style and language that have both disconcerted and disappointed some critics.[24] Berryman himself was well aware of his new style; he called it "transparent."[25] At its most distinctive, it can seem almost prosaic in its directness and its emotional nakedness; it is sharply different from Berryman's *Dream Song* style with its slang, syntactical inversions, black dialect, and other forms of linguistic play. Although not all of the later poems are devoid of these characteristics, there is little question that Berryman's style changed greatly and that profound inner causes lay behind the change. Because the dates of composition or first publication of Berryman's later poems are sometimes unknown, they will generally be considered in the order in which they appear in Berryman's three last volumes of verse (1970, 1972, 1977), a procedure that will reveal no steady progress from active alcoholism to sobriety but rather a warfare in which victories could be precarious and ambiguous.

For tracing this development, one of Berryman's most important poems is "Of Suicide."[26] Freed of the persona of Henry and its accoutrements, it is written in Berryman's new style. It depicts a poet almost as desperate as a trapped animal, still looking for ways to avoid a final reckoning with his alcoholism but clearly running out of options. I quote here all but the third and sixth stanzas of this seven-stanza poem:

> Reflexions on suicide, & on my father, possess me.
> I drink too much. My wife threatens separation.
> She won't "nurse" me. She feels "inadequate."
> We don't mix together.
>
> It's an hour later in the East.
> I could call up Mother in Washington, D.C.
> *But* could she help me?
> And all this postal adulation & reproach?
>
> .   .   .   .
>
> I still plan to go to Mexico this summer.
> The Olmec images! Chichén Itzá!
> D. H. Lawrence has a wild dream of it.

> Malcolm Lowry's book when it came out I taught to
> my precept at Princeton.
>
> I don't entirely resign. I may teach the Third Gospel
> this afternoon. I haven't made up my mind.
> It seems to me sometimes that others have easier jobs
> & do them worse.
>
> .   .   .   .
>
> Rembrandt was sober. There we differ. Sober.
> Terrors came on him. To us too they come.
> Of suicide I continually think.
> Apparently he didn't. I'll teach Luke.

Suicide, especially his father's but also his own, is one of Berryman's major preoccupations; nowhere else in the poetry is the thought of it linked more directly to his drinking. If the final line affords a frail affirmation in Berryman's decision to go on, to "teach Luke," this is certainly threatened by the next-to-last line. The middle sections of the poem disclose a number of major unresolved problems that almost certainly abetted Berryman's drinking and therefore his continual thoughts of suicide. There is a distinct note of self-pity, one of the most harmful vices of the alcoholic, in Berryman's complaint that "others have easier jobs / & do them worse"; such a feeling, of course, can readily supply the alcoholic with an excuse to get drunk (*AA*, pp. 61–62). Even more definitively symptomatic of alcoholism is Berryman's expectation, though currently frustrated, that his wife perform the service that AA calls "enabling": it might consist of literal nursing, as Berryman suggests without elaboration, but it can also be any function—sympathy for his hangovers, acceptance, calling an employer with an excuse for why the alcoholic cannot come to work—that helps him to continue his alcoholic drinking and to avoid confronting it. F. Scott Fitzgerald found several women to fill this role after the more or less permanent hospitalization of Zelda and the onset of his worst alcoholism in the 1930s. Because Berryman's wife refuses this part, the poet then considers telephoning his mother. Although he refrains from this appalling transference of dependence,[27] his mind, still seeking ways to evade his alcoholic problem, leaps to the prospect of a geographical cure, a vacation in Mexico. But the reference to Malcolm Lowry's *Under the Volcano*, which memorializes Lowry's colossal Mexican drunkenness, exposes the futility of this cure. So, although Berryman's struggles to evade his alcoholism are not encouraging, there is hope in the sense conveyed by the poem that he is close to exhausting ways of dodging his problem.

That Berryman's movement toward sobriety was a curve of ups and downs can be seen by juxtaposing two poems from 1970. "Death Ballad," written either during or shortly after Berryman's hospitalization for alcoholism in the spring of 1970 and first published on 22 July 1970,[28] is about two people in the psychiatric ward, Tyson and Jo. Its last stanza expresses affectionate concern that amounts almost to a prayer:

> take up, outside your blocked selves, some small thing
> that is moving
> & wants to keep on moving
> & needs therefore, Tyson, Jo, your loving.

By evincing his care for Tyson and Jo in writing the poem, Berryman was also and perhaps even consciously escaping "the bondage of self," an important stage in the recovery from alcoholism (*AA*, p. 63). Nevertheless, Berryman relapsed into drinking and was hospitalized again in the fall of 1970. "He Resigns," though written not long after "Death Ballad," manifests such great remorse and despondency that the resumption of drinking was utterly predictable:

> Age, and the deaths, and the ghosts.
> Her having gone away
> in spirit from me. Hosts
> of regrets come & find me empty.
>
> I don't feel this will change.
> I don't want any thing
> or person, familiar or strange.
> I don't think I will sing
>
> any more just now;
> or ever. I must start
> to sit with a blind brow
> above an empty heart.[29]

The "resigns" of the title is ambiguous; it could simply mean that Berryman wishes to resign from living. But if it may also indicate a

John Berryman and Drinking

form of acceptance, this and the emptiness of the poem could suggest Berryman's readiness to try sobriety and Alcoholics Anonymous again, because AA stresses the importance of an admission of powerlessness over alcohol and a surrender to the help of a higher power in achieving sobriety.[30]

Assuming that the next three poems of *Delusions* (excluding only "Ecce Homo") stand in the order in which they were written, they illustrate a fascinating development from "He Resigns." "No" (p. 41) reveals a common obstinacy of the alcoholic: although he may admit his alcoholism, he is not necessarily willing to take action against it. "She says: *Seek help!*" almost certainly refers to Berryman's wife; and the help she means is almost as certainly AA or at least a hospital with a program of therapy. But much of the remainder of the poem is a series of images of revulsion—"putrid olives, / stench of the Jersey flats, the greasy clasp / crones in black doorways afford their violent clients"—vehemently signifying Berryman's rejection of his wife's demand and his disgust for a life without alcohol. If he must act, Berryman indicates his preference "for some soft & solid & sudden way out," such as the "hemlock" of Socrates. By this time in his drinking career Berryman was familiar enough with AA to know of its warning against seeking an "easier, softer way" to sobriety (*AA*, p. 58). In his first adjective Berryman may not only be echoing that phrase, one of the most often cited by AA members, but also implying that, in spite of AA's rejection of ease, death is both easier and better than sobriety. "Mutinous," the opening word of the next poem, "The Form" (pp. 42–43), aptly describes Berryman's frame of mind in "No." Naturally enough for an alcoholic, this leads to a bender ("through sixteen panicked nights / a trail of tilted bottles"), thoughts of suicide (the purchase of a gun), and feelings of divine rejection ("He has spewed me out").[31] The poem is probably based on the actual drunk that hospitalized Berryman in the fall of 1970. Surprisingly, however, the poem ends on a note of nascent surrender to God, "My light terrible body unlocked, I leaned upon You," which is reiterated and strengthened in "A Prayer After All" (pp. 45–46), a poem written shortly after his hospitalization:

> Father, Father, I am overwhelmed.
> I cannot speak tonight.
> *Do* you receive me back into Your sight?
> It seems it must be so. . . .

The experience described in the rest of the poem was apparently as sudden and powerful as the spiritual experience of Bill Wilson, co-founder of AA.[32]

This surrender did not mark the end of Berryman's difficulties. As most in AA realistically acknowledge, alcoholics are refractory and repeatedly need to submit their wills to God. Nor was this Berryman's only problem with sobriety. In an untitled poem in *Henry's Fate*, facing the difficulty of giving up the life of drinking "established 22 years ago," Berryman also faces a related difficulty: that of living "in the now. Where I must be / for years, for years, for years" (p. 45). Living in the present, a day at a time—or even a minute at a time, if this is necessary for staying sober—is one of AA's key ideas; if practiced, it prevents the corrosive discouragement and return to drinking that could well follow from the formidable difficulty of having to stay sober forever. Unfortunately, Berryman's poem shows that, rather than mastering that concept, he is dismayed by the prospect of sobriety for years on end. "The Alcoholic in the 3rd Week of the 3rd Treatment," though on the surface more hopeful of sobriety, is slightly tainted in tone by what seems a sarcastic overemphasis on the simplicity of staying sober, for which only one procedure is required: "You just never drink again all each damned day." Since the rest of the poem is serious, it is unlikely that Berryman is suddenly turning playful here; he seems genuinely resentful of the necessity of maintaining sobriety a day at a time (*Henry's Fate*, p. 86).

Ultimately, however, Berryman's problem with sobriety was profoundly spiritual. "A Prayer for the Self," whose importance to Berryman may be suggested by its being the only one of "Eleven Addresses to the Lord" to have its individual title, concludes: "Lift up / sober toward truth a scared self-estimate."[33] This is as much a prayer or exhortation to the self as it is a prayer for the self. For all its succinctness, it shows that Berryman was acutely aware of the spiritual action he must take, though with God's help. It is also extremely significant because it specifies the four elements involved in this action: sobriety, truth or a quest for it, fear, and a self-evaluation or "moral inventory," as the important Step 4 of AA terms it.[34] For Berryman, these elements were not of equal strength; consequently, although the action seems relatively simple and straightforward, it was so difficult for him that he never really accomplished it.

He certainly tried. "4th Weekend" is about his attempt to take

Step 4; if successful, he would have made a major approach to the truth about himself and the reasons for his drinking. But the poet, like Alan Severance in the early pages of *Recovery*, is somewhat too busy with his fellow patients. Although these outreach efforts are admirable in themselves, one suspects him of using them to divert himself from the pain of looking inward, for when he does, he discovers "a wilderness," the roads through it washed out by "torrents." At the end of the poem, in his hope that writing four letters may lead "toward my own awful center" (*Henry's Fate*, p. 88), one may suspect still more delusion or evasion; Step 4 is not epistolary.

By "Dry Eleven Months," written on 16 December 1971, less than a month before Berryman's death, he has evidently taken Step 4: "I've tried my self, found guilty on each charge / my self diseased." To any AA member, however, it would be significant that Berryman speaks of himself as "dry" rather than "sober." His sobriety is unhappy and therefore precarious. The ending of the preceding poem in *Henry's Fate*, "Group,"

> Each long-dry throat
> still, still with horror & passion runs
> immortal alcohols,

suggests that he and his fellow patients, despite the horror of their illness, have a perpetual, unquenchable craving for its source. Even more significant, as Berryman notes in "Dry Eleven Months," although he has made sacrifices and to the best of his ability incorporated the principles of AA in his life, he has not achieved one of the major results that the whole program promises: "I am not without a companion: there's left Fear."

What has gone wrong? The probable answer to this question comes at the end of the poem, revealing the object of Berryman's fear. When his heart stops, he says, "I'm afraid of you" (*Henry's Fate*, p. 92). Although the poem nowhere else mentions God, this could hardly refer to anyone else. Because AA's Step 3, the decision to turn one's will and life over to the care of God, precedes Step 4 as a condition for its effectiveness, the reason why this step has not brought a contented sobriety becomes clear: Berryman could scarcely surrender himself to a power he feared. AA promises that faith will conquer fear; obviously this cannot work when the object of faith is also the source of fear.[35]

"Dry Eleven Months" is not completely at odds with Berryman's other poetry concerning God. In "The Facts & Issues," written on 20 May 1971, Berryman's friend and fellow poet William Meredith notices the queer hysteria at the end, "the baffling spectacle of a man fending off torrents of a grace that has become unbearable." It is less baffling if we detect fear of God just beneath the surface of some other lines. Considering an afterlife, Berryman writes:

> I can't say I have hopes in that department
> myself, I lack ambition just just there,
> I know that Presence says it's mild, and it's mild,
> but being what I am I wouldn't care
> to dare go nearer.

Although Berryman stridently proclaims his happiness in the present, "what I am," as explained elsewhere in the poem, is a "filthy fact," a collection of "pathetic & disgusting vices." If the Redeemer is willing to forgive these, Berryman seems less sure of the "Presence" in spite of his hasty concession of its mildness.[36]

This account of Berryman's fear is admittedly something of an oversimplification of his emotional state during his final months. His fear or (more accurately) fears were so long lasting and pervasive, such a prevalent motif of his poetry,[37] that in the end they cannot be completely accounted for. But it does suggest why AA did not fully work for Berryman and why his sobriety was such an uphill struggle. The recognition of the nature of this struggle and of the profundity of Berryman's fears[38] can help one see more clearly the injustice of James Dickey's contempt for Berryman as a "timid little academic who stays drunk all the time." Given Berryman's conception of God, to work for sobriety at all required even more courage than it usually takes for other alcoholics. If the feared rejection of the "Presence" is a projection of Berryman's self-loathing, the valor of his struggle is no less real.

The next-to-last poem of *Henry's Fate*, written and dated by Berryman only two days before his suicide, is inevitably of interest for that reason. It contemplates suicide, including the means Berryman actually chose, and again expresses fear, though of a much less cosmic kind (what might happen if his suicide attempt should fail) than that expressed in "Dry Eleven Months." Although anyone claiming full understanding of the reasons for a man's suicide would only be exposing his own insufferable presumption, the last poem of the volume, "Phase Four," throws more light on the despair that may have led to that act than does the penultimate poem. If "King David Dances" is the late poem for which Berryman would perhaps most like to be remembered, the triumphal assertion of his indomitability as a poet against overwhelming odds,[39] "Phase Four" is the poem that discloses the plight of the suffering alcoholic with the greatest poignance.

> I will begin by mentioning the word
> "Surrender"—that's the 4th & final phase.
> The word. What is the thing, well, must be known
> in Heaven. "Acceptance" is the phase before;
>
> if after finite struggle, infinite aid,
> ever you come there, friend,
> remember backward me lost in defiance,
> as I remember those admitting & complying.
>
> We cannot tell the truth, it's not in us.
> That truth comes hard. O I am fighting it,
> my Weapon One: I know I cannot win,
> and half the war is lost, that's to say won.
>
> The rest is for the blessed. The rest is bells
> at sundown off across a dozen lawns,
> a lake, two stands[40] of laurel, where they come
> out of phase three mild toward the sacristy.

Much of the poem is based on the idea that there are four stages by which the alcoholic achieves sobriety: awareness of his problem, admission, acceptance, and surrender to a higher power for help in overcoming it. We have already noticed Berryman's difficulty with the stage of surrender. Here he reiterates and further illuminates this difficulty. In heaven surrender may be really achieved, but on earth it is merely verbal; all we can do is mouth "the word." If acceptance, the phase before surrender, can be achieved by some "after finite struggle, infinite aid," it will not be won by Berryman, who is "lost" in the opposite state, "defiance." There is even perhaps a touch of scorn for "those admitting & complying"—for those, that is, who only go through the motions of true acceptance, evidently incapable of the moral rigor or energy required for a searching inquiry into the meaning of these four stages. If they were capable, they might have to confront the shock with which the third stanza opens: "We cannot tell the truth, it's not in us. / That truth comes hard." Berryman is now rejecting as impossible that approach to truth whose importance he acknowledged in "A Prayer for the Self." Far more disturbing, this line and a half constitute a total rejection of the foundation of AA, which maintains both that a person can know the truth about his alcoholism and that he can then know, through AA, how to overcome it. Although in the same stanza Berryman goes on to say that he is resisting this hard truth that we cannot know the truth, its last two lines are so obscure that the shock of its beginning is not significantly reduced. "The rest"—the vision of paradisal peace in the remainder of the poem—"is for the blessed," whose number cannot include Berryman. Their condition requires that they come "mild toward the sacristy," whereas Berryman has already established his defiance.

Reading this poem, one can hardly be surprised that, as Haffenden notes, Berryman returned briefly to drinking not long before his death. [41] In view of his despair, the wonder is that he did not continue drinking until the very moment of his suicide. The poem is almost unbearably bleak: the "truth" is not accessible, and there is no compensation for that cruel discovery, at least not for Berryman, in another state. The despair becomes still more ominous if one accepts the importance of Kathe Davis's perception about Berryman: "It's difficult to avoid the impression that Berryman's often desperate belief that he could find the truth and that it would make him free—despite the accumulating evidence of his own life—was . . . what kept him going." [42] If "Phase Four" marks the end of this belief, it also brings the end of his motive or will to live. Yet one cannot withhold admiration from a man whose honesty and courage led him to this impasse, a man perhaps resembling Marlowe's Dr. Faustus as Robert Ornstein understands him: refusing to exchange defiance for compliance or submission in order to propitiate a God who, for Faustus, had already fattened on too many pious souls and who for Berryman, in the final analysis, aroused too much fear to command trust or love.[43] To be sure, a number of Berryman's later poems, in particular "A Prayer After All" and "Eleven Addresses to the Lord," appear to achieve, however tentatively, a faith in a benevolent deity. "Phase Four," however, may represent his most fundamental beliefs on this subject.

E I G H T

Jim, Jake, and Gordon
Alcohol and Comedy

The chapters up to this point have dealt mostly with alcohol as a major problem of a central character or characters and with works in which that problem receives extended treatment. Although a deft short-story writer like John Cheever can indicate the horrors of alcoholism in a few pages, the writer who regards it as a complex problem requiring thorough exploration will be most likely to put it near or at the center of a lengthy work. Of course, there are many writers (and many people) for whom drinking is not a problem but a pleasure, conducive to comedy rather than tragedy; these writers tend to give it less prominence than those for whom it constitutes a problem. This is not to say that, when reduced to a scene or an incident in a book, drinking is rendered inconsequential. This chapter will examine three comic novels where the main characters are definitely not alcoholic or problem drinkers but where a drunk scene (or, in one case, two such scenes) makes an important difference. Each scene contributes to preserving or reinforcing the comic quality of Kingsley Amis's *Lucky Jim* and *Jake's Thing* and of George Orwell's *Keep the Aspidistra Flying*.

Two connections between alcohol and comedy are worth noting at this point; one involves comic vitality, the other, a link between alcohol and satiric comedy. As Leopold Damrosch, Jr., has observed in a recent essay, the Gaelic meaning of "usquebae" (whiskey) is "'water of life'—the same substance that revives Finnegan's corpse in the ballad 'Finnegan's Wake'"; and, Damrosch adds, "Burns, with his comic vision, suggests that man is more human, not less, when liberated by drink."[1] Perceiving this connection depends on also grasping the implied contrast between the life-threatening character of tragedy and comedy as a life-giving or life-renewing force. Robert M. Polhemus, in observations somewhat more elaborate than Damrosch's, posits a

prehistoric time when wine was substituted for blood in tribal cere-
monies, for reasons probably related to the symbolic substitution of
wine for Christ's blood in the eucharist: wine is used in a festive celebration of life, in a "comic mass" that affirms the celebrant's oneness
with his fellows, at least temporarily ending his separateness and
muting his "nagging knowledge that 'I' must die."[2] At the level of
ordinary experience, Don Marquis's comic character the Old Soak
seems to confirm this theory:

> And by the time you drink the third one, somewhere away
> down deep inside of you there is a warm spot wakes up and
> kind of smiles.
> And that is your soul has waked up.
> And you sort of wish you hadn't been so mean with your wife
> when you left home, and you look around and see a friend and
> have one with him and your soul says to you away down deep
> inside of you for all you know about them old Bible stories they
> may be true after all and maybe there is a God and kind of feel
> glad there may be one.[3]

From the context of these reflections it is obvious that the Old Soak
is using them to rationalize his excessive drinking. But his vulgarity
only shows how commonplace, even trite, are the beliefs about
drinking couched in more formal language by Polhemus.

Certainly such ideas help to account for Jake's drunk to escape
awareness of incipient impotence and the drunks of Jim and Gordon
to overcome feelings of loneliness, humiliation, or acute uneasiness
in their society. But in his emphasis on drinking as a kind of commu-
nion, a quest for human solidarity, Polhemus fails to see that, when
carried to excess, drunkenness may instead be an act of aggression, a
rebellious attack on a society that the drinker is rejecting or is at least
far from sure he wants to join. Freud is important for understanding
this motive for drinking and its relation to satiric comedy. He asserts
that "a change in mood is the most precious thing that alcohol
achieves for mankind," because it "reduces the inhibiting forces . . .
and makes accessible once again sources of pleasure which were
under the weight of suppression." Although it should be added that
in this passage Freud had in mind the inducement of "a cheerful
mood" by alcohol, it seems quite legitimate to suppose that he would
also have acknowledged alcohol to assist in another sort of release

from inhibition, that which would facilitate what he calls "tendentious jokes." These are "especially favoured" as expressions of "aggressiveness or criticism . . . against persons in exalted positions who claim to exercise authority. The joke then represents a rebellion against that authority, a liberation from its pressure."[4] In other words, the lowering of inhibitions by alcohol may just as well result in aggression as in warm feelings of oneness with mankind. Freud's idea of the tendentious joke, when joined with his comments about the effects of alcohol, is particularly useful in explaining the drunken behavior of Amis's Jim Dixon. It also sheds some light on Amis's Jake Richardson and Orwell's Gordon Comstock, although Jake, older than the other two, perhaps finds less need for alcohol as a means of assertion or expression. Other connections between alcohol and various aspects of comedy can best be established as we analyze individual novels.

Lucky Jim is not one type of comedy but a complex synthesis of types. A phrase that Frank Lentricchia has recently used to characterize the goal of the criticism of Kenneth Burke also admirably summarizes Jim Dixon's major goal: "the full realization of freedom in the stream of actual historical life."[5] The phrase suggests that Dixon will not, while pursuing his aim, retreat to the "green world" of comedy described by Northrop Frye. Dixon and his beloved, Christine Callaghan, are much too occupied with struggling against an oppressive society to find leisure for any idyllic interlude. For the most part Amis is a realistic rather than a romantic observer and critic of society; in presenting the intricacies of his characters' machinations Amis writes, among other things, a twentieth-century satiric comedy of manners.[6] If Lucky Jim traces the pattern of comedy that Frye defines as "the movement from isolation to integration in the community,"[7] it is only after a protracted battle with, followed by a repudiation of, a false society, represented chiefly by Margaret Peel and the Welches. Dixon and Christine do not come to terms with the community they start with; instead, they abandon it altogether for a new and better society under the aegis of Christine's uncle, Julius Gore-Urquhart. Nevertheless, Frye's ideas help us to see what a classic, almost archetypal comedy Lucky Jim is in some ways, pitting Jim's youth (Spring) against the older, blocking character (Winter) of Professor Welch, who doubles as the rigid, mechanical character identified by Bergson as the chief object of laughter.[8] Indeed, some of the most hilarious passages in *Lucky Jim* occur when Welch, an ill-made human machine, mismanages another machine, his automobile.[9] Also older than Dixon, Margaret is a second blocking character. Her behavior is mechanical and predictable; her neurotic dependency on men makes her manipulative and calculating. Dixon, though caught in her toils till quite late in the novel, still observes that she is like an actress planning her effects (pp. 78, 114, 163).

Jim's most valuable possessions—authenticity, spontaneity, freedom, honesty—are threatened by these characters, who at least unwittingly would force on him their own "mechanical forms of repetitive behavior."[10] Although Jim is a member of the university history department that Welch chairs and is thus supposedly a colleague, when Welch deigns to notice him at all it is usually in order to employ him as academic factotum. Jim's dismissive contempt for all academic pursuits (including his own specialty, medieval history) as a giant swindle might be regarded as a sign of Amis's anti-intellectualism, but this reading is probably erroneous and certainly unnecessary. Jim's honesty reacts in proportion to the strength of the threat he feels, and because the novel affords no evidence that Welch is unrepresentative of academic leadership, how could Jim see the so-called life of the mind in a collegiate setting as anything other than a fraud?[11]

Jim's environment, in any event, seems so indifferent to him that it would deny him his very identity. This at least could be the subtle suggestion of the several false names given him: "Faulkner," more than once, by Welch; "Dickinson" by Welch's son Bertrand; "Jackson" by the college porter; "Dickerson" and "Dickenson" by Caton, a journal editor whose fraudulence neatly complements Welch's; and a formal "James" by Margaret, who thereby doubtless hopes to hold him at a convenient but easily manipulable distance. These misnomers are a small but real addition to the exasperation that Dixon already feels at being regarded, especially by the Welches, as a provincial upstart, a social and cultural inferior. But Christine soon begins to call him "Jim"; and Gore-Urquhart gets his name right the first time. The misnaming also suggests that Dixon's most profound struggle is to find his real identity and individuality.

The odds against Dixon's success seem heavy at first. Although he has a few friends and allies, they are not, until the appearance of the enigmatic Gore-Urquhart, people with much authority or influence. Jim greatly admires a fellow lodger named Atkinson "for his air of detesting everything . . . and of not meaning to let this detestation become staled by custom" (p. 36), but Atkinson is too peripheral a figure to serve as a real mentor. At one point a vision of Welch "canted over in his chair like a broken robot"(p. 80) furnishes a sinister glimpse of what Dixon could become unless he somehow frees himself from Welch and his society. This task is made still more difficult by the appearance, early in the novel, of another blocking character, Welch's son Bertrand, with whose girl, Christine, Dixon falls almost immediately in love and whom he must wrest from Bertrand in a contest that takes most of the novel.[12]

To triumph over these forces Jim needs, by his own admission, a great deal of luck. And he receives it—hence the appropriateness of the title and its epigraph, the "old song"

> Oh, lucky Jim,
> How I envy him.
> Oh, lucky Jim,
> How I envy him.

Since his satiric scorn for the society that surrounds him becomes increasingly open, he is extraordinarily lucky to avoid the fate that, according to Robert C. Elliott, sometimes befell the primitive or prehistoric satirist: that of becoming a scapegoat, of falling victim to his society's desire for revenge.[13] There are more obvious instances of his luck; his meeting and eventual winning of Christine require large increments of luck as well as Jim's persistence and a mutual attraction. As a man realistically and often resentfully aware of his social class, Jim recognizes on first meeting Christine that "women like this were never on view except as the property of men like Bertrand" (p. 41). Without the blunt questioning of Carol Goldsmith, a friendly acquaintance, as to what he intends to do about Christine (p. 127), Dixon would never have made his decisive move of taking Christine away from Bertrand at a dance and back to the Welches in a taxi. Later, Margaret suddenly and surprisingly overcomes her neurosis long enough to encourage Dixon to pursue Christine (pp. 190–91); but because he does not yet feel worthy of her and has developed something of a counterdependency on Margaret, Dixon also needs the further, almost providentially lucky assistance of Catchpole, Margaret's supposed former lover, whose disclosures about her neurotic contrivances free him. Finally, Dixon needs the luck of Welch's lateness in delivering Christine to a train station to match his own lateness in arriving there by bus. Though by then his union with Christine seems assured, he nevertheless has the uneasy feeling that it may hinge on his meeting her at the station.

Indispensable as luck is to his success, it must be abetted by some of his own strengths, particularly his cleverness, his spontaneity and freedom, and his willingness to act decisively at crucial moments. In combination with honesty, his cleverness recalls the true wit of Restoration comedy, hating and mocking sham or affectation in others—the affectation of being an artist (Bertrand) or being knowledgeable about the arts (Welch). In willingness to act, Dixon's foil is Beesley, his friend and fellow toiler in the academic vineyard, alone at the college dance and quietly getting drunk at the bar instead of attempting to fulfill any sexual desires. In contrast, Dixon, though luckier than Beesley, comes to see that his good fortune demands the support of courageous faith and commitment—that is to say, an important form of mental action. "For once in his life Dixon resolved to bet on his luck. What luck had come his way in the past he'd distrusted, stingily held on to until the chance of losing his initial gain was safely past. It was time to stop doing that" (p. 140).

In the early chapters Jim seems a long way from being able to act with resolute courage. He despises people like Welch but keeps these feelings hidden; the only outlet for his anger at being in Welch's power is fantasized violence expressed by private mimicry, which crops out with great frequency and constitutes some of the most brilliant comedy in the book. The mimicry venting anger becomes such a settled habit of expression that, when he begins to fall in love with Christine, Dixon can at first find no appropriate "face" for his emotions; he can only think of conveying them in a manner very much like one he might choose in a moment of disgust with Welch: "He wanted to implode his features, to crush air from his mouth" (p. 74).

Initially Dixon does not dare to act out his fantasies or practice his mimicry. He is inhibited by what he conceives of as the "economic necessity" of holding a job and thus continuing to work under Welch (p. 28). His behavior toward Margaret is governed by more complex considerations: pity for her recent and (he mistakenly supposes) genuine attempt at suicide; guilt at having been a possible cause of it; friendship for her; common decency; and a conventionally male sentiment that he should help a woman in distress, a sentiment that Margaret exploits to her own full advantage. Most of all, Dixon is trapped by conventional standards and desires, general but powerful: the desire to succeed at what he has undertaken and not to make a fool of himself. All these considerations check his more authentic and autonomous desires for freedom and spontaneity. They are a special threat to his honesty, which is compromised so long as it leads only the furtive half-life of secret mimicry.

Caught in the vise of powerful opposing forces of approximately equal strength, Dixon needs, in addition to luck and his native wit, another aid. This is drink. It, too, is fortuitous: the pub where Dixon goes to escape from his pugnacious dislike of Bertrand and the insufferable cultural spuriousness of Welch's party stays open half an hour later than he expected; he is therefore able to drink to an unplanned excess. The drunk is just what he needs in order to do violence to the proprieties that shackle him. To revive his vitality, he needs to become a child again, one of the benefits Freud ascribes to the influence of alcohol.[14] In part this means returning to a kind of primitive, preverbal level of behavior, at which Dixon sings loudly, expresses lust for Margaret, bellows with rage at a locked bathroom in Welch's house, clumps noisily down Welch's stairs, guzzles the better part of a bottle of Welch's liquor, lets it slop "refreshingly down his chin and under his shirt collar" (p. 61), wipes his mouth on Welch's tablecloth—and then, retiring to bed with his cigarettes, burns an astonishing array of patterns in the bedding, rug, and table of Welch's guestroom. It is quite a series of accomplishments for a man whose defiance had previously been cautiously controlled. Dixon had once wondered how Welch would react if he should "yaw drunkenly . . . in Welch's presence screeching obscenities, punching out the windowpanes, fouling the periodicals" (p. 65). Now he has actually perpetrated similar outrages, and if they are somewhat toned down from the fantasy, they have an added recklessness from having happened in Welch's home. As Dixon wakes, hung over, to the havoc of the bedroom, he likens himself to a "broken spider crab . . . spewed up . . . on the tarry shingle of the morning" (p. 64). The image may recall a similarly vivid metaphor by which Eliot's J. Alfred Prufrock regrets his own tameness and cowardice, wishing he had been "a pair of ragged claws / Scuttling across the floors of silent seas."[15] Dixon, though immobilized for the moment by his debauch, will at least not turn into a Prufrock. Though the horror he feels at the damage done to the bedroom indicates that he is hardly free of his desire to stay on Welch's good side or of his own proprieties, Dixon's drunk marks the beginning of an active rebellion from which there is no turning back.

Though horrified, Dixon at this point has a countervailing reaction of even greater power. While the whole novel is intensely and relentlessly witty, Dixon's faculty of wit, his comic observation and invention, now reaches new heights of exuberance and exhilaration. For sheer richness of hilarity, perhaps no passage in modern literature can equal Amis's description of Dixon's drunk and hangover. Here is the opening paragraph about the hangover, minus the previously quoted part about the crab:

> Dixon was alive again. Consciousness was upon him before he could get out of the way; not for him the slow, gracious wandering from the halls of sleep, but a summary, forcible ejection. He lay sprawled, too wicked to move. . . . The light did him harm, but not as much as looking at things did; he resolved, having done it once, never to move his eyeballs again. A dusty thudding in his head made the scene before him beat like a pulse. His mouth had been used as a latrine by some small creature of the night, and then as its mausoleum. During the night, too, he'd somehow been on a cross-country run and then been expertly beaten up by secret police. He felt bad. [p. 64]

While the sources of this verbal power may remain uncertain, the exhilaration may be that of victory; Dixon has disrupted the previous standoff between the force of his true self, desiring to be defiant and free, and that of his conforming self, anxious to please those with power over him. The drunk permanently tips the balance toward freedom. Dixon has committed the comic equivalent of the action of the Blakean hero who "stamps the stony law to dust."[16]

Dixon's release of his captive self through the drunk seems to lead him directly and almost as a reward to Christine Callaghan, the other character most like Dixon in spontaneity and naturalness. She, too, has her conventional side—her "dignant" self (p. 202), as Dixon calls it—just as Dixon does; each expresses love by helping to free the other from the restraints generated by this self and to develop a truer, more authentic self. Christine is in the breakfast room having a hearty meal (even in moments of unhappiness, comic characters, being natural, seldom forget that they have bodies as well as souls) when Dixon comes downstairs badly hung over. She makes useful suggestions about how to conceal his damage to the bedroom and even goes upstairs to aid him with these measures, thus initiating their relationship. Even though their laughter, a shared sense of the risible and the ridiculous, is the main source of their bond, it is also significant that they have a common attitude toward the natural use of drinking. At the end of the novel, as their love is about to be consummated, Dixon proposes a drink to her and thinks that he might "begin with an octuple whisky" (p. 253). Here, in an archetypal way, drinking clearly represents and celebrates life, joy, love, union, fertility; Christine, now confident of their love, is ready to join the drinking with Jim, whereas earlier, doubtful of the outcome of their relationship, she had insisted on tea (p. 156).

Just as his drunk almost immediately brings him to Christine, so it more sharply separates him from the Welches. Welch is, if not abstinent, abstemious—and niggardly; when Dixon arrived at his house the evening before the party, Welch served him "the smallest drink he'd ever been seriously offered" (p. 61). Though Welch keeps his liquor cabinet well stocked, it is scarcely for personal enjoyment. It is simply the thing to do, like being arty. That either Welch or his son Bertrand should ever get drunk is inconceivable. As a machine that barely functions even when sober, Welch would, if drunk, disintegrate into primal chaos. As for Bertrand, he perfectly illustrates the wisdom of the belief attributed to Humphrey Bogart that one should not trust a man who doesn't drink. The implication is, of course, that such a person is afraid to reveal himself. Bertrand does have plenty to hide: his incompetence as a painter, his duplicity with Christine while conducting an affair with Carol Goldsmith, and, most of all, his willingness to manipulate anyone in order to gain his end of living in wealth and ease. Though these and other unpleasant sides of his personality emerge in spite of himself, to lower his inhibitions and expose them by getting drunk is more of a risk than the opportunistic Bertrand cares to take.

Lucky as Dixon is in many ways, he is luckiest of all in the appearance of the wealthy Julius Gore-Urquhart, Christine's uncle and

Dixon's benefactor and employer when he beats out Bertrand for the position of Gore-Urquhart's private secretary. When Dixon first meets him, at the college dance, it is clear that they are emancipated kindred souls to whom cigarettes and drink matter: Dixon expresses delight that Gore-Urquhart has circumvented college drinking rules and obtained pints rather than half-pints (later in the dance he introduces gin).

Gore-Urquhart's role in the novel only becomes important at the time of Dixon's second drunk. This second drunk differs from, and is even more crucial than, the first, for Dixon, after experiencing success in his struggle against the Welches and Margaret, is now slipping. The occasion for his second drunk is his inability to face or to avoid the shame of acting as Welch's puppet in delivering the "Merrie England" lecture; at the same time, he feels himself losing Christine and regressing to Margaret. Three sherries at the party before the lecture, preceded by a "half-dozen measures of Bill Atkinson's whisky" (p. 217), are insufficient to buck Dixon up. To perpetrate more offenses of the sort committed during his first drunk would be another regression, a mere repetition of the rebellion already launched. This time he needs to achieve an end that he himself is not aware of.

During the party before the lecture, Gore-Urquhart queries Dixon tersely but searchingly, as if trying to determine whether Dixon is worthy of the role he is about to assume. Although *Lucky Jim* resembles an updated Restoration comedy of manners, Gore-Urquhart's self-appointed role has an almost archetypal dimension; he becomes the "benevolent grandfather, so to speak, who overrules the action set up by the blocking humor"[17]—Welch in his attempt to thwart Dixon's natural development by forcing him to deliver the Merrie England speech. But this view of Gore-Urquhart is not quite complete. Just before the lecture, when Dixon's "spirits were so low that he wanted to lie down and pant like a dog," Gore-Urquhart appears in the washroom and gives Dixon spirits: namely, a couple of stiff belts from his flask of scotch (pp. 224–25). With the punning on "spirits," the comedy tilts perceptibly toward the cosmic. Though his terseness and plain speaking keep him from becoming portentous, one can nevertheless discern in Gore-Urquhart the outlines of a spiritual father as he grips Dixon's arm in the washroom and says, cryptically but not impenetrably, "No need to worry; to hell with all this." The first part of this is, in its way, as deeply comforting as the "And all shall be well and / All manner of thing shall be well" in the "Little Gidding" section of Eliot's *Four Quartets*; the second part hints to Dixon that there is a way out of the futility of repetitive rebellion.

Much heartened by his "spirits" and encouraged during the lecture he delivers by the "loud skirling laughter" (p. 230) of Gore-Urquhart, Dixon proceeds finally to come into his own. He must first work his way to his own identity by parodying Welch's voice and mannerisms, which he now does publicly for the first time; his months of private rehearsal pay off. And, because practice has brought his talent for mimicry of all sorts to a pitch of perfection, it is fitting that Dixon should slough off the Welchian persona and its arty nattering about "Merrie England" by briefly adopting, as he continues the lecture, the counter-persona and sardonic tone of a "nazi trooper in charge of a book-burning reading out to the crowd excerpts from a pamphlet written by a pacifist, Jewish, literate communist" (p. 230). In enacting all these roles Dixon is moving toward a wholeness of self, and his means is not only mimicry but drunkenness. In this, the climactic scene of the novel, Amis chooses to afford us some serious fun by playing on the old definition of enthusiasm or insanity as possession or intoxication by God. With the spirits and inebriation provided by Gore-Urquhart, Dixon delivers a mad but inspired burlesque version of his lecture, throwing off the spirit of his false father, Welch, in the process finding both a bride and his true spiritual father, and at last becoming himself.

Jake Richardson of *Jake's Thing* might be regarded as a Jim Dixon about to turn sixty. Lacking a Gore-Urquhart, he has remained a university teacher.[18] Although he specializes in early Mediterranean history and is at least minimally conscientious about the performance of his duties as an Oxford don, it comes as a surprise that he has published four books, for he really seems no more devoted to scholarship or research than was Dixon, at one point thinking of a pending project with a kind of weary cynicism: "He must get that bit of nonsense about Syracuse off the ground again before too long."[19] Jake seems to have chosen an academic career for want of better alternatives.

There are some noteworthy differences between *Lucky Jim* and *Jake's Thing*. Especially in tone, the later novel is more astringent. Jake has suffered some loss of innocence, and the lines between wit and folly, and thus between the characters belonging in one or another of these camps, are not quite so sharply drawn. To be sure, Jake, like Jim, is recognizably the *honnête homme* and shrewd observer of the pretentious and the bogus, which are here of more nearly epidemic proportions. In their marked resemblance to Professor Welch and Margaret Peel, the Mabbotts suggest the immortality of certain species of absurdity: Geoffrey frowns "as some aspect of reality came to his attention" (p. 279); Alcestis, like Margaret in her performance of a series of roles, favors the gruff manner and voice of a retired colonel that Jake hilariously mimics *sotto voce* (p. 18). Added to these recurring types are some new ones, the most important being Ed, a group therapy leader, and his colleague, Dr. Rosenberg. But the character who makes *Jake's Thing* a more ambiguous novel than *Lucky Jim* is Jake's wife, Brenda. Though not completely blind to the weaknesses of Ed and Rosenberg, she is far more willing than Jake to see the benefits of their therapy, and early in the novel she becomes furious with Jake for his scorn of the Mabbotts, even though, as Jake notes to himself, this sentiment must have been wholly invisible and thus harmless to them. In Brenda's fondness for the Mabbotts, it is rather as if Christine in *Lucky Jim* had suddenly begun demanding of Dixon a more sympathetic treatment of Professor Welch. Brenda's partial defection from Jake and his values, a defection that increases in the course of the novel, is the most important sign that he is more nearly isolated than Dixon. The younger man has two firm friends in Atkinson and Beesley, a friendly acquaintance in Carol Goldsmith, a woman friend (though a manipulator) in Margaret, a friend and bride-to-be in Christine, and a powerful ally in Gore-Urquhart; numerically, the balance between Dixon's friends and his enemies seems about equal. In contrast, apart from Brenda with her wavering loyalty, a risky relationship with a much younger deranged woman, Kelly, and a former lover, Eve Greenstreet, whom Jake quickly offends, he has only the friendship of his fellow don Damon Lancewood, whom he evidently does not see often.

Though he is comfortable materially, Jake is a lucky Jim whose luck seems to have run low. Counting heads is the least important measure of Jake's isolation; indeed, a stronger word, alienation, would be more accurate. Not just his incipient impotence but the sexual fashions and postures of his world leave him in dismay: the women who pass him on the street wear clothes that look like "curtains, bedspreads, blankets, tablecloths, loose covers off armchairs and sofas" (p. 51); on the train to Oxford he sees a couple locked "in a loose half-embrace, eyes bent on vacancy, mouths and jaws slack to a degree that suggested heavy sedation" (p. 99). Under Dr. Rosenberg's instructions to buy a sex magazine and stimulate himself, Jake is put off by the picture of an otherwise pretty girl with a smile like President Carter's and a pudendum "like the inside of a giraffe's ear" (pp. 55–56). He carries out Rosenberg's instructions, but without much enthusiasm. What bothers Jake more than these incongruities is the pseudo-scientific jargon and mechanical qualities of the therapy. To improve their sex relations, he and his wife hold "non-genital sensate focusing sessions"; augmenting these is "interpersonal recreative sociality" (p. 143), Rosenberg's term for the Richardsons' going out together.

Jake's alienation from sex is only a microcosm of his alienation from a whole society that, he senses, is as much out of joint as his sexual life. Nothing seems to connect, to make sense. As a confirmed bus rider, Jake seems always to encounter variations on the same scene. Just as sex was once a holistic, natural act but is now threatened by a mechanical approach analyzing its separate components, so Jake in his travels through London sees not an organic city but its detritus, abandoned in senseless patterns and tableaux: "large pieces of machinery and piles of bricks stood unattended on a rather smaller stretch of mud; no one was in sight among the strange apparatuses in what might have been a playground for young Martians; a house that had stayed half-demolished since about 1970 overlooked a straight-forward bomb-site of World War II; nearer the centre, the stone face of a university building was spattered with rust-stains from scaffolding on which Jake had never seen anybody at work" (p. 35). In this milieu it is not surprising that names are zanily anomalous. Jake disembarks from his bus at a "Kevin's Kebab"; Dr. Rosenberg, against all probability, is Irish and has the even less probable first name of Proinsias (p. 47); a woman doctor who administers mechanical tests of reactions to sexual stimuli bears the exotic name of Rowena Trefusis. In the matter of names, as in the city scenes, nothing seems to fit or make sense. Jake once had a dream in which, in the army, he could not "find his boots, equipment, rifle or cap and didn't know the way to the parade ground" (p. 131). This symbolizes his disorientation in a world where the familiar markers have somehow disappeared.

Of all the sources of modern chaos, it is the confusion between public and private, amounting to a virtual annihilation of the private, that disturbs Jake the most. The chapter in which he puts his reaction to sexual stimuli on public display in the name of supposed therapy is symptomatic of this confusion. The therapists themselves appear to have no private life; they proceed from the assumption that a private self should be fully willing to go public. Another manifestation of a similar confusion of public and private is the women's demonstration for admission to Jake's college, invading the privacy of sex by subordinating it to public, political ends. As he approaches the college one day, Jake sees the demonstrators and hears several of their chants, among them "Wanker Richardson!"; though Lancewood later defines the term as meaning someone who holds a sinecure or coasts on his reputation (p. 123), it is also British slang for "masturbator." When Jake tries to enter the gate, the women simulate cries of passion; "kisses descended, breasts were rubbed against him and his crotch was grabbed at" (p. 104). The most private and intimate of shared experiences is thus degraded in a public spectacle and used as a weapon, just as, Jake soon discovers, a plastic phallus is mailed to him and "wanker" is scrawled in the margin of the library copy of one of his articles (p. 134).

Jake is all the more troubled by this confusion because, in an old-fashioned way, he knows and almost always respects the difference between the public and the private. Indeed, except when he thinks that the harm a person does outweighs the harm done to him by an attack, Jake keeps his ridicule private; his only public attack is on Ed and Rosenberg. Although he discovers himself to be a misogynist, it is in a qualified manner. Jake insists on preserving the distinction between private scorn and public decency and consideration, as instanced by his treatment of his student, Miss Calvert (pp. 113–14). In contrast, Rosenberg is oblivious to the inappropriateness of discussing private matters in a public place because he is oblivious to any difference between public and private. In a crowded pub he announces to Jake the sex photo revealed by the stimulation session to have been Jake's favorite (p. 96). Thus Jake, scornful of a variety of people, comes across as a kinder person than Rosenberg, who seems void of any capacity for contempt, public or private. If Rosenberg were aware of this discrepancy between Jake's public and private self, he would probably accuse him of repression. But, as Freud once observed, civilization is little more than the fragile surface over a volcano of savage emotions.[20] Rosenberg would replace the facade maintained by Jake's civilized kindness or decency with public exposure of all emotions, with results that would parallel the disordered wilderness of the London cityscape.

A little incident occurring quite early in the novel summarizes much of what Jake stands for and also opposes. A madwoman, after recapitulating her problems audibly, asks the other bus riders, "Don't anybody think I've been given a raw deal?" Jake is the only passenger who replies: "Yes, I do" (p. 72). His words are an example of one of the "little, nameless, unremembered, acts / Of kindness" mentioned by Wordsworth in *Tintern Abbey*. Furthermore, as the adjectives indicate, Jake's act is an assertion of the private self making a public connection with another private self in the face of public indifference; the other riders pretend that the madwoman does not exist. At the same time, the act is an assertion of the personal against the increasing mechanization of Jake's society, as manifested especially by his sex therapy. Finally, Jake may sense that he is so out of step with his society, with the powerful forces opposed to spontaneity, connection, kindness, and the private self, that he is more akin to the madwoman than to other members of this society. Like her, he is being "given a raw deal." In any event, his brief encounter with her anticipates a stronger and deeper interest in Kelly, a younger, more attractive madwoman who is participating in the group therapy that Jake and his wife enter.

The major developments of this interest are preceded by an important event, Jake's drunk, which in fact alters their character and directly or indirectly exerts an influence on most of the other developments in Jake's life. Initially, Jake's drunk may appear comparable to Dixon's first drunk in *Lucky Jim*. Just as Dixon's may seem a healthy rebellion against playing the dutiful academic, so Jake's may seem a gloriously vigorous assertion of human desire against the whole mass of forces that have alienated and isolated him. Jake's use of drunkenness as an essential aid to fornication with a former lover, Eve Greenstreet, can be viewed as a salutary attempt to reestablish his potency, just as Dixon uses his drunk to empower him in a larger sense and to activate his struggle against the constraints of his society. Comparison of the two drunk scenes appears to be validated by the hilarious descriptions of both hangovers, as if the exuberance signaled some beneficial psychological release. The passage from *Jake's Thing* surely equals the corresponding passage in *Lucky Jim*: "the bottom sheet [of the bed] had become strewn with little irregular patches of hot semi-adhesive sand. More than this, his recent struggles to breathe regularly had fucked up some neural mechanism or other so that he now seemed to be breathing by conscious control alone." When Jake hears a voice from another room announce "Tea," he struggles "up to a sitting position, having to take his time about it because of the way his head rolled about like a small baby's unless he concentrated hard." Entering the bathroom, he sees his face in the mirror looking "as if it had been seethed in a salt solution for a time and then given a brisk buffing with sandpaper" (pp. 198–99).

These similarities between the drunk scenes are misleading. Jake's drunk is not a celebration of life or even a healthy assertion of his potency. For one thing, drunkenness is unnatural to Jake; as he puts it to his friend Lancewood in a lengthy attempt to understand his behavior with Eve, "I absolutely hate being drunk" (p. 222). Unlike Dixon, who regards his drunk and its consequences with mounting amusement, Jake regards his with increasing aversion, reaching the conclusion that his conduct with Eve must reveal that he really hates women and that he is a "male chauvinist pig" (pp. 227–28). Although Lancewood demurs from the first conclusion and Jake leaves his rooms before he can reply to the second, his drunk has forced to the surface his awareness that he takes no interest in women except as "sexual pabulum" or "creatures to go to bed with" (pp. 130, 192)—a judgment that, after his treatment of her, Eve seconds (p. 200). Moreover, Jake's sleeping with Eve constitutes a betrayal of two of his most cherished standards. As adultery, it is wanton violation of the private relationship between Eve and her husband; as the use of a woman for his pleasure without regard for hers, it is as much a mechanization of sex as any of the therapeutic gimmickry and jargon employed by Rosenberg. In short, Jake's drunken enactment of the part of Restoration libertine—a part he has enacted sober with more than a hundred women over two decades, he has previously told Rosenberg (p. 43)—is the very opposite of comic and is antithetical to the associations between procreation and comedy that Cornford and other writers have noted.

Yet Jake's intoxication and subsequent copulation with Eve could be characterized as a significant comic reenactment of the fortunate fall, for they effect several major changes in him. Ironically, after he demonstrates his potency with Eve, such performance no longer matters to him; his recognition that its reassertion lay in hatred of women and male chauvinism liberates him from caring about it, a freedom symbolized by his destruction of the plastic male organ (p. 228). In a curious way this discovery confirms the old adage *in vino veritas*; his drunk brings the revelation of an extremely unpleasant side of his true self. This discovery, in turn, helps to facilitate the growth of a better self, particularly in Jake's relationship with Kelly.

Even before he is able to articulate his disturbing discovery to Lancewood, Jake's behavior toward her seems to be changing as a result of his drunken experience. Before that, he could scarcely be said to have had a relationship with her: he has met and observed her at a therapy workshop, been appalled by her maniacal fit, but also felt the stirrings of a nascent sexual interest in her. After Kelly pays a surprise visit to their home, Brenda, detecting her interest in Jake, gives him permission to reciprocate it (p. 188). Then occurs the drunken fling with Eve, followed the next day by another surprise visit from Kelly, this time to his rooms at Oxford, with the quickly stated intention of having sex with him. He thus has an easy opportunity to repeat his conquest of Eve, and his decision enables the reader to determine whether he fully deserves the accusation of male chauvinism that he hurls at himself in the next chapter.

Learning and recoiling from his drunken irresponsibility toward Eve, he responsibly refuses to take advantage of the psychotic younger woman. As becomes clear later in the novel, at the time of her suicide attempt, it is not Jake but Ed and Rosenberg who have been Kelly's brutally indifferent exploiters, practicing a kind of psychological rape by their ignorance of her problems and how to treat them. Though likewise ignorant of any cure, Jake comes closer to understanding, to establishing a connection with her (as he has with the earlier madwoman) than do Ed or Rosenberg. Perhaps it is by virtue of his wit to madness near allied and his *sotto voce* verbal lunacies; perhaps it is because, as the only one in the novel who works hard at maintaining a civilized sanity, he is the only one who can really apprehend its opposite. But the major difference between him and the therapists, the major sign of his ability to change as a result of his drunken experience and the disproof of his chauvinism, is that he begins to care about Kelly. As he walks back to his Oxford rooms after the visit from Kelly and his session with Lancewood, he reflects on his feelings: "He didn't think he felt any affection for her . . . his main feeling for her was pity. She certainly aroused his interest, genuine interest as opposed to the testosterone-fed substitute that had graced his sometime dealings with Eve" (p. 228).

The last thing Amis wants to do is to simplify Jake or turn him into a sentimental hero. During the scene with Kelly in his rooms, a number of practical considerations may restrain him, including continuing fears of impotence, fear of sexual involvement with a psychotic nymphomaniac, the lingering effects of his hangover, and, most likely, his sudden and honest realization that he just does not want sex any longer "with anybody" (p. 219). As a wit, Jake is his own shrewdest self-critic: he is not even sure whether his new interest is in Kelly as a phenomenon or as a person (p. 228). But as Lancewood points out (though in a different context), Jake tends to be too hard on himself (p. 227). The undeniable sign of his caring humanity is that he "shrank" from Kelly's having to walk to the Oxford railroad station and sees to it that she gets a taxi (p. 220).

Following out the chain of events and the changes in Jake that originate in his debauch, at Kelly's urging he attends an out-of-town therapeutic workshop but fails to heed her appeal to come to her room at an appointed time of night. Jake does not possess perfect foresight: she attempts suicide. But his reaction demonstrates his sense of responsibility, an old-fashioned conscience, and the attempt prompts him to combat several of the forces oppressing him throughout the novel. Surmounting isolation and alienation, he makes something really work by loosing a devastating talent for satire on Ed and Rosenberg. In so doing, Jake effects the exposure of Ed that Kelly had only been able to fantasize about. Moreover, in Ed's proposal to cover up the suicide attempt, Jake finds the superbly appropriate occasion to address the disjunction between private and public: his private passion for honesty and responsibility finds its proper public vehicle in a satiric attack on Ed and Rosenberg. Qualities far superior to potency or the ability to lust after a woman have thus been restored to Jake—or, rather, given him for the first time.

As the novel moves toward a conclusion after its climactic scene of satire, Jake seems resigned to accepting the limits of a man turning sixty. Remaining are his friend Lancewood, his honesty, and his clarity of vision; they seem to be enough. Jake quite easily accepts his wife's sudden announcement that she is leaving him for Geoffrey; perhaps he recognizes the justice in this, for his attempts to show her affection have largely failed. The last chapter of the novel effaces any residual melancholy from this separation. Jake is visiting Dr. Curnow, the same one who referred him to Rosenberg in Chapter 1, thereby setting in motion the whole train of events. Only instead of potency, Jake's complaint now is "excessive shitting" (p. 283), perhaps indicative of his final attitude toward the world. And Jake is content to leave it at that. When Curnow informs him of a simple new cure for impotence, Jake declines it, after reflecting in misogynist fashion on all the faults of women. As in the story of Sophocles at eighty, he seems glad to be delivered from the tyranny of sex.

At least until the closing chapters of *Jake's Thing*, however, his drunken fornication is probably the key scene of the second half of the novel. Though it may seem strictly a negative act, it provides Jake with his major motivation for change and, ultimately, with a major motivation for effectively counteracting those aspects of modern life that have most oppressed him. From his drunk he learns the worst about his deep-seated attitudes toward women; reacting against these, he redeems himself by learning to care for Kelly as something more than a potential object of lust. Acting as a kind of surrogate for her in levelling against Ed and Rosenberg the attack that she could only contemplate, he achieves a wholeness of self. If the *disjecta membra* of modern society refuse to unite, he can at least make his own connections and find his own function, venting private convictions through the impassioned public voice of the satirist.

George Orwell's *Keep the Aspidistra Flying* is, in some respects, a perplexing novel. Most of the difficulties center around the hero, Gordon Comstock. Definitely comic in its outcome, *Aspidistra* is nevertheless a comedy of an exceedingly strange kind, one in which the hero is (or seems) both old and young, both winter and spring, both the blocking character, the aged humorist or impostor, and the youth who overthrows this character. During the protracted struggle between them, the blocking part of Gordon's character assumes such an extreme Bergsonian rigidity that it is tempting to dismiss him in exasperation. Yet there is little doubt that Orwell wished also to keep in sight the youthful, more sympathetic Gordon, who finally learns to choose what William McCollom calls the "divine average"—in Gordon's case, middle-class life and values—rather than the exceptionality of his blocking views.[21]

The reaction of many readers to Gordon, however, is likely to be even more perplexed than this, for the blocking side of Gordon's character represents some of the favorite notions of the modern liberal intelligentsia. He has devoted himself to poetry and rejected the world of money and commercial success. To the extent that this dedication seems admirable, Gordon's complete abandonment of it by the end of the novel will be difficult to accept—perhaps even to credit. His reversal could scarcely be more complete: Gordon throws down a sewer a long poem he had been writing for two years, returning to the advertising agency to write copy for a new campaign involving "P. P."—which stands for "Pedic Perspiration."[22] To be sure, Gordon undergoes this metamorphosis somewhat reluctantly, but at the same time with a hopefulness born of his new (or newly admitted) faith in the middle-class values of work and family. Because Gordon has inveighed most passionately and persistently against money, his changed attitude toward it is likely to be the most unsettling to some readers: "He had blasphemed against money, rebelled against money, tried to live like an anchorite outside the money-world; and it had brought him not only misery, but also a frightful emptiness, an inescapable sense of futility. To abjure money is to abjure life. Be not righteous over much; why shouldst thou die before thy time?" (p. 237).

The problem for the reader may lie not so much in accepting these changes singly as in countenancing their totality and their extremity. It is rather as if Molière's Alceste had surrendered his misanthropy and become a courtier. A reader who has shared the passionate disgust of such a denunciation as Gordon's "to settle down, to Make Good, to sell your soul for a villa and an aspidistra!" (p. 48) may even feel betrayed by Gordon's willing embrace of exactly these goals, the aspidistra of the novel's title being the major recurring symbol of middle-class standards and a chief object of Gordon's antipathy. The novel brings so complete a revolution that even at the end an astonished reader may lag somewhat behind Gordon. Because the sustained intensity of Gordon's rejection of the money-code seems to isolate him from society, Orwell's belated attempt to explain him as an

Everyman figure—"Everyone rebels against the money-code, and everyone sooner or later surrenders" (p. 238)—may be the cause of another serious strain on the reader's credence.

The reader's difficulties may come primarily from an awareness, nagging if fitful, that there are really two Gordons who never quite coalesce: the individualized Gordon whose rebellion against society, however exasperating at times, may endow him with almost heroic determination; and the other Gordon, overlapping but distinct, who is the vehicle in a didactic novel of ideas. By marrying Rosemary, who is already pregnant by him, he gives the final turn to his individuality, merging it with middle-class society in a recognizably comic affirmation of renewal and fertility. He is not, as he had thought he was, the last of the dying family of Comstocks. At the same time, however, he may retain the lineaments of another sort of comic figure, the Bergsonian; he may swing too rigidly from one faith or set of beliefs to another: from a fanatical opposition (which at one point he specifically thinks of as "religion") to the "filthy money-world," he swings to a new religion, a belief in the middle-class decencies that somehow redeem or transmute this money world (pp. 194, 239).

Rosemary, an instrument essential to Gordon's changes, is even more didactically conceived than he is. Though endowed with a good deal of personal charm and touching in her loyalty to her beloved, even magnanimously transcending her middle-class respectability on the occasion when she sleeps with Gordon (it is the only way she knows to lift him from the profound apathy into which he has fallen), Rosemary is perhaps, in her extraordinary strength and good sense, too much the foil for Gordon and too close to the Woman envisioned by George Meredith as the fountain of comedy.[23] She is a better Célimène, accepting Gordon and finally winning him to her values by her love, rather than spurning him.

If the foregoing comments accurately reflect some problems of the novel, even they probably fail to do justice to the complexity of the reader's likely reactions to Gordon. Orwell evidently wished to present Gordon's criticisms of society as generally valid; although replaced or superseded by the more vital concerns of procreation and making a living, the criticisms are not cancelled out.[24] Where Gordon errs is not in having strong principles but in the stubborn intransigence of trying to live wholly by them. Had Gordon been a poet of genius, Orwell might have represented as justified his rejection of society for the sake of dedication to his art. But because Gordon has no such talent, this is a moot point. Certainly Orwell has limited patience with the kind of failed artist or bohemian that Gordon is rapidly becoming, the kind who, in a rage because of his failure and futility, projects his self-hatred onto society. Even the reader who shares Gordon's implicit belief in the redemptive power of art and who sympathizes with his invectives against the corrupting power of money will find many disturbing details in the first two chapters, and beyond. Emphasized from the outset are the frailty of Gordon's appearance and his "moth-eaten" look, suggesting infertility or impotence. Likewise, the qualities most emphasized in the bookstore where Gordon works are dryness, desiccation, the deadness of nearly all the wares he is supposed to sell; even the novels of the lending library, which at least circulate, image death in their appearance of immurement, of "bricks laid upright" (p. 4). The effect of such imagery is strongly reinforced by Chapter 3, an elaboration on the meaning of the characterization of Gordon in the first chapter as the "last member of the Comstock family" (p. 3). Of the twelve children of his paternal grandfather, only one, Gordon's father, married and produced children; and neither Gordon nor his sister, Julia, seems likely to marry. Although Orwell mentions Rosemary and a friend of Gordon's named Ravelston early in *Aspidistra*, the novel is remarkable for the belatedness of meaningful dialogue involving the central character; apart from superficial chat with bookshop patrons and Gordon's rejection of an invitation from a fellow boarder, Flaxman, to accompany him to a pub, Gordon has no real companionship until his conversation with Ravelston in Chapter 5—by which point the novel is nearly one-third over. Lack of money is responsible for this delay; Gordon is ashamed to appear before Ravelston or Rosemary without money in his pocket, a scarce possession because of his meager wages. Likewise, lack of money, with the powerful sense of helpless rage and weakness it generates, is responsible for his most viciously hate-filled fantasy of "enemy aeroplanes flying over London; the deep threatening hum of the propellers, the shattering thunder of the bombs. . . . It was a sound which, at that moment, he ardently desired to hear" (pp. 16–17, 21). Not only does this seem prophetic of World War II; it also seems to lay bare the psychological roots of war in the despair turned to destructive rage of millions of hopeless persons such as Gordon. This glimpse of apocalypse, however, does not fit the novel as a whole. Unlike the rage and desperation of the victims of the Great Depression, Gordon's emotions are avoidable because his poverty is self-induced. As long as his opposition to money is based on obsessive principle, he is susceptible to such fantasies as a relief from the futility of his hatred. And, given his apparent inability to mitigate the fierceness of his hatred, he seems trapped in an impasse.

As early as Chapter 2, drinking comes to seem a possible solvent, a means of escape. As the novel progresses, alcohol has two kinds of effects on Gordon. One is mild and incontrovertibly desirable; it touches on but remains distinct from a second, more violent series of changes that at first appear negative but ultimately come to seem good.

Flaxman's drinking at a pub called the Crichton Arms becomes for Gordon a symbol of warmth, gregariousness, fellowship, innocent fun and laughter—the sort of life that at times he yearns for intensely. On a night of solitary, nearly penniless wandering, he passes three women, "red-armed," standing with mugs of beer outside a pub door (p. 73); these women may anticipate the woman with "brawny red forearms" hanging out clothes in 1984, a moving symbol of working-class sturdiness and ruddy health.[25] During an initially idyllic day together in the country, Gordon and Rosemary notice those aspects of nature that we may associate with the fecundity of comedy: "All round them the beech-trees soared, curiously phallic"; they pass a field in which "innumerable rabbits were browsing" (pp. 126–27). Although the restaurant where they stop for lunch is like a "dreary aquarium" and its food is overpriced, a bottle of wine warms and relaxes them; as it does so, the sun, reemerging, seems to act as its ally and encourages Gordon's intentions of having sex with Rosemary in a field on the way back to the train. What thwarts him is Rosemary's reluctance and, perhaps even more, his consciousness that the lunch cost more than he could afford. In fact, in a conflict between obvious symbols of fertility and impotence, "the warmth of the wine, and the hateful feeling of having only eightpence left, warred together in his body" (p. 138). Gordon's failure to bring a contraceptive causes Rosemary's reluctance. Because he also fears the trap of a subsequent forced marriage almost as much as the trap of money, believing that marriage would necessarily chain him to slaving for wages, the wine is clearly not powerful enough to dissolve Gordon's fears and constraining rigidities.

As explored thus far, drinking in *Aspidistra* seems a symbol of an unambiguously beneficent vitality. But Gordon's saturnalian drunk is quite different and, it at first appears, much darker in its effects. Although it is immediately triggered by his celebrating the arrival of fifty dollars from an American magazine that has accepted one of his poems, there are some foreshadowings of it. Gordon tends to associate drinking and women, not always innocently: for example, when Flaxman, who lives in Gordon's boarding house because he has been ejected by his wife for adultery, goes to the Crichton Arms, Gordon knows that part of the reason is to tell obscene jokes and pinch the bum of the barmaid, a "blonde cutie" (p. 74). This vision of the pub, which almost entices Gordon to enter, has been preceded by the red-armed women outside another pub and, a page before that, by his fleeting encounter with a prostitute. The three distinct scenes seem related in Gordon's mind.

Flaxman's behavior in the Crichton Arms is innocent compared to Gordon's on his drunk. The fifty dollars from the American magazine having gone to his head, Gordon insists on treating Ravelston and Rosemary to dinner at an expensive restaurant. Even before they leave, Gordon is drunk, and as the imagery of the rest of the chapter indicates, the night becomes his descent into hell. In drunken lust, right on the street he "thrust his hand . . . into the front of" Rosemary's dress (p. 167); naturally enough, her response is to desert him for the rest of the night. Ravelston, still protective of his friend, is dragged by Gordon to a pub that seems more like a place of the damned than the warm, cheerful Crichton Arms. The whores who next accost Gordon and take him to their apartment are certainly no figures from the green world of comedy. As the evening and the chapter end, Gordon is draining a bottle of chianti, overwhelmed by the wine flowing down his throat and into his nose (p. 177). The next day, vilely hung over, Gordon finds himself in jail for having hit a policeman.

Bailed out by Ravelston, Gordon manifests the first of several changes resulting from his drunk by feeling mostly apathy and bored indifference to his situation. Although dismissed from his old job because of his drunk, he is not in much hurry to find a new one; his former aversion to accepting charity from Ravelston, with whom he lives temporarily, has greatly abated. He finds a position similar to his old one, yet worse: he manages a lending library consisting only of the trashiest books, his wages are even lower than formerly, and both the library and his room are in a more squalid quarter of London. But he thinks he has fulfilled the only desire that still matters to him, that of sinking into a netherworld "where decency no longer mattered. . . . where failure and success have no meaning" (p. 203).

Gordon properly feels his drunken night to be of such importance that it "marked a period in his life" (p. 203). The trouble is that he does not look deeply enough into what kind of period. Quite early in the novel Gordon thinks of his aged Uncle Walter as being typical of those family members who never made a "stab at life": at most, Gordon imagines, his uncle may have had "a few furtive . . . frolics" as a young man, "a few whiskies in dull bars . . . a little whoring on the Q. T." (p. 58). Gordon's drunk, however, is recklessly flamboyant, not furtive; as drunks go, it is probably more like some experiences of the robust Flaxman, who, accompanying Ravelston to bail Gordon out of prison, glances about him as if at familiar surroundings (p. 182). Getting drunk as he does, then, is Gordon's boldest assertion of vitality against the dying Comstocks, even though its first consequence seems to be a lassitude and a poverty worse than theirs. His resistance to change, moreover, had been so intransigent that he needed the extremity of his drunk to blast him loose. This done, further changes become possible.

Probably the most important of these changes is the end of Gordon's pretensions to innocence. In his drunkenness he virtually attempts to ravish Rosemary, but that he achieves his own deflowering probably explains the listlessness into which he plunges after his drunk. He knows himself to be a man who needs a religion, but, as a result of the reckless spending on his drunk, he realizes that he is as much a prey to the temptations of money and to vulgar display as the worst devotee of the money-god could possibly be.[26] Gordon's behavior with the whores, moreover, resembles the adulteries for which Flaxman's wife breaks "cut-glass whisky decanters" (p. 104) over his head and turns him out of the house: both signify a world of guilty reality from which Gordon has previously managed to hold himself aloof, maintaining a fragile purity. Now, thanks to his drunk, his illusion of innocence is shattered, and when he recovers from the lethargy into which the shock of his experience has temporarily thrown him, his transition to a new view of money and his acceptance of a decency that is compromised by reality, rather than untenably pure, will be easier.

As in *Jake's Thing*, then, the drunk scene of *Keep the Aspidistra Flying* is ultimately a fortunate fall. To complete Gordon's changes, other assistance is even more important, in particular the devotion and the pregnancy of Rosemary.[27] But although Gordon's drunk appears to lead away from the green world of comedy, the actions it entails and his subsequent realizations enable him to break the grip of the dying Comstocks and, even more important, to abandon the sterile purity of his obsessive war against money, freeing him to enter the world of renewal, fertility, and ordinary, practicable decency.

Epilogue

I n concluding this book, I want to attempt a broad speculation—so broad, in fact, that it can probably never be fully demonstrated or refuted. The speculation is this: To an important extent, the attitudes toward or treatments of drinking studied in this book are manifestations of literary modernism; to the extent that these attitudes or treatments show signs of change or evolution, they may indicate significant changes in modernism. I advance even so tentative a hypothesis with uneasiness, fully aware of the difficulty of defining anything as complex as modernism and having already regarded with skepticism the adequacy of one historical phenomenon (Prohibition, its aftermath, and the attitudes toward drinking that stemmed from them) for explaining the views discussed in the preceding chapters. It is even possible that reactions to Prohibition were one source of American literary modernism. Nevertheless, though without attempting anything so grandiose as a full account of modernism, let me explain my hypothesis. If two of the leading characteristics of modernism are a radical dissatisfaction with commonplace reality[1] and a consequent attempt to undermine conventional reality by greatly altering traditional states of consciousness, the fundamental challenges to and ruptures of these states offered by heavy drinking may seem desirable from a modernist viewpoint. Moreover, if one sees the roots of modernism in the Romantic movement, one may trace back to it not only the beginnings of the modernist discontent with traditional modes of consciousness but also the beginnings of a radical experimentation with this consciousness through the use of drugs—the opium experimentation undertaken by more than one Romantic writer and discussed by M. H. Abrams and Alethea Hayter.[2] One could argue that, just as early modernism is marked by a willingness to alter consciousness or perception by the use of opium, so late modernism is marked by a similar willingness to use alcohol.

The particular experience of the individual writers or works assessed in my book may seem too varied to be part of the broad development outlined above. In an important sense, of course, this objection is valid: the literary work and the view of drinking that it expresses are uniquely valuable in themselves, not as part of some cultural movement. Yet it can be instructive to see that, for all their ineffable differences, these works may be part of the larger whole called modernism and may even reveal something important about its ultimate fortunes. The whole modernist ethic and aesthetic, including the desirability of a constant search for ways of altering or destroying traditional modes of perception, may be under increasingly severe critical examination. Certainly the works considered here are for the most part highly cautious, to say the least, about embracing alcoholism or heavy drinking as a desirable solvent of commonplace reality or a means (to adapt Ezra Pound's phrase) of making it new. *Under the Volcano*, for example, is ambivalent on this score. Although the Consul's alcoholic hallucinations represent a stunning addition to the modernist imagination, this achievement is darkened by our awareness of the extreme price paid by the Consul (and, implicitly, by Lowry), so that in the end the reader may question whether any work of art is worth the sacrificial destruction of the artist. When the illness of alcoholism may weaken the integrity or honesty of the work of a major writer, as it seems to have done with F. Scott Fitzgerald, the question about the price exacted by alcoholism becomes still more disturbing. Although Cheever appears to decide that in some instances an alcoholic defiance or transcendence of society is worth this price, and although Waugh definitely suggests that the price of Sebastian's alcoholism is small because it is a means to his salvation, even these writers fully expose the destructive ravages of the disease; and of the large cast of alcoholic characters in *The Iceman Cometh*, Larry alone sanely rejects drunkenness and, in so doing, escapes the insidious, dehumanizing comfort of alcoholic pipe dreams.

John Berryman's poetic accomplishment might be a test case of whether alcoholism will seem worth the price to future writers and readers. As strong and almost obsessive as his concern for fame was, Berryman's death is too recent for his permanent rank among modern poets to be clear. But there can be little doubt that Berryman forged a distinctive poetic style, and there is just as little doubt that his heavy drinking contributed to the development of this style—to its jazzy, jagged rhythms, its incoherences, its uninhibited (though of course calculated) use of colloquialisms and slang. Nor can there be much doubt that Berryman's alcoholism was an important source for much of the emotional ambience of the *Dream Songs*: for the sometimes raucous defiance, or for a more pervasive quality that is not self-pity (as Donald Newlove has claimed) but a strong current of grieving, a haunting consciousness of loss sometimes centering on Berryman's father, a suicide, but more fundamentally if unwittingly emanating from Berryman himself, a grieving for the talents he has squandered by his alcoholism.

In his poems after the *Dream Songs*, however—numerous, but so far largely neglected by the critics—we find a marked tendency toward contrition, toward a penitential spirit quite similar to that of a seventeenth-century poet like George Herbert. Both Berryman's poetic form, which is extremely simple, and his mood become antithetical to modernism, and the major impetus to repentance is Berryman's deep remorse for his alcoholism.

It is too soon to know whether Berryman signifies any kind of turning point in modernist attitudes toward the uses of alcohol. Two writers more nearly contemporary than Berryman, James Dickey and Raymond Carver, resemble Berryman in their willingness to show alcohol as a means to freedom from dull conventionality or the enslavement of the quotidian; however, neither writer evinces the kind of romantic enchantment with drinking that Fitzgerald once did in *The Great Gatsby*, or the blindness to its deleterious effects that both Fitzgerald and Berryman often maintained. Dickey remarks in his journals that he is "sick of the petty wildness and the phony ecstasy of drinking"[3]—a remark particularly worth noting from a drinking writer, suggesting that awareness of the liabilities of heavy drinking has advanced so far that a restoration of the bibulous glamor of Gatsby's parties is no longer possible. If this is so, then a chief modernist means of deconstructing conventional ways of seeing, and thus perhaps a major support of modernism itself, is no longer usable.

Oddly enough, to see more clearly what may be happening to attitudes toward alcohol, we would do well to look at the contrasting attitudes toward drinking of the eighteenth-century writers James Boswell and Samuel Johnson. Somewhat arbitrarily, but for reasons that I hope will become clear and defensible, let me call Boswell's attitudes on this subject "modern" and Johnson's "postmodern"—that is to say, Johnson's are a possible indication of what our attitudes are evolving toward, or back to.

Boswell displays an ambivalence toward drinking that seems characteristic of modern writers such as Dickey, Cheever, and Berryman. On one hand there is the public Boswell, most evident in his *Life of Johnson*: despite occasional worries and fears about his own drinking, Boswell here generally upholds moderate drinking as a means to truth (*in vino veritas*), a release from oppressive cares, a source of vivacity and high spirits.[4] In such passages he bears some resemblance to the Dickey of "Bums, On Waking," the Berryman of Dream Song 232, and the Amis who provided Jim Dixon with alcohol to throw off the shackles of self and society. If in his support of moderate drinking Boswell's public self might disapprove of the more extreme views of these writers and of a character like Cheever's Gee-Gee, whose alcoholism is some sort of life spirit, Boswell nevertheless shares their sentiment that alcohol can be a vital, beneficent force.

But Boswell's own drinking, most fully displayed in his journals, leaves a much different impression. Even a glance at the indexes shows the extent and seriousness of Boswell's drinking problem: in three volumes of the published journals—*Boswell: The Ominous Years 1774–1776, Boswell in Extremes 1776–1778,* and *Boswell Laird of Auchinleck 1778–1782*—index entries such as "drinks heavily, intoxicated" and "ill after drinking" under Boswell's name swarm with page references. On one occasion Boswell narrowly missed enacting the shameful part of wife-beater; in fact, he was deterred only by his extreme intoxication and his resulting inability to direct with accuracy the chairs and walking stick with which he assaulted his wife. Naturally, he condemned himself for this behavior: "What a monstrous account of a man!" Less than two years later he experienced a longer period of despondency from what can only be called a protracted bender. From 2 June until 24 July 1777 Boswell records being drunk sixteen times (there are seven days when he made no entries in his journal); indeed, he seems to have got drunk at virtually every opportunity and despite his concern for his wife's consumption, which eventually killed her.[5] Like Dickey in the previously quoted journal entry, Boswell manifests strong disgust with himself; and, like Cheever in many of his stories, Boswell in his journal was well aware of the domestic strife and misery caused by his drinking. Following

Boswell on the subject of drinking from the *Life of Johnson* to his journals is an enlightening study in contrasts, rather like reading Berryman's *Dream Songs* and then turning to his later poems. The more inward or private the reflections of the two writers, the more they perceive the liabilities of drinking to outweigh any benefits.

Samuel Johnson's attitude toward drinking may be aptly characterized as resulting from his awareness of the disproportion of drawbacks to benefits. Regarding Johnson as "postmodern" in any sense may at first glance seem ludicrous, but if we remember his famous injunction to "clear your *mind* of cant,"[6] we may be better able to see that, in his remarks on and attitudes toward drinking, Johnson practices a form of deconstruction on much of the cant or rationalization about drinking in his own age. This analysis is just as powerful when applied to the delusions or self-deceptions of a Fitzgerald or a Berryman as it was against men like Boswell, or Joshua Reynolds. The painter contended on one occasion "that moderate drinking makes people talk better." Johnson replied, "No, Sir; wine gives not light, gay, ideal hilarity; but tumultuous, noisy, clamorous merriment." When Reynolds suggested that the sober Johnson felt envy of drinkers, he countered, "Perhaps, contempt." Discoursing on this subject on another occasion, Johnson granted that the ability of wine to make "a man better pleased with himself" was a real boon; he added, however, that "the danger is, that while a man grows better pleased with himself, he may be growing less pleasing to others. Wine gives a man nothing. It neither gives him knowledge nor wit; it only animates a man, and enables him to bring out what a dread of the company has repressed. It only puts in motion what has been locked up in frost. . . . A man should cultivate his mind so as to have that confidence and readiness without wine, which wine gives."[7]

Johnson reached these conclusions largely because of two qualities for which he is famous, his empiricism and his honesty. Rather than accept, for example, the stock belief that drinking makes men more convivial, Johnson insisted on thinking and observing for himself; when he did, this, along with most of the other benefits claimed for drinking, seemed illusory. Among the most painfully influential of his observations was Johnson's awareness of how drink changed his once affectionate wife, who today would almost certainly have been regarded as alcoholic. Increasingly cut off from Johnson by her drunkenness, she for years refused to have sexual relations with him.[8] Above all, however, Johnson's analysis of drinking derives its trenchancy from a rigorously honest *self*-examination, one that corroborated and strengthened his empirical discovery that most people lose more than they gain by drinking. Recognizing the value of being pleased with oneself, he also recognized that drink involves a price that, ultimately, Johnson's many years of abstinence suggest he was unwilling to pay: the price of irrationality, of loss of control, of delusion, of increased melancholy.[9] No important thinker before the advent of Alcoholics Anonymous subjected the attractions of drinking to such skeptical and damaging attention as did Johnson.

Although some artists will doubtless always wish to experiment with the heavy use of alcohol or drugs, in my view such experimentation will increasingly come to be regarded as an exercise in futility. For one thing, writers like Malcolm Lowry and John Berryman have probably demonstrated all that drinking can do to enlarge the writer's repertoire of experiences and perceptions; further attempts of this sort would probably only sound like a mediocre imitation, a harsh phrase that nevertheless accurately characterizes the relationship of, for example, Kerouac's *Big Sur* to *Under the Volcano*. For another, there are signs of an increasing reluctance among modern writers like Carver, Dickey, and Berryman to see a martyrdom to alcohol as somehow warranted by the resulting work of art. In his final years Berryman attempted to draw back from this abyss and to find a poetic style freed from the dislocations of alcohol, even though this effort ended in suicide and in only partial artistic success or change.

Samuel Johnson's deromanticizing of drinking, his remarkably honest and shrewd observations that have been generally substantiated by Alcoholics Anonymous and by modern science, may indicate the nature of a developing "postmodern" attitude toward alcohol: an attitude skeptical of its benefits, cognizant of the high cost of heavy or alcoholic drinking, doubtful that any achievements can ever justify the payment of such a price, and devastatingly inimical to the kind of willful blindness or self-deception that some alcoholic writers only a generation or two ago could use to deny their illness and its effects. Like most major changes, however, this one has been gradual and quiet.

Notes

INTRODUCTION

1. Among the many examples of this type of listing are "Booze," pp. 25–33, and Kazin, "'Giant Killer,'" pp. 44–50. With little argument or supporting evidence, one or both of these sources include the following modern writers as either heavy or alcoholic drinkers: F. Scott Fitzgerald, Jack London, Ring Lardner, Dylan Thomas, John P. Marquand, John O'Hara, Evelyn Waugh, Hart Crane, Edwin Arlington Robinson, Wallace Stevens, Philip Barry, Brendan Behan, Edna St. Vincent Millay, Dorothy Parker, Dashiell Hammett, Theodore Roethke, Robert Benchley, John Berryman, William Saroyan, Conrad Aiken, Truman Capote, Norman Mailer, Tennessee Williams, James Dickey, Edmund Wilson, Allen Tate, William Styron, Irwin Shaw, James Jones, Sinclair Lewis, Eugene O'Neill, William Faulkner, Ernest Hemingway, John Steinbeck, E. E. Cummings, Thomas Wolfe, W. H. Auden, and Malcolm Lowry.

2. Kazin, "'Giant Killer,'" p. 44.

3. Goodwin, "Alcoholism of Fitzgerald," pp. 86–90.

4. Newlove, *Drinking Days*, p. 125.

5. Ibid., p. 146.

6. Bergreen, *James Agee*.

7. Jeffs, *Brendan Behan*, pp. 16–18, 93–95, 121, 155, 167.

8. "*Pass It On*," p. 83.

9. Newlove, *Drinking Days*, p. 125, attributes this claim to Kerouac's biographer John Clellon Holmes.

10. Roth, "'Milk of Wonder.'"

11. Lentricchia, *Criticism*, pp. 123–32.

12. Lowry, *Volcano*, pp. xi–xxx.

13. Fuchs, *Saul Bellow*, pp. 45–48.

14. Alcoholics Anonymous regards alcoholism as a threefold illness, physical, mental, and spiritual. See "*Pass It On*," p. 82.

15. Dickey, "Bums, On Waking," pp. 153–55.

16. Carver, "Drinking While Driving," p. 35.

17. James, *Varieties*, pp. 377–78.

18. Mann, *Doctor Faustus*, p. 242.

19. Kurtz, *Not-God*, p. 208.

20. See for example Gellman, *Sober Alcoholic*, p. 121; Sagarin, *Odd Man*, pp. 45–55; Pattison, "Rehabilitation," p. 620; and Davies, "Stabilized Addiction," p. 372.

21. For a short list of such figures see Fitzgibbon, *Drink*, p. 166.

CHAPTER 1

1. For some comment on these two aspects of Lowry, see Cross, *Malcolm Lowry*, pp. ix–x, 11–12, 18–19, 26–27, 53, 61, 129n50, 130–31n57; Grace, "Malcolm Lowry," pp. 94–95; Bradbrook, "Intention and Design," p. 153; Markson, *Lowry's "Volcano*," pp. 3–9 passim; Kilgallin, *Lowry*, pp. 199–200; Costa, *Malcolm Lowry*, pp. 21–44; Dodson, *Malcolm Lowry*, pp. 28–33; Dorosz, *Lowry's Infernal Paradise*, pp. 12–13; Epstein, *Private Labyrinth*, pp. 47–55; Corrigan, "Malcolm Lowry," pp. 425–26; and Bareham, "Paradigms of Hell," pp. 113–27.

2. Lowry said that "the idea I cherished in my heart was to create a pioneer work in its own class, and to write at last an authentic drunkard's story" (from "Preface to a Novel" in the French translation of *Under the Volcano*, p. 15).

3. Of the handful of essays that deal with or touch meaningfully on the novel as a study of an alcoholic, Edmonds, "Mescallusions," pp. 277–88, mostly concerns itself with the amount and type of alcohol consumed by the Consul; Edmonds, "*Under the Volcano*," pp. 95–96, appreciatively notes the vividness of some hallucinations but does not attempt to assess their importance for the novel as a whole; Brooke-Rose, "Mescalusions," p. 104, says without elaboration that Lowry's mescalusions (by which she probably means the Consul's hallucinations) are "the best things" in *Under the Volcano*, but she finds little else to recommend it; finally, in an article that despite its general title is solely concerned with Lowry and the Consul, Hill, "The Alcoholic," pp. 33–48, is excellent on *Under the Volcano* as a study of the patterns and peculiarities of the alcoholic mind, but has nothing to say about hallucinations.

4. Lowry, *Letters*, pp. 61–62. Edmonds, "Mescallusions," p. 279, points out that "there is no essential difference between mescal and tequila." Thus the Consul's (and Lowry's—see *Letters*, p. 71) apparent assumption that mescal is the liquid equivalent of the hallucinogenic drug mescalin is erroneous. But the assumption explains why the Consul dreaded the great potency of mescal and why, after he begins drinking it, his hallucinations seem to increase in frequency and intensity.

5. Lowry, *Letters*, p. 63.

6. Day, *Malcolm Lowry*, p. 350.

7. Of course there is nothing accidental about Lowry's particular mingling of hallucinations and angelic voices. Many have noted that "spirits" is one name for alcohol and that drinking, rightly used, leads to enhanced spiritual awareness or bliss. Abuse of alcohol, however, by polluting spirit, would lead to awareness, sometimes in hallucinatory form, of dark or diabolical powers. See Dorosz, *Lowry's Infernal Paradise*, pp. 51–56, 83; Clinebell, "Philosophical-Religious Factors," p. 479; and the letter from C. G. Jung to Bill Wilson (cofounder of Alcoholics Anonymous) printed in Thomsen, *Bill W.*, pp. 362–63.

8. The classic study of drug-induced hallucinations is Klüver, "Mechanisms of Hallucinations," pp. 175–207. For a longer essay, an extension and elaboration of Klüver, see Siegel and Jarvik, "Drug-Induced Hallucinations," pp. 81–161.

9. See, e.g., Curran, "Personality Studies," pp. 654–63; Wolff and Curran,

"Nature of Delirium," pp. 1181–92, 1202–3, 1205, 1215; Davies, Scott, and Malherbe, "Resumed Normal Drinking," pp. 188–91; Davidson, "Syndrome of Hallucinosis," pp. 467, 471–78; Deiker and Chambers, "Structure and Content," pp. 1835, 1838; Róheim, "Alcoholic Hallucinations," pp. 450–77, 479; Mott, Small, and Anderson, "Comparative Study," pp. 596, 598–600; Ditman and Whittlesey, "Comparison of LSD-25," pp. 54–56; Karlan, "Alcoholism and Hallucinosis," pp. 64–67; Burton-Bradley, "Alcoholic Hallucinosis," p. 10; Rosenberg, "Psychogenesis," pp. 317–20; Richards, "Diplopic and Triplopic," p. 630; Brune and Busch, "Anticonvulsive-Sedative," p. 337; Isbell et al., "Etiology of 'Rum Fits,'" pp. 12, 22–25; May and Ebaugh, "Pathological Intoxication," pp. 205, 211, 214–24; Thomas, "Alcoholism and Mental Disorder," pp. 68–71, 77; Norman, "Alcoholic Hallucinatory States," pp. 565–70; Mitchell, "Alcoholic Insanity," pp. 252, 255–65, 268–69, 271; Schilder, "Psychogenesis of Alcoholism," pp. 280–81, 284; Wortis, "Delirium Tremens," p. 255; Victor and Hope, "Auditory Hallucinations," p. 659; Wolin, "Hallucinations," pp. 308-11, 313–16; Trapp and Lyons, "Dream Studies," pp. 253, 256–62, 264; Gross et al., "Sleep Disturbances," pp. 493, 498–500, 508; Bromberg and Schilder, "Castration and Dismembering," pp. 207, 209–23; Brierre de Boismont, *Hallucinations*, pp. 163–69; and Krafft-Ebing, *Text-Book of Insanity*, pp. 518, 520–21, 525–26, 528–30, 533–40.

10. Dynes, "Survey of Alcoholic Patients," pp. 195, 197.

11. See Day, *Malcolm Lowry*, pp. 234–44, and Lowry's letters to John Davenport, Juan Fernando Marquez, Conrad Aiken, and James Stern in *Letters*, pp. 11–15, 29, which probably misdates the letter to Davenport. Day makes it clear that there are other relevant letters, unpublished, in the Lowry collection at the University of British Columbia. He also makes it clear that Lowry's descent into paranoia (and perhaps hallucinations) may have begun as early as October 1937, when the discovery of an extra copy of a magazine on his coffee table was, he thought, evidence that thieves had visited his house (Day, p. 229).

12. Lowry, *Under the Volcano*, p. 342. Most future references to this novel will appear in parentheses in the text. A somewhat similar catalogue of remembered and anticipated hallucinations occurs in Lowry's novella *Lunar Caustic*. Bill Plantagenet, its hero, recites to Dr. Claggart the horrors that await him in New York City when he leaves the hospital where he finds himself because of his alcoholism: "it's all there waiting for me: the ghosts on the window blind, the scarlet snowshoe, the whispering of lost opportunities, and all the fury, the anguish, the remorse, the voices, voices, voices; the doll that turns to Ruth [Plantagenet's wife], the brownstone—brimstone—fronts transformed into judges, the interminable helpful but—alas—non-existent conversations." I quote from the text in *Malcolm Lowry: Psalms*, p. 295; the story can also be found in *The Paris Review* 8 (Winter-Spring 1963): 15–72. In its alcoholic hero and its use of hallucinations, this has a greater similarity to *Under the Volcano* than does any of Lowry's other work.

13. For other hallucinations of Hugh or Yvonne, see pp. 256–58, 279, 324, 333, 335–36.

14. For a notable exception, see Costa, *Malcolm Lowry*, pp. 74–80.

15. Bowman and Jellinek, "Alcoholic Mental Disorders," p. 332, observes that alcoholics are occasionally able to view their hallucinations "with a tinge of whimsical humor."

16. Kilgallin, *Lowry*, p. 200, notes that the first phrase is a parody of the final line of Yeats's "The Magi": "The uncontrollable mystery on the bestial floor." This allusion gives the vision a more than comic resonance and depth.

17. The pimp seems to be an elaboration of the "stool pigeon"—himself perhaps a combination of hallucination, reality, and invention—whom Lowry describes in one of his letters (*Letters*, p. 29) recounting his experiences in a Mexican jail: "I learned the true derivation of the word *stool pigeon*. A stool pigeon is one who sits at stool all day in prison and inveigles political prisoners into conversation, then conveys messages about them. If he's lucky, he gets a bit of buggery thrown in on the side. So simple, but to think that I might have lived my life without knowing to what heights humanity could rise."

18. Day, *Malcolm Lowry*, p. 234.

19. See also Markson, *Lowry's "Volcano,"* pp. 28, 56–57, for other evidence of *Don Quixote* in Lowry's novel.

20. Cross, *Malcolm Lowry*, p. 72, supposes that the Consul's sexual intercourse with Maria may have "biographical foundation," basing his supposition on the fact that one of Lowry's other autobiographical characters, Sigbjørn Wilderness in *Dark as the Grave Wherein My Friend Is Laid*, says that after the breakup of his marriage he slept with one prostitute after another in an attempt to find meaning in his suffering. It would be difficult, however, to discover any such motive in the Consul's coupling with Maria; and one prostitute is not many. Though all of the major characters of Lowry's fiction are doubtless autobiographical in many respects, his letters provide more reliable sources for speculating about what these respects are.

21. See, e.g., Freedman et al., "Imagery," p. 108; Solomon and Mendelson, "Hallucinations," p. 142; and Dement et al., "Hallucinations and Dreaming," p. 335.

22. For confirmation that the Consul refers in this phrase to his hallucinations, see Miller, *Malcolm Lowry*, p. 26.

23. Cross, *Malcolm Lowry*, p. 79.

24. Matson, "Second Encounter," p. 100.

25. *Dr. Faustus* 5.2.1979. I follow the interpretation of Ornstein, "Marlowe and God," p. 1384.

26. That this is a hallucination rather than an imaginative vision seems certain from the passage immediately preceding it: "He had peered out at the garden, and it was as though bits of his eyelids had broken off and were flittering and jittering before him, turning into nervous shapes and shadows, jumping to the guilty chattering in his mind, not quite voices yet, but they were coming back, they were coming back" (pp. 144–45).

27. On the tendency of his characters to be aspects of a single "human spirit," see Lowry's letter to Cape, *Letters*, pp. 60, 66.

28. Lowry himself refers to a "hint of redemption" at the end (*Letters*, p. 85);

Cross, *Malcolm Lowry*, p. 43, locates another and similar hint as early as p. 140 of the novel, in the little allegory of the insect escaping from the jaws of a cat.

29. Parallels between the Consul and Christ begin at least as early as p. 200, where the Consul recalls a beggar who took him for the Savior. These multiply near the end of the novel when the Consul is accused of being Jewish and his corpse is given a kind of cloacal crucifixion by being thrown into the barranca. See Kilgallin, *Lowry*, p. 186; Markson, *Lowry's "Volcano,"* p. 201, who thinks that the police's anti-Semitic questioning is "the first of the detailed Christ equations"; and Epstein, *Private Labyrinth*, p. 215, who says of the Consul that "in his physical self-sacrifice he becomes the Messiah for one short but eternal moment."

CHAPTER 2

1. Waugh, *Handful*, p. 93.

2. Waugh, *Brideshead*, p. 114. Most future references to this novel will appear in parentheses in the text.

3. Some maintain that the traits or personalities of alcoholics are no different from those of nonalcoholics: see, e.g., Mann, *Marty Mann Answers*, p. 58, and Bowman, "Treatment of Alcoholism," p. 320. An authoritative and exceptionally thorough work, Vaillant, *Natural History of Alcoholism*, esp. pp. 49–51 and 71–79, lends support to this view. Nevertheless, many other studies claim that certain characteristics often produce alcoholism and attempt to identify those characteristics. The following include one or more of Sebastian's prominent qualities in their assessment of the definitive characteristics of the alcoholic: White, "Personality among Alcoholics," p. 1139; Lisansky, "Etiology of Alcoholism," p. 329; Bowman and Jellinek, "Alcohol Addiction," pp. 107, 118; Strecker, "Chronic Alcoholism," pp. 13–14; Hampton, "Alcoholism and Personality," pp. 26, 33; Chafetz, Blane, and Hill, *Frontiers of Alcoholism*, p. 19; Catanzaro, "The Disease: Alcoholism," p. 16; Blum, *Alcoholism*, p. 87–88; Tiebout, "Syndrome of Alcohol Addiction," p. 541; Zimering and Calhoun, "Alcoholic Personality?," p. 101; *12 & 12*, pp. 46, 53; AA, p. 545.

4. See, e.g., Ray, *Drugs*, p. 140, and Vaillant, *Natural History of Alcoholism*, p. 51.

5. Johnson, *I'll Quit Tomorrow*, pp. 2–3.

6. Johns Hopkins University Hospital formulated thirty-five questions designed to help its patients decide whether they are alcoholic. One of these questions appears in two different forms in AA pamphlet literature: "Do you turn to lower companions and an inferior environment when drinking?" (*A.A. and the Alcoholic Employee*, p. 15) and "Do you turn to an inferior environment since drinking?" (*At last . . . AA*, p. 4). At the end of the list of thirty-five questions, *At last . . . AA* states: "If you have answered YES to any one, there is a definite warning that you may be an alcoholic. If YES to any two, the chances are you are—and to three or more you DEFINITELY are an alcoholic" (p. 4).

7. *12 & 12*, p. 48: "We had made the invention of alibis [for drinking] a fine art."

8. See *AA*, Ch. 9, "The Family Afterward."

9. On alcoholic defiance and rebellion, see Lisansky, "Etiology of Alcoholism," p. 335; *12 & 12*, pp. 28, 31–32; *AA*, pp. 265, 524.

10. Recognition that alcoholism is at least in part a spiritual illness is quite common: see Kurtz, *Not-God*, pp. 205, 208–9; Stewart, *Adventure of Sobriety*, p. ix; Clinebell, "Pastoral Counseling," pp. 197–98, and "Philosophical-Religious Factors," p. 476; *12 & 12*, "Foreword" and p. 46; and *AA*, pp. 64, 219, 457, 473. The first two references of this last source suggest that alcoholism is more a spiritual than a physical or mental illness. Waugh would probably have agreed.

11. Vaillant, *Natural History of Alcoholism*, esp. pp. 64–71, marshals and evaluates the growing body of scientific evidence that children with one or two biological parents who are alcoholic have a significantly greater chance of becoming alcoholic than other children.

12. That alcoholism results in withdrawal from people or society, isolation, and profound loneliness has been frequently observed. See, e.g., Sillman, "Chronic Alcoholism," p. 134; Gerard, "Intoxication and Addiction," p. 691; Bowman and Jellinek, "Alcohol Addiction," p. 116; Hampton, "Alcoholism and Personality," p. 29; U.S. Department of HEW, *First Special Report*, p. 73; *12 & 12*, pp. 55, 58; *AA*, pp. 21, 109–10, 119, 151, 177, 247, 284, 290, 301, 306, 410–11, 455, 467, 478.

13. *12 & 12*, pp. 58–59, 79, 113, 119–21, 128–29; *AA*, "Foreword to Third Edition," p. xxi; "The Doctor's Opinion," p. xxv; pp. 14–15, 17, 63, 89, 152–53, 229, 296, 312, 516.

14. The critical consensus seems to be that, under the Flyte influence, Charles at last acquires faith and is converted: see, e.g., Delasanta and D'Avanzo, "Truth and Beauty," p. 141, and Hardy, "*Brideshead Revisited*," pp. 159–60. In the prologue to the novel, Hooper's remark to Charles when he discovers a Catholic service taking place in the chapel at Brideshead—"More in your line than mine" (pp. 16–17)—may appear to confirm this position. For a view skeptical of this position see Powell, "Uncritical Perspective," pp. 64–65.

15. Augustine, *Confessions*, 1:29. Heath comments that "like Augustine, Sebastian is redeemed in North Africa" (*Picturesque Prison*, p. 306n26).

16. In the wartime epilogue to the novel, Nanny Hawkins tells Charles that Julia, Cordelia, and Bridey are all in Palestine (p. 349).

17. As Cosman, "Nature and Work," p. 440, aptly observes, "It is as if Waugh were an anchorite looking upon this life as a preparation for the next."

18. Thomsen, *Bill W.*, p. 363.

19. Pope, "Epistle to Arbuthnot," p. 331, l. 132.

20. Though it is much too complex a poem to fit neatly or completely into the *contemptus mundi* tradition, see Eliot, *Four Quartets*, p. 128: "The whole earth is our hospital." As references to cold accumulate in *Brideshead*, Sebastian may be said to be experiencing "frigid purgatorial fires," in Eliot's phrase (p. 128). There is no question that Eliot's influence on Waugh was far reaching and profound. It would be both tenable and enlightening to argue that some of Waugh's early nov-

els, particularly *A Handful of Dust*, were his *Waste Land* and that *Brideshead Revisited* was his *Ash Wednesday* and *Four Quartets*. For evidence of this influence and Waugh's admiration for Eliot, see Waugh, *Diaries*, pp. 242, 666; Sykes, *Evelyn Waugh*, p. 315; Waugh, *Letters*, p. 447; Joost, "*Handful of Dust*," pp. 180–81, 194; and especially Crawford, "Evelyn Waugh," pp. 49–63.

21. In a summary of *Brideshead* for prospective Hollywood producers, Waugh seems to imply that Sebastian's alcoholism was a form of grace. See Lane, *Evelyn Waugh*, pp. 99 and 168n11, who cites as his source Heath, "*Brideshead*," pp. 226–27. For other comment on the operations of grace in *Brideshead* see Doyle, *Evelyn Waugh*, pp. 26–27, and Heath, *Picturesque Prison*, pp. 178, 182.

22. For Waugh's interest in such matters as martyrdom, sainthood, and holiness, see especially his *Helena*, *Ronald Knox*, and *Edmund Campion*. In the preface (p. 14) to the life of Knox, Waugh writes, "But genius and sanctity do not thrive except by suffering." This sounds much like the connection Cordelia wishes to see between Sebastian's alcoholic suffering and his holiness.

23. Burns, "Holy Willie's Prayer," 1:76; and Butler, *All Flesh*, pp. 228–29.

24. Dyson maintains that Sebastian's fate is characteristic of Waugh's novels in "Evelyn Waugh," pp. 72–79.

25. In World War II, during a long and tedious mission with Tito's forces in Yugoslavia, Waugh and the Earl of Birkenhead endeavored to silence an egomaniacal, frequently intoxicated Churchill by betting him ten pounds each that he could not read the Bible through in two weeks. The effort failed to produce peaceful silence; one of Churchill's favorite comments on his reading was "God, isn't God a shit" (*Diaries*, p. 591). Waugh is plainly disgusted with Churchill, but he is just as obviously fascinated by his rampaging irrepressibility. Although he remembers the bet as fifty pounds each and omits Churchill's four-letter word, Birkenhead records the incident in "Fiery Particles," pp. 161–62, referring to Churchill's "appalling garrulity," his "engulfing river of talk" (p. 161).

26. The only other study of *Brideshead* that considers Sebastian's alcoholism in any detail is Eagleton, *Exiles*, pp. 60–67. Eagleton's complaint is that, for various reasons, the alcoholism is insufficiently explained or accounted for. As I have tried to indicate, I believe that the major problems in Waugh's treatment of the alcoholic lie elsewhere.

CHAPTER 3

1. O'Neill, *Iceman Cometh*, p. 236. Future references to this work will appear in parentheses in the text. The play was written in 1939 and first published in 1946. O'Neill's only published short story, "Tomorrow" (1917), anticipates the play in several respects. For details of O'Neill's drinking and the causes of his abstinence, see Boulton, *Long Story*, pp. 126–38, 144–67; Goodwin, "Alcoholism of O'Neill," pp. 99–104; and Sheaffer, "Eugene O'Neill," pp. 106–10. Sheaffer believes that O'Neill drew on his experience as a periodic alcoholic in his depiction of Hickey (p. 109). Like Hickey, O'Neill avoided mixing work and alcohol: see Goodwin, p. 101, and Gelb, *O'Neill*, pp. 375–76, 963.

2. At a few points in the play it may seem that Hickey acts to defeat his purpose of helping the others to gain sobriety. When he first arrives at Harry's for the birthday celebration, he exhorts them to drink (p. 78); he himself even drinks a toast to Harry (pp. 143–44); late in the play he once again encourages drinking (p. 225). But the first two instances are tactical: he wishes to retain the sympathies of the men, more specifically of Larry, who has accused Hickey of being afraid to drink, so that he may put his message across; and on the last occasion he is beginning to be exasperated with the others for not changing as rapidly as he expected them to. In all three instances Harry's birthday celebration sanctions the drinking. When this event is past, Hickey persists in believing, his message will be heeded: having achieved peace by seeing their pipe dreams as such and abandoning them, the rest will no longer require the solace or escape of alcohol.

3. *AA*, p. xxi: "Each day, somewhere in the world, recovery begins when one alcoholic talks with another alcoholic, sharing experience, strength, and hope."

4. *AA*, p. 64: "Our liquor was but a symptom. So we had to get down to causes and conditions."

5. Tiebout, "Act of Surrender," p. 54, seems to state quite exactly the result that Hickey claims can stem from the surrender of alcoholic fantasies or "pipe dreams" as he has surrendered his: "an inner peace and serenity, the possession of which frees the individual from his compulsion to drink. In other words, an act of surrender is an occasion when the individual no longer fights life but accepts it." To those who practice its principles, AA extends the promise that they "will comprehend the word serenity and . . . will know peace" (*AA*, pp. 83–84).

6. Step 3 of the twelve steps central to AA's program for sobriety is "made a decision to turn our will and our lives over to the care of God *as we understood Him*."

7. These principles are commonly referred to in AA as the "twelve steps" (*AA*, pp. 59–60): 1. We admitted we were powerless over alcohol—that our lives had become unmanageable. 2. Came to believe that a Power greater than ourselves could restore us to sanity. 3. Made a decision to turn our will and our lives over to the care of God *as we understood Him*. 4. Made a searching and fearless moral inventory of ourselves. 5. Admitted to God, to ourselves, and to another human being the exact nature of our wrongs. 6. Were entirely ready to have God remove all these defects of character. 7. Humbly asked Him to remove our shortcomings. 8. Made a list of all persons we had harmed, and became willing to make amends to them all. 9. Made direct amends to such people wherever possible, except when to do so would injure them or others. 10. Continued to take personal inventory and when we were wrong promptly admitted it. 11. Sought through prayer and meditation to improve our conscious contact with God *as we understood Him*, praying only for knowledge of His will for us and the power to carry that out. 12. Having had a spiritual awakening as the result of these steps, we tried to carry this message to alcoholics, and to practice these principles in all our affairs.

8. Johnson, *I'll Quit Tomorrow*, pp. 117–18.

9. *AA*, p. 90, explicitly enjoins those who would help an alcoholic not to force themselves or their ideas upon him if he does not wish to stop drinking.

10. Here may be noted another parody of an AA idea, which states that the alcoholic seeking sobriety must be prepared to "go to any length to get it" (*AA*, p. 58). In pointing out these various parodies and travesties, of course, I in no way mean to imply that they were conscious or that O'Neill knew anything about AA or its principles; there is no evidence that he did.

11. Johnson, *I'll Quit Tomorrow*, pp. 2–3, 53, 85–86. One great value of Johnson's book is that it is based on first-hand experience with many alcoholics; in 1966 he began working out his own alcohol treatment program, which has since been adopted by a number of hospitals (p. 6). For much different views of the inhabitants of Hope's saloon, see Frazer, *Love as Death*, p. 21, and Scheibler, *Late Plays*, pp. 195–202.

12. The severely divided character was a recurring feature of O'Neill's dramas and reflected his pessimism about the possibility of human wholeness or integration. Sometimes the split is so great that O'Neill embodies it in separate characters. See, e.g., *Days without End*, in which opposite sides of the same self are played by different actors, John and Loving, who resume one identity at the play's implausible end. Similarly, Dion Anthony and Billy Brown, of *The Great God Brown*, represent opposing halves of an allegorical Everyman. Bogard, *Contour in Time*, p. 304, notices that the male characters of *Strange Interlude* "are really partial aspects of a whole male personality." A character perhaps more like Hickey than any of those mentioned above, Emma Crosby of O'Neill's *Diff'rent*, suffers such an irreconcilable split between the demands of her id and her superego that sane, coherent action is finally impossible.

13. Freud, *Ego and Id*, pp. 78–79. Driver, "On the Late Plays," pp. 117–18, provides a psychological interpretation of Hickey that is similar to mine though less elaborated. Driver, however, views Hickey's ego as the source of a death wish. For another discussion of Hickey's divided personality, see Scheibler, *Late Plays*, p. 164.

14. As Hickey tells his story, Evelyn, though never appearing in the play, assumes the importance of a character. Although she lacks roundedness, she is more than an abstract, dehumanized superego. Our major disadvantage in evaluating her is that we see her only through Hickey's increasingly hostile eyes. Thus she may seem to resemble the type of spouse who in AA lore is sometimes called the "enabler": one who, while seeming to help the alcoholic, may in fact impede his chances of recovery by too readily offering excuses, sympathy, and forgiveness for his drinking. One supposed though unconscious motive of such a spouse is to enjoy and maintain dominance in the relationship, because an alcoholic becomes progressively less able to discharge his responsibilities and it is tempting to treat him as a froward child. Hickey, his mind clouded by the unreconciled polarities of love and hate, at times approaches this view of Evelyn; and possibly one may trace something of O'Neill in or behind it, for his second wife is said to have "confided to a friend that she had fallen in love with O'Neill and married him because he was drunk all the time and needed her help"

(Goodwin, "Alcoholism of O'Neill," p. 103; Gelb, *O'Neill*, p. 626). For studies of the spouse who seems to wish to help her alcoholic husband but who may actually want him to remain drunk, see Igersheimer, "Group Psychotherapy," p. 83; Macdonald, "Group Psychotherapy," p. 125; and "The Sufferer" and "The Waverer" portraits in Whalen, "Wives of Alcoholics," pp. 634–36, 638–39. (If such flawed spouses are usually women, the male spouses of alcoholic women may be said to be even more greatly flawed; for they more often leave their wives than sober wives leave alcoholic husbands. See Sandmaier, *Invisible Alcoholics*, pp. 20, 226–27.) It is precisely because of Hickey's distortions that his views of Evelyn are suspect. Whatever her motives for marrying Hickey—and he is silent about these—she may well have been an unusually sympathetic, forbearing, forgiving wife without any ulterior or sinister motives. At any rate, her virtues are not automatic or cloyingly easy: on the repeated occasions when Hickey stumbled home after one of his binges, he "could see disgust having a battle in her eyes with love" (p. 237).

15. Although Hickey "believes that his father's 'religious bunk' never affected him, the truth is that it made an indelible impression upon him. His reform wave in Hope's saloon testifies to this: it is performed in his father's spirit" (Törnqvist, *Drama of Souls*, p. 228).

16. A hard-drinking protagonist in another late O'Neill play, Con Melody of *Touch of the Poet*, resembles Hickey in the sharp division between id and superego and in the resolution of this split with the victory of the id. Unlike Hickey, however, this victory leads not to murder but to a strengthened love for Con's wife, Nora, whose peasant stock represents the roots to which Con's id returns, his superego of gentlemanly pretensions overthrown. Moreover, Con's resolution of conflict produces not Hickey's hectic burst of activity followed by the peace of death but a renewed and, we are to believe, lasting flow of purposeful energy. But Con's personality and its change seem less subtly and plausibly drawn than Hickey's.

17. By his approval of Parritt's death, Larry also breaks out of what AA calls "the bondage of self" (*AA*, p. 63), the self-centeredness that AA regards as a chief obstacle to recovery from alcoholism.

18. In the illustrative inventory given in *AA* (p. 65), fear appears to be the cause of all other character defects. See also p. 67: "the fabric of our existence was shot through with" fear.

19. Boswell, *Life of Johnson*, 2:435–36n7. As the note acknowledges, Johnson's comment was recorded by Stockdale, *Memoirs* (1809), 2:189.

20. Goodwin, "Alcoholism of O'Neill," p. 101, remarks that O'Neill "succumbed to pneumonia in a Boston hotel" at age sixty-five "after years of wanting to die and being unable to do so." O'Neill's resemblance to Larry is well brought out in a letter he wrote to his friend Kenneth Macgowan as he was falling in love with Carlotta Monterey, for whom he was to divorce Agnes, although still feeling loyalty and love toward her: "I envy those simple souls to whom life is always either this *or* that. It's the this *and* that . . . that slow-poisons the soul with complicated contradictions." This letter is quoted in part in Sheaffer, *O'Neill*, p. 237.

O'Neill's resemblance to Larry is also remarked on by Brustein, "*Iceman Cometh*," pp. 101–2, and by Watson, "The Theater," pp. 237–38.

CHAPTER 4

1. For indications that this familiarity derives from first-hand alcoholic experience, see Hersey, "Talk with Cheever," p. 27; Schickel, "Cheever Chronicle," p. 31; Santana, "Tripping," p. 61; "Inescapable Conclusions," p. 125; Clemons, "Cheever's Triumph," p. 62. These sources, however, have been generally superseded by Susan Cheever's memoir of her father, *Home Before Dark*; on Cheever's alcoholism, see esp. pp. 161–63, 181–201.

2. Cheever, *Bullet Park*, pp. 6, 8.

3. Cheever, *Wapshot Scandal*, p. 239.

4. Cheever, "President of Argentine," p. 44; *Wapshot Scandal*, pp. 83–86.

5. Cheever, *Stories*, p. 469. Except when otherwise noted, this is the text of Cheever's short stories used throughout; hereafter, most page references will appear in parentheses in the text.

6. See Rupp, "Upshot of Wapshot," p. 31: "Life, Cheever seems to be saying, is a familial enterprise, a social enterprise." Although Rupp makes this remark specifically about *The Wapshot Chronicle*, it has wider relevance to Cheever's work. See also Morace, "John Cheever," p. 91, who notes Cheever's belief, as evidenced in his stories, "that the individual who separates himself from his family and community must learn to reintegrate himself in the group." Finally, Waldeland, *John Cheever*, pp. 142–43, although terming Cheever a romantic, comments that "one of Cheever's most frequently chosen subjects is family relationships."

7. For a well-reasoned defense of Cheever's authorial intrusions and manipulations, see Molyneux, "Affirming Balance," pp. 35–40.

8. See, e.g., "The Housebreaker of Shady Hill," *Stories*, pp. 260–61, in which Johnny Hake, the son of divorced parents, recalls meeting his father at the Plaza Hotel when he was fifteen after not seeing him for ten years; the father, drunk, takes him to a musical comedy and then offers to arrange to let him "have" any girl in the chorus. In *Bullet Park*, pp. 27–28, Nailles recalls that, when he brought his college roommate home in his freshman year, his father got drunk, took them to a hotel dining room, made a grab at a waitress, and then conducted the orchestra. Although everyone else seemed much amused, Nailles, "had he possessed a pistol, would have shot his father in the back." Hammer, the other main character of the novel, is born out of wedlock and does not see his father for many years. One Christmas holiday he decides to look him up and locates him in a hotel room "in a poleaxed, drunken sleep, naked" and alone although the "two unmade beds . . . had seen some venereal mileage" (p. 164). He decides not to increase the embarrassment by waking his father. In *The Wapshot Scandal*, Coverly recalls the time that his father, drunk, smoked a cigarette in church: "a lot of people had seen him. What I wanted then was to be the son of Mr. Pluzinski the farmer" (p. 21). Although the relationship in Cheever's

Falconer is between brothers and Eben may not be drunk on the occasions referred to, nevertheless, like the father of "Reunion," he offends waiters and embarrasses his brother, Farragut, the novel's protagonist (pp. 62, 204). Farragut also remembers a scene from his childhood in which he searches for his father, who has supposedly gone off to commit suicide. In an interesting variation on Cheever's pattern of embarrassment, Farragut finds his father on an amusement-park roller coaster, only "pretending to drink from an empty bottle" and to threaten suicide "from every rise"; like Nailles's father in *Bullet Park*, he has an amused and admiring audience (pp. 62–64). See also "The Seaside Houses," discussed below, esp. pp. 487–88. Cheever, *Home Before Dark*, p. 210, quoting from a letter by her father about his father, shows that Cheever unquestionably drew on his father's drunken escapades for his fiction. But see also pp. 203–4, which indicate that in some ways the father of "Reunion" resembles Cheever's brother, Fred, who also drank too much and deeply embarrassed John.

9. Although certainly not devoid of skill, one of Cheever's early stories, "Peril in the Streets," is relatively crude as a portrayal of a drunk and helps one more fully to appreciate his artistry in "Reunion." "Peril" can be found in Cheever's first collection of stories, *Way Some People*, pp. 235–39; none of these is in the later collected *Stories*.

10. Cheever, *Home Before Dark*, p. 43.

11. See Blythe and Sweet, "Perverted Sacraments," p. 394.

12. Bunyan, *Pilgrim's Progress*, pp. 213, 218.

13. Ibid., p. 212.

14. Graves's assertion that Neddy has a drinking problem may lack sufficient evidence in the story but seems not far from the truth. See her "Dominant Color," p. 4. See also Auser, "Cheever's Myth," pp. 18–19.

15. For a higher estimate of Neddy, see Moore, "The Hero," pp. 149–50. See also Coale, *John Cheever*, p. 47, for a conclusion similar to mine about "The Swimmer": "Suburbia may be limited in its moral scope and social pretensions, but outside its pale all remains darkness and dissolution."

16. Elliott, *Power of Satire*, pp. 138–39.

17. See Waugh, *Decline and Fall*, p. 269, for Paul Pennyfeather's eulogy to Grimes on hearing of his supposed drowning in a bog: "Paul knew that Grimes was not dead. Lord Tangent was dead; Mr. Prendergast was dead; the time would even come for Paul Pennyfeather; but Grimes, Paul at last realized, was of the immortals. He was a life force. Sentenced to death in Flanders, he popped up in Wales; drowned in Wales, he emerged in South America; engulfed in the dark mystery of Egdon Mire, he would rise again somewhere at sometime, shaking from his limbs the musty integuments of the tomb." Philbrick and Fagan are two other characters in *Decline and Fall* with remarkable powers of survival and recuperation, but they have less constant identities than Grimes or Gee-Gee.

18. In one scene of *Bullet Park*, Marietta Hammer, who is apparently drunk at the time, may bear a distant resemblance to Gee-Gee because of her outspokenness (pp. 53–56). Unlike Gee-Gee, however, none of her interesting potential is developed; she simply seems unreasonably abusive toward her husband.

19. Cheever, "Leaves," pp. 195–96.

20. Cheever, *Home Before Dark*, pp. 173–78, 206–8.

21. Cheever, *Falconer*, pp. 51, 7. Other citations appear in parentheses in the text.

22. This man seems to be a descendant of the Depression era drunks who disgust the landlady and whom she evicts when she can afford to in "Brooklyn Rooming House," an uncollected story that appears to be Cheever's first in *The New Yorker*.

23. Johnson, "Moral Structure," p. 26.

CHAPTER 5

1. Bellow, *Humboldt's Gift*, pp. 6–8.

2. Bellow, *The Victim*, pp. 78, 80. Subsequent references to the novel will appear in parentheses in the text.

3. Snyder, *Alcohol and the Jews*, p. 160, prints this song in full (in English, not Yiddish) and suggests that it is one of the best known of various Jewish stories, songs, or sayings whose theme is that sobriety is a Jewish virtue and inebriety a Gentile vice (p. 159). The heart of Snyder's study consists of data derived from interviews with seventy-three Jews living in New Haven. When one interviewee professed ignorance of this song, a relative exclaimed to him, "Aw, come on—everybody knows that!" (p. 160). Snyder was aware that, even as he was conducting his study, traditional reasons for Jewish hostility toward excessive drinking were being eroded. But it is worth noting that the date of his study is close to the first publication of Bellow's novel (1947); that Leventhal grew up in Hartford, not far from New Haven; and that, like most of those interviewed by Snyder, Leventhal is a Russian or Polish Jew.

4. Snyder, *Alcohol and the Jews*, p. 174.

5. McSheehy, *Skid Row*, p. 37, has a comment on the lighting of flophouse cubicles that confirms Leventhal's reverie. They have, he says, "no electrical outlets; a 25 watt bulb suspended from chicken wire is the only source of light." He also has interesting comments (p. 43) on the clerks in hotels for "transients": they are expected to maintain order, usually live in the hotel, work twelve hours a day seven days a week, and are paid $8.00 to $12.00 per day or $.67 to $1.00 per hour. (McSheehy gathered his data when the minimum wage was $1.60 an hour.)

6. Zettler, *The Bowery*, p. 146.

7. As Gordon, "'Pushy Jew,'" p. 132, aptly sums it up, "Allbee is Leventhal's anti-self, everything that Leventhal most fears he could himself become: self-destructive, a failure, a drifter, a drunkard, a man who has lost his wife, a lecher, and a madman."

8. Baumbach, *Landscape of Nightmare*, p. 42, makes a similar point.

9. There have been many claims that alcohol enhances spiritual perception. For a few discussions, see Clinebell, "Philosophical-Religious Factors," pp. 474–76, 480, and "Pastoral Counseling," pp. 197–98; Kurtz, *Not-God*, pp. 205, 208; Jellinek, "Symbolism of Drinking," pp. 854–58; MacAndrew and Edgerton,

Drunken Comportment, pp. 40, 98; and Stewart, "Meaning of Intoxication," pp. 132–33.

10. Allbee's thinking here is remarkably like the idea of Alcoholics Anonymous that, to stop drinking for good, the alcoholic must have reached his bottom—that is, he must have experienced so much pain and misery that he cannot bear to continue his drinking. It is not likely, however, that Bellow would have derived this idea from AA in 1947, at which time it was still relatively little known; and of course the idea is not original with AA.

11. As Bradbury, "Saul Bellow," p. 82, puts it, Leventhal is "forced to experience Allbee's state as if it were his own." I would, however, reject the notion that Leventhal is forced into this experience.

12. *AA*, p. 21. For abundant evidence of the typicality of blackouts for the alcoholic, see the personal stories in this volume, pp. 171–561.

13. Rats and mice are among the most commonly hallucinated animals in the enormous literature on alcoholic delusions. Jackson's *Lost Weekend*, which made a considerable stir at its publication only three years before *The Victim*, has as the climactic incident of one long section its alcoholic hero's hallucination of a bat attacking and devouring a mouse.

14. See Bahr, *Skid Row*, p. 64, for quoted reactions to the smell of the derelicts in this library.

15. See Scheer-Schäzler, *Saul Bellow*, p. 21: when Leventhal "gets drunk it is more an act of identification [with Allbee] than of helplessness and despair."

16. Leventhal "had the strange feeling that there was not a single part of him on which the whole world did not press with full weight, on his body, on his soul, pushing upward in his breast and downward in his bowels. . . . He put out all his strength to collect himself, beginning with the primary certainty that the world pressed on him and passed through him" (pp. 257–58). Allbee, as I have already said, is for Leventhal the chief representative of this oppressive world. Later in the chapter Leventhal takes a bath, after which "he felt freshened and almost cheerful" (p. 265).

17. Although most commentators on *The Victim* appear skeptical that Leventhal experiences significant growth, I share the view of Clayton, *Saul Bellow*, p. 141, that Leventhal is "essentially changed" by the end of the novel. Clayton likewise recognizes the importance of Leventhal's entering Allbee (pp. 160–61). If he is rather sketchy about the particulars of this process and the resemblances between the two men, Clayton's is in general the most comprehensive, detailed, and sound analysis of *The Victim*.

CHAPTER 6

1. The alcoholic "is a real Dr. Jekyll and Mr. Hyde": *AA*, p. 21; Graham, *Real Fitzgerald*, esp. Ch. 6, "The Drinker," pp. 96–115. Although Graham asserts that Fitzgerald was "completely sober during his last thirteen months" (p. 11), in an earlier book, *College*, pp. 152–53, she acknowledges that Frances Kroll, Fitzgerald's loyal and admiring secretary, disputes this belief.

2. Graham, *Real Fitzgerald*, p. 97; Bruccoli, *Epic Grandeur*, p. 143, notes that Fitzgerald's suspension from the Club occurred in 1920 because of his and Zelda's behavior during a visit.

3. Graham, *Real Fitzgerald*, pp. 98, 105, 109, 114. For versions of some of the same stories about Fitzgerald's drinking, see also Graham and Frank, *Beloved Infidel*. For the alcoholic's tendency to seek out low company as his illness progresses, see also Susan Cheever's memoir of her father, *Home Before Dark*, p. 189, where she records that during the worst of his alcoholism, in Boston in 1974, John Cheever once lay "down on the grass in the Public Garden to share a bottle of hooch in a paper bag with a bum who suddenly seemed to be a friend." Fitzgerald once told Tony Buttitta of his hallucinations, a frequent occurrence in the late stages of alcoholism (*After the Good*, p. 155). Latham (*Crazy Sundays*, p. 5) relates a story from the '20s of how Fitzgerald—drunk, of course—tried to kill Zelda and Anita Loos by throwing a candelabrum and other heavy objects at them in the dining room of his Great Neck, New York, home. He had locked the doors but was finally restrained by a butler who broke a glass pane in one of the doors and entered. A large collection of Fitzgerald's drunken episodes is found in Donaldson's *Fool for Love* in the chapter entitled "Demon Drink." Although some allowance should perhaps be made for her exaggeration, Zelda, in an extremely long letter of 1930 after her hospitalization for a nervous breakdown, presents a blunt and mordant history of Fitzgerald's increasing drunkenness during the 1920s. See Fitzgerald, *Correspondence*, pp. 245–51.

4. I ignore the many Fitzgerald stories in which drinking figures casually or incidentally, as well as such stories as "The Camel's Back" and "May Day" (both 1920), in which drinking, though given some prominence, should probably be seen as having minor interest. In "The Camel's Back," for instance, the drunkenness of Perry Parkhurst is simply the mechanism that moves the story toward its extended gag and happy ending; and in "May Day," the drunkenness of "Mr. In" and "Mr. Out," though certainly displaying Fitzgerald's keen observation of (if not intimate familiarity with) intoxicated behavior, is of less interest in itself than as a means of counterpointing and complementing the drunkenness of Gordon Sterrett, Gus Rose, and Carrol Key, all of which is intended to testify not so much to the prevalence of drinking as to the degeneration or decay at all levels of American society after World War I.

5. See Roulston, "*Beautiful and Damned*," p. 157. I am not persuaded by the psychoanalytic argument suggested in Roulston's subtitle. Wasserstrom, "Goad of Guilt," pp. 300–303, also advances some psychological explanations of Fitzgerald's drinking.

6. Fitzgerald, *Beautiful and Damned*, p. 241. Other citations of this novel will appear in parentheses in the text.

7. Roth, "'Milk of Wonder.'"

8. Ibid., p. 6; *Great Gatsby*, p. 43. The same appearance of drink without human agency also occurs on pp. 11 and 40.

9. Roth, "'Milk of Wonder,'" p. 11; *Great Gatsby*, p. 47.

10. Fabricant, "Medical Profile," p. 148; Mizener, *Far Side*, pp. 195–97; Bruccoli, *Epic Grandeur*, p. 185; Eble, "Touches of Disaster," p. 48. Eble's comprehen-

sive, indispensable article on the subject of alcoholism in Fitzgerald's short stories will hereafter be cited in parentheses in the text. These estimates of when Fitzgerald's drinking became alcoholic are conservative; the frequency of his drunken escapades before *Gatsby* would support a strong argument for dating the change about 1920, or even earlier.

11. In spite of growing public awareness of the dangers of alcoholism and the means of overcoming it, the usual estimate is that only one alcoholic in ten will achieve permanent sobriety. Because help is nowadays widely known to be available and effective, the alcoholic's "denial system" more than any other single reason is probably responsible for the appallingly poor recovery rate. Mann, *Marty Mann*, p. 73, regards denial as the "outstanding characteristic of alcoholics": "almost without exception alcoholics deny their condition and continue to do so long after it has become apparent to everyone around them."

12. Graham, *Real Fitzgerald*, p. 113.

13. Hemingway, *Moveable Feast*, pp. 152–53; Hemingway's vignette is quoted by Mizener, *Far Side*, pp. 196–97.

14. See Bruccoli, *Epic Grandeur*, p. 489: "Alcoholic cardiomyopathy, or enlargement of the heart chambers, which occurs in chronic alcoholics, may result in heart failure."

15. Mizener, *Far Side*, p. 197; Fitzgerald, *Notebooks*, p. 190.

16. See Fitzgerald, *Letters*, pp. 230, 306; Fitzgerald, *As Ever*, pp. 207–10; Bruccoli, *Epic Grandeur*, pp. 306–7; Fitzgerald, *Correspondence*, pp. 241–43.

17. Bruccoli, *Epic Grandeur*, p. 439.

18. Bruccoli, *Composition*, pp. 4–5, notes that of the twenty-four reviews of the novel he has found, eight complained "that Doctor Diver's collapse was insufficiently documented." These eight include some of the most thoughtful reviewers of the 1930s: Clifton Fadiman in *The New Yorker*, William Troy in *The Nation*, and D. W. Harding in *Scrutiny*. Troy observes that a reader is confused about the reasons for Diver's disintegration; Harding goes even further and claims that Fitzgerald gives no reason for Diver's crack-up (Bruccoli, pp. 6–7). Although Bruccoli himself vehemently disagrees with this kind of assessment, it perhaps continues to be the leading reaction to Diver. See Ellis, "Fitzgerald's Fragmented," p. 127: "Critics who examine *Tender Is the Night* usually agree that the motivation for Dick Diver's collapse is vague. Though the novel, they say, describes his destruction, it does not satisfactorily explain the causes for the deterioration of a man so gifted as he has been made to appear."

19. Fitzgerald, "One Trip Abroad," pp. 262, 270–71.

20. "Family" was first published, like many of Fitzgerald's stories, in *The Saturday Evening Post* (4 June 1932; Mizener, *Far Side*, p. 405); it was collected in *Taps at Reveille* (1935). One problem in dealing with Fitzgerald's stories is that there is no standard collected edition.

21. First published in *Esquire*, December 1939 (Mizener, *Far Side*, p. 407).

22. Balliett, "Even His Feet," p. 32.

23. Step 2 of AA clearly implies the insanity of the drinking alcoholic: "Came to believe that a Power greater than ourselves could restore us to sanity" (*AA*, p. 59).

24. First published in *The Saturday Evening Post* (4 July 1931; Mizener, *Far Side*, p. 405).

25. Graham, *Real Fitzgerald*, p. 115. In response to Fitzgerald's comment that he did not like to baby women, Laura Hearne perceptively noted in her diary: "No, I thought, you like them to baby *you*" (p. 236). Her diary, dealing with her relations with Fitzgerald in Asheville, North Carolina, in the summer of 1935, has been printed in *Esquire* as "Summer with Fitzgerald." As a headnote says, Hearne acted as "secretary, companion, nurse, and confidential agent" to Fitzgerald.

26. Raleigh, "O'Neill's *Long Day's*," p. 137.

27. Buttitta, *After the Good*, p. 160.

28. *The Saturday Evening Post* (21 February 1931; Mizener, *Far Side*, p. 405).

29. Citing several other critics, Donaldson, *Fool for Love*, p. 151, notes both the omission of alcoholism from Fitzgerald's account and the probable reason for the omission: the alcoholic's denial of his illness. Fitzgerald's essay actually consists of three parts, each with its own title: "The Crack-Up," general title and title of the first part (February 1936); "Handle with Care," title of the second part (March 1936); "Pasting It Together," title of the third part (April 1936). All three parts first appeared in *Esquire*.

30. The friend was Laura Hearne. Her estimate of Fitzgerald's peak consumption is in "Summer with Fitzgerald," p. 164. On p. 252, she records that Fitzgerald "was not sober at all" for a month before he was hospitalized on 19 September. Another published reminiscence of the same summer (Peeples, "Twilight," p. 171) confirms Fitzgerald's astonishing consumption of beer. In a letter to Hearne of 29 July 1935 announcing his reasons for leaving his hotel in North Carolina, Fitzgerald himself really verifies these two accounts: "I'm such a wreck physically that I expect the heart, liver and lungs to collapse again at a moments notice—six weeks of late hours, beer and talk, talk, talk." Late hours and talk never hurt anyone's liver. In the sentence preceding this, Fitzgerald characteristically tries to displace the responsibility for his drinking: "Dont women have anything more to do than to sit around and make love & drink beer?" (*Correspondence*, p. 417). See also Fitzgerald's letter of August to his lover of that summer, Beatrice Dance, in which he mentions the effects of his excessive smoking and beer drinking (p. 419). Finally, Fitzgerald's ledger for 1935 almost certainly belies his claim of a long spell of dryness before his crack-up. Under October he mentions his "1st gloom article" and, under December, "two more gloom articles," in all probability the three-part "Crack-Up" that *Esquire* published in early 1936. So Fitzgerald wrote the first part only one month after his hospitalization, a fact that he records in his ledger for September 1935 and that the entry for August hints was caused by drinking. See Fitzgerald, *Ledger*, "Appendix."

31. Fitzgerald does not give the title of Seabrook's book—*Asylum*.

32. *The Saturday Evening Post* (3 November 1934; Mizener, *Far Side*, p. 406).

33. *American Mercury* (October 1932; Mizener, *Far Side*, p. 405).

34. *AA*, p. 21, notes as one of the definitive traits of an alcoholic that "he has a positive genius for" getting drunk just when it is crucial that he should not. This

is exactly what Fitzgerald did at the Thalberg gathering. Eble clearly implies a direct connection between Fitzgerald's getting drunk at the Thalbergs and his being fired by MGM; this view agrees with LeVot, *Fitzgerald*, p. 264: "Thalberg, who had watched [Fitzgerald's] performance from across the room and who despised alcoholics, fired him at the end of the week." In contrast, Bruccoli, *Epic Grandeur*, p. 323, suggests that, having finished his assignment, Fitzgerald left Hollywood voluntarily because of worry about Zelda's health. That opinion was probably based on a retrospective letter Fitzgerald wrote to his daughter, Scottie, in which he even says that he was asked to stay in Hollywood but "I wanted to get East when the contract expired to see how your mother was" (letter of [July 1937] in *Scott Fitzgerald*, p. 26). Perhaps the truth of the matter can never be ascertained; but, given Fitzgerald's inclination to deny his drinking problem, it is not likely that he would admit—especially in a letter to his teenaged daughter—that he had been fired for drinking. In any event, his shame over getting drunk at the party would have been almost as great even if it had not resulted in his being fired.

35. Oddly enough, Coles's drink count as given by Fitzgerald agrees with an estimate of the number of drinks Fitzgerald had at the Thalberg party; in *Joy Ride*, p. 243, Dwight Taylor, who went to the party with Fitzgerald, says that Fitzgerald could have had only one or two drinks while out of his sight and before insulting Robert Montgomery. Taylor adds, however, that Fitzgerald was "as drunk as a man who had been swilling for half the night"—a condition that Coles is far from exhibiting in the story. It does not seem to occur to Taylor that, to become as drunk as he reports, Fitzgerald must have managed to sneak quick drinks at the party or to be mostly drunk before ever arriving, each of these ploys being familiar to many alcoholics.

36. Fitzgerald, *Pat Hobby*, p. ix. Hereafter cited in parentheses in the text.

37. Eastman, *Enjoyment of Laughter*, p. 192; Boughner, *Braggart*, p. 10; Cornford, *Attic Comedy*, pp. 129, 134.

38. Raleigh, "O'Neill's *Long Day's*," p. 137.

39. "Teamed with Genius," "On the Trail of Pat Hobby," "Two Old-Timers"; "Fun in an Artist's Studio," p. 128.

40. Graham and Frank, *Beloved Infidel*, p. 279.

41. The possibility of this connection is also seen by Rees, "Pat Hobby," p. 556.

42. Graham, *College*, p. 136.

CHAPTER 7

1. Vidal, "Immortal Bird," p. 5.

2. Bell, "Meaning of *PR*," p. 34. Atlas, *Delmore Schwartz*, p. 302, notes Schwartz's "ominous injunction" that the poet would have to be destroyed or sacrificed in the service of his art.

3. Hyde, "Alcohol & Poetry," p. 9.

4. Crane, "Critical Principles," p. 97. After characterizing Berryman as "blind"

to the way his alcoholism shaped his poems and "lost" in alcoholism, Hyde nevertheless asserts that he was not "trapped" by it (pp. 9, 11), a qualification that appears inconsistent with his deterministic views. Although generally more plausible, another critic who approves of Hyde's deterministic thinking and abets it is Hall. In *Remembering Poets*, p. 29, Hall claims that "in our culture an artist's self-destructiveness" is substantially increased by a self-hating bourgeois society that believes that this tendency is admirable because "if we did what we really wanted . . . we would be drunk all the time or addicted to heroin or at least suicidal."

5. Dickey, *Sorties*, pp. 52, 85. It should be added, however, that in a brief "Afterword to the New Ecco Edition," *Babel to Byzantium*, p. 296, Dickey speaks more affirmatively of what he now calls Berryman's "poetry of the will." Arpin also discusses Berryman's playfulness in *Poetry of Berryman*, p. 4.

6. In Berryman's unfinished novel, *Recovery*, p. 160, Alan Severance, who bears a close resemblance to Berryman, recalls that at one point in his therapy for alcoholism he felt primarily bewildered and confused. Because his years of drinking have thoroughly distorted his natural responses and feelings, the alcoholic often has more than the problem of denying his alcoholism; though this is real, it is also made possible by a genuine loss of ability to know his innermost feelings, including those about his alcoholism.

7. Berryman perhaps modified this absolute position somewhat in an interview with Stitt, "Art of Poetry," p. 193: "Henry both is and is not me, obviously. We touch at certain points."

8. I agree (at last) with Hyde, "Alcohol & Poetry," p. 11, that Berryman's separation of himself from Henry was "a poet's whim" and should be disregarded. The similarity of Berryman and Henry is also maintained by Conarroe, *John Berryman*, p. 95. Other critics, however, insist on their difference: see, e.g., Rosenblatt, "'Confessional Mode,'" pp. 158–59; Hoffman, "Impersonal Personalism," p. 695; and Arpin, *Poetry of Berryman*, pp. 61–62. I strongly disagree with Arpin's conclusion that because of this difference "we never get a realistic, specific picture of Henry's alcoholism" such as we find in Lowry's *Under the Volcano*. The difference between Berryman and Lowry is unrelated to any separation of Berryman from Henry and has to do, simply, with the difference between poetry and fiction. Berryman, though lacking neither realism nor specificity, was practically required by the brevity of individual Dream Songs to achieve these qualities tersely or elliptically; the massive specificity of the novelist (it would be a mistake to think of *Under the Volcano* as primarily realistic) was simply not available in the kind of poetic form chosen by Berryman for the *Dream Songs*.

9. Simpson, *Poets*, p. 157. See also Haffenden, *Life of Berryman*, pp. 167–95.

10. *Berryman's Sonnets*, pp. 33, 37, 93.

11. Berryman, *Dream Songs*, p. 372. Other citations will appear in parentheses in the text.

12. Boswell, *Life of Johnson*, 1:468.

13. Haffenden, *John Berryman*, p. 117.

14. Haffenden, "Drink as Disease," p. 574.

15. Although exhaustion was the official medical reason for the hospitaliza-

tion in 1958 during which Berryman wrote this poem, his alcoholism could well have been an important contributing cause: see Haffenden, *Life of Berryman*, pp. 266, 268. According to Stefanik, *John Berryman*, p. 255, Dream Song 54 was first published on 22 April 1960.

16. Barbera comments in detail on Song 225 in "Under the Influence," pp. 56–65.

17. *AA*, pp. 6, 65, 67. See also the classic early essay on alcoholism by Jellinek, "Phases of Alcohol Addiction," pp. 682–83. This article is essentially an abridgment of a much longer one by Jellinek, "Phases in Drinking History," pp. 1–88.

18. This seems also to be an instance of rationalization, another leading characteristic of the alcoholic mentioned by Jellinek, "Phases of Alcohol Addiction," p. 680.

19. Ibid., p. 681. In Berryman, *Recovery*, p. 124, Alan Severance includes "remorse without respite" in a long list of alcoholic traits.

20. Heyen, "John Berryman," p. 54; Haffenden, "Drink as Disease," p. 570; Simpson, *The Maze*, p. 142.

21. Luks, *Four Authors Discuss*, p. 20.

22. Berryman, *Recovery*, p. 96. In his interview with Peter Stitt, Berryman discoursed on the poet's need to suffer. Haffenden, *Life of Berryman*, quotes this portion of the interview at length (pp. 381–82), cogently citing it as "fantastically hubristic" and as evidence of Berryman's "deludedness" during the interview, when he was once again (October 1970) hospitalized for alcoholism. Haffenden also says that Berryman told Ernest Samuels in 1967 that without alcohol he would commit suicide—perhaps because without it he would lose his source of inspiration. Writing in his journal on 18 August 1971, however, Berryman rejected a connection between his art and drinking (*Life of Berryman*, p. 414).

23. Meredith reports on meeting Berryman in May 1971: "He who would never wear decorations was wearing a rosette: the badge of three months' abstinence, from Alcoholics Anonymous" ("Foreword," p. xiv).

24. Among the critics disappointed by Berryman's changed style in his later poems is Oberg, "John Berryman," p. 86: "The complexities of lyric, elegy, blues, ballad, minstrelsy, and vaudeville [in the *Dream Songs*] dwindle to something less than art." See also Vendler, "Ammons, Berryman, Cummings," p. 425, and Kazin, review of *Henry's Fate*, p. 35.

25. Haffenden, *Life of Berryman*, p. 417.

26. *Love & Fame*, pp. 69–70. Haffenden, *Life of Berryman*, p. 378, shows that this poem was composed in the spring of 1970.

27. On the typicality of sick alcoholic dependence, see *12 & 12*, pp. 54–55: "The primary fact that we fail to recognize is our total inability to form a true partnership with another human being. . . . Either we insist upon dominating the people we know, or we depend upon them far too much. If we lean too heavily on people, they will sooner or later fail us, for they are human, too, and cannot possibly meet our incessant demands. In this way our insecurity grows and

festers." "The Recognition" (*Henry's Fate*, p. 89), written during one of Berryman's hospitalizations for alcoholism in 1970, also demonstrates Berryman's dependence. At a time when he should have been concentrating entirely on the therapy for his alcoholism, his fears that his wife had become indifferent to him or was preparing to leave him—fears totally unwarranted, as the poem makes clear—could only distract him from therapy and thus reduce his chances of recovery.

28. *Love & Fame*, pp. 75–76; Stefanik, *John Berryman*, p. 258.

29. *Delusions*, p. 40. Haffenden, *Life of Berryman*, p. 417, dates this 4 August 1970. For a similar poem, quoted from by Saul Bellow in his headnote to *Recovery*, see "Despair," *Love & Fame*, p. 72.

30. Steps 1 and 3 of AA read: "We admitted we were powerless over alcohol—that our lives had become unmanageable" and "Made a decision to turn our will and our lives over to the care of God *as we understood Him*" (*AA*, p. 59).

31. "Spewed" suggests that Berryman might have had in mind Christ's words in Rev. 3:15–16: "I know thy works, that thou art neither cold nor hot: I would thou wert cold or hot. So then because thou art lukewarm, and neither cold nor hot, I will spue thee out of my mouth."

32. "*Pass It On*," pp. 120–21; Haffenden, *Life of Berryman*, p. 385.

33. *Love & Fame*, p. 93; first published 25 September 1970, according to Stefanik, *John Berryman*, p. 259.

34. "Made a searching and fearless moral inventory of ourselves" (*AA*, p. 59).

35. *12 & 12*, p. 108. C. G. Jung's hope of combatting alcoholic spirits with the divine spirit would not have worked for Berryman, either. Of an alcoholic identified only as Roland H., Jung wrote, "His craving for alcohol was the equivalent, on a low level, of the spiritual thirst of our being for wholeness, expressed in medieval language: the union with God. . . . You see, 'alcohol' in Latin is 'spiritus' and you use the same word for the highest religious experience as well as for the most depraving poison. The helpful formula therefore is: *spiritus contra spiritum*" (letter to Bill Wilson, cofounder of AA, in Thomsen, *Bill W.*, pp. 362–63).

36. *Delusions*, pp. 68–69; Meredith, "Foreword," p. xix; Haffenden, *Life of Berryman*, p. 397. Barbera, "Pipe Dreams," p. 128n16, mentions another foreboding reference to the "Presence" in Berryman's *Recovery*.

37. E.g., two of the four epigraphs to *His Toy, His Dream, His Rest*, which became part of the *Dream Songs*, concern fear: "No interesting project can be embarked on without fear. I shall be scared to death half the time" and "For my part I am always frightened, and very much so. I fear the future of all engagements." See also Pooley, "Berryman's Last Poems," p. 292.

38. Haffenden, *Life of Berryman*, p. 420.

39. *Delusions*, p. 70; written, according to Haffenden (*John Berryman*, p. 156), on 17 April 1971. Berryman would of course have known that David is a traditional symbol of the poet.

40. *Henry's Fate* prints "strands"; but in a letter to me of 26 July 1985, John Haffenden has kindly pointed out that this is a typographical error and has provided the correct reading.

41. An autopsy revealed no trace of alcohol in his body, although Berryman

had briefly returned to drinking before his suicide on 7 January 1972; before
that, he had gone nearly a year since his last drinking (Haffenden, *Life of
Berryman*, pp. 393, 418).

42. Davis, "Li(v)es of the Poet," p. 59. The entire article is of great importance
for understanding Berryman.

43. Ornstein, "Marlowe and God," p. 1384. For conclusions about Berryman
that are similar to mine, see the review of *Recovery* entitled "The Sodden Soul,"
p. 1465. In the letter to me of 26 July 1985 Haffenden says that "Phase Four" was
placed last in *Henry's Fate* at the publisher's suggestion "for artistic reasons," because it has "a quality of appeasement or acceptance," but that it was written at
the same time as the group of poems beginning with "Some Women in Here"—
meaning during one of Berryman's hospitalizations in 1970. Although I obviously disagree with Haffenden's interpretation of "Phase Four," his grouping of
it indicates that it was not literally Berryman's final word on the subject of God.
But Berryman's fear of God is certainly expressed in one of his last poems, "Dry
Eleven Months," dated less than a month before his death; and "Phase Four"
seems to offer the best explanation of the source of this fear.

CHAPTER 8

1. Damrosch, "Burns, Blake," p. 648.

2. Polhemus, *Comic Faith*, pp. 60, 76–79. Another study of symbolic meanings and uses of alcohol is Jellinek, "Symbolism of Drinking," pp. 849–66.

3. Marquis, *Old Soak*, p. 46.

4. Freud, *Jokes*, pp. 105, 127.

5. Lentricchia, *Criticism*, p. 58.

6. See Hirst, *Comedy*, pp. 1–2.

7. Heilbrun interpreting Frye in "Profession and Society," p. 410.

8. Frye, "Mythos of Spring," pp. 163–86; Bergson, *Laughter*, pp. 10, 16, 29,
37, 58, 87.

9. See esp. the description of Dixon's first drive with Welch in Ch. 1. Other
citations of the novel will appear in parentheses in the text.

10. McFadden, *Discovering the Comic*, p. 170. This is from a passage interpreting Frye's theory of comedy.

11. Although Amis warns that "Dixon resembles Larkin in not the smallest
particular," it is still tempting to see in Dixon something of the irreverence of
Philip Larkin, the English poet and Amis's friend at Oxford, toward the university and many of the readings required of undergraduates. The irreverence is
described in Amis's "Oxford and After," pp. 23–30, a tribute to the poet. Amis's
reference to Larkin's outstanding quality of "total honesty" (p. 29) also suggests
Dixon, the completeness of whose honesty is the more striking because he has to
struggle against repressive fears within himself.

12. Bertrand is also an example of the *alazon* as impostor: he is incompetent at
his vocation, painting, and is not really in love with Christine. On the impostor,
see Frye, "Mythos of Spring," p. 172, and Cornford, *Attic Comedy*, p. 129.

13. Elliott, *Power of Satire*, pp. 135, 138–39.

14. Freud, *Jokes*, p. 127.

15. Eliot, "Love Song," p. 5.

16. Blake, *Marriage*, p. 102.

17. Frye, "Mythos of Spring," p. 171. Fallis also discusses the mythic and archetypal elements of the novel in "*Lucky Jim*," pp. 65–72. Gindin, "Amis' Funny Novels," p. 39, contains similar comment on *Lucky Jim*.

18. Wilson makes almost exactly this point in "Jim, Jake," p. 55.

19. Amis, *Jake's Thing*, p. 100. Further citations of the novel will appear in parentheses in the text. For an extended comparison of *Lucky Jim* and *Jake's Thing*, see Gardner, *Kingsley Amis*, pp. 106–7. This is the only booklength study of Amis's work.

20. See the following from Freud, *Civilization*, p. 58: "men are not gentle creatures . . . . their neighbour is for them not only a potential helper or sexual object, but also someone who tempts them to satisfy their aggressiveness on him, to exploit his capacity for work without compensation, to use him sexually without his consent, to seize his possessions, to humiliate him, to cause him pain, to torture and to kill him. *Homo homini lupus*," which Freud borrows from Plautus's *Asinaria* and which translates: "Man is a wolf to man."

21. McCollom, *Divine Average*, p. 7. For the very different view that Orwell satirizes Gordon as a "repulsive, intolerable fool," see Greenblatt, *Three Modern Satirists*, pp. 53–57. The most extensive study of Orwell as a novelist, Lee, *Orwell's Fiction*, also claims that Orwell took a dim view of Gordon, "picturing him as a self-pitying adolescent of twenty-nine" (p. 52).

22. Orwell, *Aspidistra*, p. 242. Other references to the novel will appear in parentheses in the text. Among the critics who find the completeness of Gordon's change difficult to credit are Wain, "Lower Binfield," p. 76; Alldritt, *Making of Orwell*, pp. 35–36; Lodge, *Modes of Modern*, p. 190; and Hammond, *Orwell Companion*, p. 112.

23. Meredith, *Essay on Comedy*, p. 92.

24. Eagleton, *Exiles*, pp. 93, 98; Lee, *Orwell's Fiction*, p. 65. Eagleton's Marxist analysis of Orwell's novel is greatly at variance with my own.

25. Orwell, *1984*, p. 139.

26. Lee, *Orwell's Fiction*, p. 58, shrewdly notices that Gordon's spending "proves three facts: that Gordon is under the affective power of money; that his attitudes are sham; that he shares the same lower-middle-class values he so fanatically condemns."

27. Guild, "Dubious Battle," p. 54.

EPILOGUE

1. The antipathy of modernism to reality is discussed by Lentricchia, *After the New Criticism*, pp. 53–55.

2. Abrams, *Milk of Paradise;* Hayter, *Opium and Romantic*.

3. Dickey, *Sorties*, p. 101.

4. Boswell, *Life of Johnson*, 2:188, 193; 3:327n2.
5. *Boswell: The Ominous Years*, p. 178; *Boswell in Extremes*, pp. 129–35.
6. Boswell, *Life of Johnson*, 4:221.
7. Ibid., 3:41, 327.
8. Bate, *Samuel Johnson*, pp. 236–37, 263.
9. Boswell, *Life of Johnson*, 1:103–5n3, 446; 3:41, 169, 245, 327, 389.

Bibliography

A.A. and the Alcoholic Employee. New York: Alcoholics Anonymous World Services, 1962.

Abrams, M. H. *The Milk of Paradise: The Effect of Opium Visions on the Works of DeQuincey, Crabbe, Francis Thompson, and Coleridge.* New York: Harper & Row, Perennial Library, 1970.

Alcoholics Anonymous: The Story of How Many Thousands of Men and Women Have Recovered from Alcoholism. 1939. 3d ed. New York: Alcoholics Anonymous World Services, 1976.

Alldritt, Keith. *The Making of George Orwell: An Essay in Literary History.* London: Edward Arnold, 1969.

Amis, Kingsley. *Jake's Thing.* 1978. New York: Penguin Books, 1980.

————. *Lucky Jim.* 1953. New York: Viking, Compass Books, 1958.

————. "Oxford and After." In *Larkin at Sixty,* edited by Anthony Thwaite, pp. 23–30. London: Faber and Faber, 1982.

Arpin, Gary Q. *The Poetry of John Berryman.* Port Washington, N.Y.: Kennikat Press, 1978.

Atlas, James. *Delmore Schwartz: The Life of an American Poet.* New York: Farrar, Straus and Giroux, 1977.

At Last . . . AA. Atlanta: Metro Atlanta Alcoholics Anonymous, n.d.

Augustine, Saint. *The Confessions. Basic Writings of Saint Augustine.* Edited by Whitney J. Oates. 2 vols. New York: Random House, 1948.

Auser, Cortland P. "John Cheever's Myth of Man and Time: 'The Swimmer.'" *CEA Critic* 29 (March 1967): 18–19.

Bahr, Howard M. *Skid Row: An Introduction to Disaffiliation.* New York: Oxford University Press, 1973.

Balliett, Whitney. "Even His Feet Look Sad." In *Such Sweet Thunder: Forty-nine Pieces on Jazz.* Indianapolis: Bobbs-Merrill, 1966.

Barbera, Jack Vincent. "Pipe Dreams, Games, and Delusions." *Southern Review* (Australia): *Literary and Interdisciplinary Essays* 13 (1979–80): 120–28.

————. "Under the Influence." *John Berryman Studies* 2 (Winter 1976): 56–65.

Bareham, T. "Paradigms of Hell: Symbolic Patterning in *Under the Volcano.*" In *On the Novel: A Present for Walter Allen on His 60th Birthday from His Friends and Colleagues,* edited by B. S. Benedikz, pp. 113–27. London: J. M. Dent, 1971.

Bate, W. Jackson. *Samuel Johnson.* New York: Harcourt Brace Jovanovich, 1975.

Baumbach, Jonathan. "The Double Vision: *The Victim* by Saul Bellow." Ch. 3 in *The Landscape of Nightmare: Studies in the Contemporary American Novel.* New York: New York University Press, 1965.

Bibliography

Bell, Pearl. "The Meaning of *PR*." Review of *The Truants: Adventures among the Intellectuals*, by William Barrett. *New Republic*, 17 March 1982, 32–35.

Bellow, Saul. *Humboldt's Gift*. New York: Avon, 1976.

———. *The Victim*. 1947. New York: New American Library, A Plume Book, 1974.

Bergreen, Lawrence. *James Agee: A Life*. New York: Dutton, 1984.

Bergson, Henri. *Laughter: An Essay on the Meaning of the Comic*. Translated by Cloudesley Brereton and Fred Rothwell. New York: Macmillan, 1937.

Berryman, John. *Berryman's Sonnets*. New York: Farrar, Straus and Giroux, 1967.

———. *Delusions, Etc*. New York: Farrar, Straus and Giroux, 1972.

———. *The Dream Songs*. New York: Farrar, Straus and Giroux, 1969.

———. *Henry's Fate & Other Poems, 1967–1972*. Introduced by John Haffenden. New York: Farrar, Straus and Giroux, 1977.

———. *Love & Fame*. New York: Farrar, Straus and Giroux, 1970.

———. *Recovery*. New York: Farrar, Straus and Giroux, 1973.

Birkenhead, Frederick, second Earl of. "Fiery Particles." In *Evelyn Waugh and His World*, edited by David Pryce-Jones, pp. 138–63. Boston: Little, Brown, 1973.

Blake, William. *The Marriage of Heaven and Hell*. In *Blake's Poetry and Designs*. Edited by Mary Lynn Johnson and John E. Grant. New York: W. W. Norton, A Norton Critical Edition, 1979.

Blum, Eva Maria, and Blum, Richard H. *Alcoholism: Modern Psychological Approaches to Treatment*. San Francisco: Jossey-Bass, 1967.

Blythe, Hal, and Sweet, Charlie. "Perverted Sacraments in John Cheever's 'The Swimmer.'" *Studies in Short Fiction* 21 (1984): 393–94.

Bogard, Travis. *Contour in Time: The Plays of Eugene O'Neill*. New York: Oxford University Press, 1972.

"Booze & the Writer." *Writer's Digest*, October 1978, 25–33.

Boswell, James. *Boswell in Extremes 1776–1778*. Edited by Charles McC. Weis and Frederick A. Pottle. The Yale Editions of the Private Papers of James Boswell. New York: McGraw-Hill, 1970.

———. *Boswell Laird of Auchinleck 1778–1782*. Edited by Joseph W. Reed and Frederick A. Pottle. The Yale Editions of the Private Papers of James Boswell. New York: McGraw-Hill, 1977.

———. *Boswell: The Ominous Years 1774–1776*. Edited by Charles Ryskamp and Frederick A. Pottle. The Yale Editions of the Private Papers of James Boswell. New York: McGraw-Hill, 1963.

———. *Boswell's Life of Johnson*. Edited by George Birkbeck Hill and L. F. Powell. 6 vols. Oxford: Clarendon Press, 1934–50.

Boughner, Daniel C. *The Braggart in Renaissance Comedy: A Study in Comparative Drama from Aristophanes to Shakespeare*. Minneapolis: University of Minnesota Press, 1954.

Boulton, Agnes. *Part of a Long Story*. Garden City, N.Y.: Doubleday, 1958.

Bowman, Karl M. "The Treatment of Alcoholism." *Quarterly Journal of Studies on Alcohol* 17 (1956): 318–24.

———, and Jellinek, E. Morton. "Alcohol Addiction and Its Treatment."
Quarterly Journal of Studies on Alcohol 2 (1941–42): 98–176.

———. "Alcoholic Mental Disorders." *Quarterly Journal of Studies on Alcohol* 2
(1941–42): 312–90.

Bradbrook, M. C. "Intention and Design in *October Ferry to Gabriola*." In *The
Art of Malcolm Lowry*, edited by Anne Smith, pp. 144–55. London: Vision
Press, 1978.

Bradbury, Malcolm. "Saul Bellow and the Naturalist Tradition." *A Review of
English Literature* 4, no. 4 (1963): 80–92.

Brierre de Boismont, Alexandre-Jacques-François. "Of Hallucinations in
Delirium Tremens." Ch. 9 in *Hallucinations: or, The Rational History of
Apparitions, Visions, Dreams, Ecstasy, Magnetism, and Somnambulism*. 1853.
Reprint, New York: Arno Press, 1976.

Bromberg, Walter, and Schilder, Paul. "Psychologic Considerations in Alcoholic
Hallucinosis—Castration and Dismembering Motives." *International Journal
of Psycho-analysis* 14 (1960): 206–24.

Brooke-Rose, Christine. "Mescalusions." *London Magazine* 7 (April 1967):
100–105.

Bruccoli, Matthew J. *The Composition of "Tender Is the Night": A Study of the
Manuscripts*. Pittsburgh: University of Pittsburgh Press, 1963.

———. *Some Sort of Epic Grandeur: The Life of F. Scott Fitzgerald*. New York:
Harcourt Brace Jovanovich, 1981.

Brune, F., and Busch, H. "Anticonvulsive-Sedative Treatment of Delirium
Alcoholicum." *Quarterly Journal of Studies on Alcohol* 32 (1971): 334–42.

Brustein, Robert. "*The Iceman Cometh*." In *Twentieth Century Interpretations of
"The Iceman Cometh*," edited by John Henry Raleigh, pp. 92–102.
Englewood Cliffs, N.J.: Prentice-Hall, 1968.

Bunyan, John. *Pilgrim's Progress*. In *Grace Abounding to the Chief of Sinners* and
The Pilgrim's Progress from This World to That Which Is to Come. Edited by
Roger Sharrock. London: Oxford University Press, 1966.

Burns, Robert. "Holy Willie's Prayer." In *The Poems and Songs of Robert Burns*.
Edited by James Kinsley. 3 vols. Oxford: Clarendon Press, 1968.

Burton-Bradley, B. G. "Aspects of Alcoholic Hallucinosis." *Medical Journal of
Australia* 2 (1958): 8–11.

Butler, Samuel. *The Way of All Flesh*. New York: Holt, Rinehart and Winston,
1960.

Buttitta, Tony. *After the Good Gay Times: Asheville—Summer of '35: A Season
with F. Scott Fitzgerald*. New York: Viking, 1974.

Carver, Raymond. "Drinking While Driving." In *Fires: Essays, Poems, Stories*.
Santa Barbara: Capra Press, 1983.

Catanzaro, Ronald J. "The Disease: Alcoholism." In *Alcoholism: The Total
Treatment Approach*, ed. Catanzaro, pp. 5–25. Springfield, Ill.: Charles C.
Thomas, 1968.

Chafetz, Morris E.; Blane, Howard T.; and Hill, Marjorie J., eds. "The
Alcoholic: Psychodynamics and Personality Structure." In *Frontiers of
Alcoholism*, pp. 5–29. New York: Science House, 1970.

Cheever, John. "The Angel of the Bridge." In *Stories*, pp. 490–97.

———. "Artemis, the Honest Well Digger." In *Stories*, pp. 650–71.

———. "The Brigadier and the Golf Widow." In *Stories*, pp. 498–511.

———. "Brimmer." In *Stories*, pp. 386–95.

———. "Brooklyn Rooming House." *New Yorker*, 25 May 1935, 76–77.

———. *Bullet Park*. New York: Knopf, 1969.

———. "The Day the Pig Fell into the Well." In *Stories*, pp. 219–35.

———. "An Educated American Woman." In *Stories*, pp. 521–35.

———. *Falconer*. New York: Random House, Ballantine Books, 1977.

———. "The Five-Forty-Eight." In *Stories*, pp. 236–47.

———. "The Fourth Alarm." In *Stories*, pp. 645–49.

———. "Goodbye, My Brother." In *Stories*, pp. 3–21.

———. "The Housebreaker of Shady Hill." In *Stories*, pp. 253–69.

———. "The Leaves, The Lion-Fish and the Bear." *Esquire*, November 1974, 110.

———. "A Miscellany of Characters That Will Not Appear." In *Stories*, pp. 467–72.

———. "The Peril in the Streets." In *The Way Some People Live*. New York: Random House, 1943.

———. "The President of the Argentine." *Atlantic Monthly*, April 1976, 43–45.

———. "Reunion." In *Stories*, pp. 518–20.

———. "The Scarlet Moving Van." In *Stories*, pp. 359–69.

———. "The Seaside Houses." In *Stories*, pp. 482–89.

———. "The Sorrows of Gin." In *Stories*, pp. 198–209.

———. *The Stories of John Cheever*. New York: Knopf, 1978.

———. "The Swimmer." In *Stories*, pp. 603–12.

———. *The Wapshot Scandal*. New York: Bantam Books, 1965.

Cheever, Susan. *Home Before Dark*. Boston: Houghton Mifflin, 1984.

Clayton, John Jacob. *Saul Bellow: In Defense of Man*. 2d ed. Bloomington: Indiana University Press, 1979.

Clemons, Walter. "Cheever's Triumph." *Newsweek*, 14 March 1977, 61.

Clinebell, Howard J., Jr. "Pastoral Counseling of the Alcoholic and His Family." In *Alcoholism: The Total Treatment Approach*, edited by Ronald J. Catanzaro, pp. 189–207. Springfield, Ill.: Charles C. Thomas, 1968.

———. "Philosophical-Religious Factors in the Etiology and Treatment of Alcoholism." *Quarterly Journal of Studies on Alcohol* 24 (1963): 473–88.

Coale, Samuel. *John Cheever*. New York: Frederick Ungar, 1977.

Conarroe, Joel. *John Berryman: An Introduction to the Poetry*. Columbia Introductions to Twentieth-Century American Poetry. New York: Columbia University Press, 1977.

Cornford, Francis Macdonald. *The Origin of Attic Comedy*. Edited by Theodor H. Gaster. Garden City, N.Y.: Doubleday, Anchor Books, 1961.

Corrigan, Matthew. "Malcolm Lowry: The Phenomenology of Failure." *Boundary* 2 3 (1975): 407–42.

Bibliography

Cosman, Max. "The Nature and Work of Evelyn Waugh." *Colorado Quarterly* 4 (1956): 428–41.

Costa, Richard Hauer. *Malcolm Lowry*. New York: Twayne, 1972.

Crane, R. S. "Critical and Historical Principles of Literary History." In *The Idea of the Humanities and Other Essays Critical and Historical*, 2:45–156. 2 vols. Chicago: University of Chicago Press, 1967.

Crawford, Fred D. "Evelyn Waugh: A Handful of Dust." Ch. 4 in *Mixing Memory and Desire: "The Waste Land" and British Novels*. University Park: Pennsylvania State University Press, 1982.

Cross, Richard K. *Malcolm Lowry: A Preface to His Fiction*. Chicago: University of Chicago Press, 1980.

Curran, Frank J. "Personality Studies in Alcoholic Women." *Journal of Nervous and Mental Disease* 86 (1937): 645–67.

Damrosch, Leopold, Jr. "Burns, Blake, and the Recovery of Lyric." *Studies in Romanticism* 21 (1982): 637–60.

Davidson, G. M. "The Syndrome of Acute (Alcoholic) Hallucinosis." *Psychiatric Quarterly* 13 (1939): 466–97.

Davies, D. L. "Stabilized Addiction and Normal Drinking in Recovered Alcohol Addicts." In *Scientific Basis of Drug Dependence: A Symposium*, edited by Hannah Steinberg, pp. 363–73. Biological Council, The Co-ordinating Committee for Symposia on Drug Action. London: J. & A. Churchill, 1969.
———; Scott, D. F.; and Malherbe, M. E. L. "Resumed Normal Drinking in Recovered Psychotic Alcoholics." *International Journal of the Addictions* 4 (1969): 187–94.

Davis, Kathe. "The Li(v)es of the Poet." *Twentieth Century Literature* 30 (1984): 46–68.

Day, Douglas. *Malcolm Lowry: A Biography*. New York: Oxford University Press, 1973.

Deiker, Thomas, and Chambers, H. E. "Structure and Content of Hallucinations in Alcohol Withdrawal and Functional Psychosis." *Journal of Studies on Alcohol* 39 (1978): 1831–40.

Delasanta, Rodney, and D'Avanzo, Mario L. "Truth and Beauty in *Brideshead Revisited*." *Modern Fiction Studies* 11 (1965–66): 140–52.

Dement, William, et al. "Hallucinations and Dreaming." *Perception and Its Disorders*, edited by David A. Hamburg, Karl H. Pribram, and Albert J. Stunkard, pp. 335–59. Research Publications of the Association for Research in Nervous and Mental Disease, vol. 48. Baltimore: Williams & Wilkins, 1970.

Dickey, James. "Afterword to the New Ecco Edition." *Babel to Byzantium: Poets & Poetry Now*. 1968. New York: Ecco Press, 1981.
———. "Bums, On Waking." In *The Early Motion: Drowning with Others* and *Helmets*. Middletown, Conn.: Wesleyan University Press, 1981.
———. *Sorties*. Garden City, N.Y.: Doubleday, 1971.

Ditman, Keith S., and Whittlesey, John R. B. "Comparison of the LSD-25 Experience and Delirium Tremens." *A.M.A. Archives of General Psychiatry* 1 (1959): 47–57.

Dodson, Daniel B. *Malcolm Lowry.* Columbia Essays on Modern Writers, no. 51. New York: Columbia University Press, 1970.

Donaldson, Scott. *Fool for Love: F. Scott Fitzgerald.* New York: Congdon & Weed, 1983.

Dorosz, Kristofer. *Malcolm Lowry's Infernal Paradise.* Studia Anglistica Upsaliensia, no. 27. Stockholm: Almqvist & Wiksell, 1976.

Doyle, Paul A. *Evelyn Waugh: A Critical Essay.* Contemporary Writers in Christian Perspective. Grand Rapids, Mich.: William B. Eerdmans, 1969.

Driver, Tom F. "On the Late Plays of Eugene O'Neill." In *O'Neill: A Collection of Critical Essays,* edited by John Gassner, pp. 110–23. Englewood Cliffs, N.J.: Prentice-Hall, 1964.

Dynes, John B. "Survey of Alcoholic Patients Admitted to the Boston Psychopathic Hospital in 1937." *New England Journal of Medicine* 220 (1939): 195–98.

Dyson, A. E. "Evelyn Waugh and the Mysteriously Disappearing Hero." *Critical Quarterly* 2 (1960): 72–79.

Eagleton, Terry. *Exiles and Émigrés: Studies in Modern Literature.* New York: Shocken Books, 1970.

Eastman, Max. *Enjoyment of Laughter.* New York: Simon and Schuster, 1936.

Eble, Kenneth E. "Touches of Disaster: Alcoholism and Mental Illness in Fitzgerald's Short Stories." In *The Short Stories of F. Scott Fitzgerald: New Approaches in Criticism,* edited by Jackson R. Bryer, pp. 39–52. Madison: University of Wisconsin Press, 1982.

Edmonds, Dale. "Mescallusions or the Drinking Man's *Under the Volcano.*" *Journal of Modern Literature* 6 (1977): 277–88.

———. "*Under the Volcano*: A Reading of the 'Immediate Level.'" *Tulane Studies in English* 16 (1968): 63–105.

Eliot, T. S. *Four Quartets.* In *Complete Poems and Plays 1909–1950.* New York: Harcourt, Brace & World, 1971.

———. "The Love Song of J. Alfred Prufrock." In *Complete Poems and Plays 1909–1950.* New York: Harcourt, Brace & World, 1971.

Elliott, Robert C. *The Power of Satire: Magic, Ritual, Art.* Princeton: Princeton University Press, 1960.

Ellis, James. "Fitzgerald's Fragmented Hero: Dick Diver." In "*Tender Is the Night*": *Essays in Criticism,* edited by Marvin J. LaHood, pp. 127–37. Bloomington: Indiana University Press, 1969.

Epstein, Perle S. *The Private Labyrinth of Malcolm Lowry: "Under the Volcano" and the Cabbala.* New York: Holt, Rinehart and Winston, 1969.

Fabricant, Noah D. "A Medical Profile of F. Scott Fitzgerald." In *13 Famous Patients.* Philadelphia and New York: Chilton, 1960.

Fallis, Richard. "*Lucky Jim* and Academic Wishful Thinking." *Studies in the Novel* 9 (1977): 65–72.

Fitzgerald, F. Scott. "An Alcoholic Case." In *The Stories of F. Scott Fitzgerald: A Selection of 28 Stories.* Introduced by Malcolm Cowley. New York: Scribner's, 1951.

———. *As Ever, Scott Fitz—Letters between F. Scott Fitzgerald and His Literary*

Agent Harold Ober 1919–1940. Edited by Matthew J. Bruccoli with the
assistance of Jennifer McCabe Atkinson. Philadelphia: Lippincott, 1972.
————. "Babylon Revisited." In *Babylon Revisited and Other Stories*. New York:
Scribner's, 1960.
————. *The Beautiful and Damned*. 1922. New York: Scribner's, 1950.
————. *Correspondence of F. Scott Fitzgerald*. Edited by Matthew J. Bruccoli and
Margaret M. Duggan, with the assistance of Susan Walker. New York:
Random House, 1980.
————. "The Crack-up." In *The Crack-Up. With Other Uncollected Pieces, Note-
Books and Unpublished Letters*, edited by Edmund Wilson, pp. 69–84. 1945.
New York: New Directions, New Directions Paperbook, 1956.
————. "Crazy Sunday." In *Babylon Revisited and Other Stories*. New York:
Scribner's, 1960.
————. *F. Scott Fitzgerald's Ledger: A Facsimile*. Introduced by Matthew J.
Bruccoli. Washington: NCR / Microcard Editions, 1972.
————. "Family in the Wind." In *Taps at Reveille*. New York: Scribner's, 1935.
————. *The Great Gatsby*. 1925. New York: Scribner's, 1953.
————. "Her Last Case." In *The Price Was High: The Last Uncollected Stories of
F. Scott Fitzgerald*. Edited by Matthew J. Bruccoli. New York: Harcourt Brace
Jovanovich/Bruccoli Clark, 1979.
————. *The Letters of F. Scott Fitzgerald*. Edited by Andrew Turnbull. New
York: Scribner's, 1963.
————. "The Lost Decade." In *The Stories of F. Scott Fitzgerald: A Selection of 28
Stories*. Introduced by Malcolm Cowley. New York: Scribner's, 1951.
————. "A New Leaf." In *Bits of Paradise: 21 Uncollected Stories by F. Scott and
Zelda Fitzgerald*. Selected by Scottie Fitzgerald Smith and Matthew J.
Bruccoli. London: The Bodley Head, 1973.
————. *The Notebooks of F. Scott Fitzgerald*. Edited by Matthew J. Bruccoli. New
York: Harcourt Brace Jovanovich/Bruccoli Clark, 1972.
————. "One Trip Abroad." In *The Bodley Head Scott Fitzgerald*. Vol. 6, *Short
Stories*. Selected and introduced by Malcolm Cowley. London: The Bodley
Head, 1963.
————. *The Pat Hobby Stories*. Introduced by Arnold Gingrich. New York:
Scribner's, 1962.
————. *Scott Fitzgerald: Letters to His Daughter*. Edited by Andrew Turnbull
and introduced by Frances Fitzgerald Lanahan. New York: Scribner's, 1963.
————. *Tender Is the Night: A Romance*. New York: Scribner's, 1934.
Fitzgibbon, Constantine. *Drink*. Garden City, N.Y.: Doubleday, 1979.
Frazer, Winifred Dusenbury. *Love as Death in "The Iceman Cometh."* University
of Florida Monographs, Humanities, no. 27. Gainesville: University of
Florida Press, 1967.
Freedman, Sanford J., et al. "Imagery in Sensory Deprivation." In
Hallucinations, edited by Louis Jolyon West, pp. 108–17. New York: Grune
& Stratton, 1962.
Freud, Sigmund. *Civilization and Its Discontents*. Translated and edited by James
Strachey. New York: W. W. Norton, 1961.

————. *The Ego and the Id.* Translated by Joan Riviere. 1927. 4th ed. The International Psycho-analytical Library, no. 12. London: The Hogarth Press and The Institute of Psychoanalysis, 1947.

————. *Jokes and Their Relation to the Unconscious.* Translated and edited by James Strachey. New York: W. W. Norton, Norton Library, 1963.

Frye, Northrop. "The Mythos of Spring: Comedy." In *Anatomy of Criticism: Four Essays.* Princeton: Princeton University Press, 1957.

Fuchs, Daniel. *Saul Bellow: Vision and Revision.* Durham, N.C.: Duke University Press, 1984.

Gardner, Philip. *Kingsley Amis.* Boston: Twayne, 1981.

Gelb, Arthur, and Gelb, Barbara. *O'Neill.* 2d ed. New York: Harper & Row, 1974.

Gellman, Irving Peter. *The Sober Alcoholic: An Organizational Analysis of Alcoholics Anonymous.* New Haven, Conn.: College and University Press, 1964.

Gerard, Donald L. "Intoxication and Addiction: Psychiatric Observations on Alcoholism and Opiate Drug Addiction." *Quarterly Journal of Studies on Alcohol* 16 (1955): 681–99.

Gindin, James. "Kingsley Amis' Funny Novels." Ch. 3 in *Postwar British Fiction: New Accents and Attitudes.* Berkeley: University of California Press, 1962.

Goodwin, Donald W., M.D. "The Alcoholism of Eugene O'Neill." *Journal of the American Medical Association* 216 (1971): 99–104.

————. "The Alcoholism of F. Scott Fitzgerald." *Journal of the American Medical Association* 212 (1970): 86–90.

Gordon, Andrew. "'Pushy Jew': Leventhal in *The Victim.*" *Modern Fiction Studies* 25 (1979): 129–38.

Grace, Sherrill E. "Malcolm Lowry and the Expressionist Vision." In *The Art of Malcolm Lowry,* edited by Anne Smith, pp. 93-111. London: Vision Press, 1978.

Graham, Sheilah. *College of One.* New York: Viking, 1967.

————. *The Real F. Scott Fitzgerald Thirty-five Years Later.* New York: Grosset & Dunlap, 1976.

————, and Frank, Gerold. *Beloved Infidel: The Education of a Woman.* New York: Henry Holt, 1958.

Graves, Nora Calhoun. "The Dominant Color in John Cheever's 'The Swimmer.'" *Notes on Contemporary Literature* 4 (March 1974): 4–5.

Greenblatt, Stephen Jay. *Three Modern Satirists: Waugh, Orwell, and Huxley.* New Haven: Yale University Press, 1965.

Gross, Milton M., et al. "Sleep Disturbances and Hallucinations in the Acute Alcoholic Psychoses." *Journal of Nervous and Mental Disease* 142 (1966): 493–514.

Guild, Nicholas. "In Dubious Battle: George Orwell and the Victory of the Money-God." *Modern Fiction Studies* 21 (1975): 49–56.

Haffenden, John. "Drink as Disease: John Berryman." *Partisan Review* 44 (1977): 565–83.

————. *John Berryman: A Critical Commentary*. New York: New York University Press, 1980.

————. *The Life of John Berryman*. Boston: Routledge & Kegan Paul, 1982.

Hall, Donald. *Remembering Poets: Reminiscences and Opinions: Dylan Thomas, Robert Frost, T. S. Eliot, Ezra Pound*. New York: Harper & Row, 1978.

Hammond, J. R. *A George Orwell Companion: A Guide to the Novels, Documentaries and Essays*. New York: St. Martin's, 1982.

Hampton, Peter J. "Representative Studies of Alcoholism and Personality: IV. Psychoanalytic Studies." *Journal of Social Psychology* 35 (1952): 23–35.

Hardy, John Edward. "*Brideshead Revisited*: God, Man, and Others." Ch. 9 in *Man in the Modern Novel*. Seattle: University of Washington Press, 1964.

Hayter, Alethea. *Opium and the Romantic Imagination*. Berkeley: University of California Press, 1968.

Hearne, Laura Guthrie. "A Summer with F. Scott Fitzgerald." *Esquire*, December 1964, 160.

Heath, Jeffrey M. "*Brideshead*: The Critics and the Memorandum." *English Studies* 56 (1975): 222–30.

————. *The Picturesque Prison: Evelyn Waugh and His Writing*. Kingston: McGill-Queen's University Press, 1982.

Heilbrun, Carolyn G. "The Profession and Society, 1958–83." *PMLA* 99 (1984): 408–13.

Hemingway, Ernest. *A Moveable Feast*. New York: Scribner's, 1964.

Hersey, John. "Talk with John Cheever." *New York Times Book Review*, 6 March 1977, 1.

Heyen, William. "John Berryman: A Memoir and an Interview." *Ohio Review* 15 (Winter 1974): 46–65.

Hill, Art. "The Alcoholic on Alcoholism." *Canadian Literature*, no. 62 (1974): 33–48.

Hirst, David L. *Comedy of Manners*. The Critical Idiom, no. 40. London: Methuen, 1979.

Hoffman, Steven K. "Impersonal Personalism: The Making of a Confessional Poetic." *ELH* 45 (1978): 687–709.

Hugo, Richard. *Making Certain It Goes On: The Collected Poems of Richard Hugo*. New York: W. W. Norton, 1984.

Hyde, Lewis. "Alcohol & Poetry: John Berryman and the Booze Talking." *American Poetry Review* 4 (January 1975): 7–12.

Igersheimer, Walter W., M.D. "Group Psychotherapy for Nonalcoholic Wives of Alcoholics." *Quarterly Journal of Studies on Alcohol* 20 (1959): 77–85.

"Inescapable Conclusions." *Time*, 16 October 1978, 122.

Isbell, Harris, et al. "An Experimental Study of the Etiology of 'Rum Fits' and Delirium Tremens." *Quarterly Journal of Studies on Alcohol* 16 (1955): 1–33.

Jackson, Charles. *The Lost Weekend*. New York: Farrar & Rinehart, 1944.

James, William. *The Varieties of Religious Experience: A Study in Human Nature*. New York: Modern Library, 1902.

Jeffs, Rae. *Brendan Behan: Man and Showman*. Cleveland: World, 1968.

Jellinek, E. M. "Phases in the Drinking History of Alcoholics." *Quarterly Journal of Studies on Alcohol* 7 (1946–47): 1–88.

———. "Phases of Alcohol Addiction." *Quarterly Journal of Studies on Alcohol* 13 (1952): 673–84.

———. "The Symbolism of Drinking: A Culture-Historical Approach," edited by Robert E. Popham and Carole D. Yawney. *Journal of Studies on Alcohol* 38 (1977): 849–66.

Johnson, Glen M. "The Moral Structure of Cheever's *Falconer.*" *Studies in American Fiction* 9 (1981): 21–31.

Johnson, Vernon E. *I'll Quit Tomorrow.* Rev. ed. San Francisco: Harper & Row, 1980.

Joost, Nicholas. "A Handful of Dust: Evelyn Waugh and the Novel of Manners." *Papers on Language & Literature* 12 (1976): 177–96.

Karlan, Samuel C. "Alcoholism and Hallucinosis." *Psychiatric Quarterly* 15 (1941): 64–67.

Kazin, Alfred. "'The Giant Killer': Drink & the American Writer." *Commentary*, March 1976, 44–50.

Kazin, Cathrael. Review of *Henry's Fate and Other Poems, 1967–72*, by John Berryman. *New Republic*, 4 June 1977, 34–35.

Kennedy, William. *Ironweed.* New York: Viking, 1983.

Kerouac, Jack. *Big Sur.* New York: McGraw-Hill, 1962.

Kilgallin, Tony. *Lowry.* Erin, Ontario: Press Porcepic, 1973.

Klüver, Heinrich. "Mechanisms of Hallucinations." In *Studies in Personality: Contributed in Honor of Lewis M. Terman*, pp. 175–207. New York: McGraw-Hill, 1942.

Krafft-Ebing, Richard von. "Part Fourth. Chapter 1. Chronic Alcoholism and Its Complications." In *Text-Book of Insanity. Based on Clinical Observations for Practitioners and Students of Medicine.* Translated by Charles Gilbert Chaddock. Philadelphia: F. A. Davis, 1905.

Kurtz, Ernest. *Not-God: A History of Alcoholics Anonymous.* Center City, Minn.: Hazelden Educational Services, 1979.

Lane, Calvin W. *Evelyn Waugh.* Boston: Twayne, 1981.

Latham, Aaron. *Crazy Sundays: F. Scott Fitzgerald in Hollywood.* New York: Viking, 1971.

Lee, Robert A. *Orwell's Fiction.* Notre Dame, Ind.: University of Notre Dame Press, 1969.

Lentricchia, Frank. *After the New Criticism.* Chicago: University of Chicago Press, 1980.

———. *Criticism and Social Change.* Chicago: University of Chicago Press, 1983.

LeVot, André. *F. Scott Fitzgerald: A Biography.* Translated by William Byron. Garden City, N.Y.: Doubleday, 1983.

Lisansky, Edith S. "The Etiology of Alcoholism: The Role of Psychological Predisposition." *Quarterly Journal of Studies on Alcohol* 21 (1960): 314–43.

Lodge, David. *The Modes of Modern Writing: Metaphor, Metonymy, and the Typology of Modern Literature.* Ithaca, N.Y.: Cornell University Press, 1977.

Bibliography

Lowry, Malcolm. "Lunar Caustic." In *Malcolm Lowry: Psalms and Songs*, edited by Margerie Lowry, pp. 259–306. New York: New American Library, A Meridian Book, 1975.

————. "Lunar Caustic." *The Paris Review* 8 (Winter-Spring 1963): 15–72.

————. "Preface to a Novel." In *Malcolm Lowry: The Man and His Work*, edited by George Woodcock, pp. 9–15. Vancouver: University of British Columbia Press, 1971.

————. *Selected Letters of Malcolm Lowry*. Edited by Harvey Breit and Margerie Bonner Lowry. Philadelphia: Lippincott, 1965.

————. *Under the Volcano*. Introduced by Stephen Spender. 1947. New York: New American Library, A Plume Book, 1971.

Luks, Allan, moderator. *Four Authors Discuss: Drinking and Writing*. New York: New York City Affiliate of the National Council on Alcoholism, 1980.

MacAndrew, Craig, and Edgerton, Robert B. *Drunken Comportment: A Social Explanation*. Chicago: Aldine, 1969.

McCollom, William G. *The Divine Average: A View of Comedy*. Cleveland: Press of Case Western Reserve University, 1971.

Macdonald, Donald E. "Group Psychotherapy with Wives of Alcoholics." *Quarterly Journal of Studies on Alcohol* 19 (1958): 125–32.

McFadden, George. *Discovering the Comic*. Princeton: Princeton University Press, 1982.

McSheehy, William. *Skid Row*. Boston and Cambridge, Mass.: G. K. Hall and Schenkman, 1979.

Mann, Marty. *Marty Mann Answers Your Questions about Drinking and Alcoholism*. New York: Holt, Rinehart and Winston, 1970.

Mann, Thomas. *Doctor Faustus: The Life of the German Composer Adrian Leverkühn as Told by a Friend*. Translated by H. T. Lowe-Porter. 1948. New York: Random House, Vintage Books, 1971.

Markson, David. *Malcolm Lowry's "Volcano": Myth, Symbol, Meaning*. New York: Times Books, 1978.

Marquis, Don. *The Old Soak* and *Hail and Farewell*. New York: Doubleday, Page, 1921.

Matson, Norman. "Second Encounter." In *Malcolm Lowry: Psalms and Songs*, edited by Margerie Lowry, pp. 97–101. New York: New American Library, A Meridian Book, 1975.

May, Philip R. A., and Ebaugh, Franklin G. "Pathological Intoxication, Alcoholic Hallucinosis, and Other Reactions to Alcohol." *Quarterly Journal of Studies on Alcohol* 14 (1953): 200–227.

Meredith, George. *An Essay on Comedy and the Uses of the Comic Spirit*. Edited by Lane Cooper. Ithaca, N.Y.: Cornell University Press, 1956.

Meredith, William. "Foreword. In Loving Memory of the Late Author of 'The Dream Songs.'" In *John Berryman: A Checklist*, compiled by Richard J. Kelly, pp. xi–xx. Metuchen, N.J.: Scarecrow Press, 1972.

Miller, David. *Malcolm Lowry and the Voyage That Never Ends*. London: Enitharmon Press, 1976.

Mitchell, H. W. "Types of Alcoholic Insanity, with Analysis of Cases." *American Journal of Insanity* 61 (1904–5): 251–74.

Mizener, Arthur. *The Far Side of Paradise: A Biography of F. Scott Fitzgerald.* Boston: Houghton Mifflin, Sentry Edition, 1965.

Molyneux, Thomas. "The Affirming Balance of Voice." *Shenandoah* 25 (Winter 1974): 27–43.

Moore, Brian. *The Lonely Passion of Judith Hearne.* Boston: Little, Brown, An Atlantic Monthly Press Book, 1955.

Moore, Stephen C. "The Hero on the 5:42: John Cheever's Short Fiction." *Western Humanities Review* 30 (1976): 147–52.

Morace, Robert A. "John Cheever." *Dictionary of Literary Biography.* Vol. 2, *American Novelists since World War II,* edited by Jeffrey Helterman and Richard Layman, pp. 88–100. Detroit: Bruccoli Clark/Gale Research Co., 1978.

Mott, Richard H.; Small, Iver F.; and Anderson, John M. "Comparative Study of Hallucinations." *Archives of General Psychiatry* 12 (1965): 595–601.

Newlove, Donald. *Those Drinking Days: Myself and Other Writers.* New York: Horizon, 1981.

Norman, Jacob P. "Alcoholic Hallucinatory States." *Quarterly Journal of Studies on Alcohol* 5 (1944–45): 563–74.

Oberg, Arthur. "John Berryman: 'The Horror of Unlove.'" Ch. 2 in *Modern American Lyric: Lowell, Berryman, Creeley, and Plath.* New Brunswick, N.J.: Rutgers University Press, 1978.

O'Neill, Eugene. *Days without End.* New York: Random House, 1934.

———. *Diff'rent.* In *The Emperor Jones, Diff'rent, The Straw.* New York: Boni and Liveright, 1921.

———. *The Great God Brown.* In *The Great God Brown, The Fountain, The Moon of the Caribbees, and Other Plays.* New York: Boni and Liveright, 1926.

———. *The Iceman Cometh.* New York: Random House, Vintage Books, 1946.

———. *Long Day's Journey into Night.* New Haven: Yale University Press, 1955.

———. "Tomorrow." *The Seven Arts* 2 (1917): 147–70.

———. *A Touch of the Poet.* New Haven: Yale University Press, 1957.

Ornstein, Robert. "Marlowe and God: The Tragic Theology of *Dr. Faustus.*" *PMLA* 83 (1968): 1378–85.

Orwell, George. *Keep the Aspidistra Flying.* 1936. New York: Harcourt, Brace & World, Harbrace Paperbound Library, 1956.

———. *Nineteen Eighty-four.* New York: Harcourt, Brace, 1949.

Parker, Dorothy. "Big Blonde." In *The Portable Dorothy Parker.* Revised and enlarged edition. New York: Penguin, 1973.

"Pass It On": The Story of Bill Wilson and How the A. A. Message Reached the World. New York: Alcoholics Anonymous World Services, 1984.

Pattison, E. Mansell. "Rehabilitation of the Chronic Alcoholic." Ch. 17 of *The Biology of Alcoholism.* Vol. 3, *Clinical Pathology.* Edited by Benjamin Kissin and Henri Begleiter. New York: Plenum Press, 1974.

Peeples, Edwin A. "Twilight of a God: A Brief, Beery Encounter with F. Scott Fitzgerald." *Mademoiselle,* November 1973, 170.

Polhemus, Robert M. *Comic Faith: The Great Tradition from Austen to Joyce.* Chicago: University of Chicago Press, 1980.

Pooley, Roger. "Berryman's Last Poems: Plain Style and Christian Style." *Modern Language Review* 76 (1981): 291–97.

Pope, Alexander. *Epistle to Dr. Arbuthnot.* In *Poetical Works.* Edited by Herbert Davis. London: Oxford University Press, 1966.

Powell, Anthony. *Afternoon Men.* 1931. London: William Heinemann, 1952.

Powell, Robert S. "Uncritical Perspective: Belief and Art in *Brideshead Revisited.*" *Critical Quarterly* 22 (Autumn 1980): 53–67.

Raleigh, John Henry. "O'Neill's *Long Day's Journey into Night* and New England Irish-Catholicism." In *O'Neill: A Collection of Critical Essays,* edited by John Gassner, pp. 124–41. Englewood Cliffs, N.J.: Prentice-Hall, 1964.

Ray, Oakley. *Drugs, Society, and Human Behavior.* 2d ed. St. Louis, Mo.: C. V. Mosby, 1978.

Rees, John O. "Fitzgerald's Pat Hobby Stories." *Colorado Quarterly* 23 (1974–75): 553–62.

Richards, Gomer. "Diplopic and Triplopic Hallucinations in Delirium Tremens." *Journal of Nervous and Mental Disease* 75 (1932): 630–31.

Róheim, Géza. "Alcoholic Hallucinations." *Quarterly Journal of Studies on Alcohol* 5 (1944–45): 450–82.

Rosenberg, Ralph. "Psychogenesis in Delirium Tremens." *Psychiatric Quarterly* 19 (1945): 316–21.

Rosenblatt, Jon. "The Limits of the 'Confessional Mode' in Recent American Poetry." *Genre* 9 (1976–77): 153–59.

Roth, Martin. "'The Milk of Wonder': Fitzgerald, Alcoholism, and *The Great Gatsby.*" Paper presented at the annual meeting of the Modern Language Association of America, New York, December 1983.

Roulston, Robert. "*The Beautiful and Damned*: The Alcoholic's Revenge." *Literature and Psychology* 27 (1977): 156–63.

Rupp, Richard H. "John Cheever: The Upshot of Wapshot." Ch. 2 in *Celebration in Postwar American Fiction 1945–1967.* Coral Gables: University of Miami Press, 1970.

Sagarin, Edward. *Odd Man In: Societies of Deviants in America.* Chicago: Quadrangle Books, 1969.

Sandmaier, Marian. *The Invisible Alcoholics: Women and Alcohol Abuse in America.* New York: McGraw-Hill, 1980.

Santana, Hubert de. "Tripping, Then Stumbling upon the Light Fantastic." *Maclean's,* 4 December 1978, 61–62.

Scheer-Schäzler, Brigitte. *Saul Bellow.* New York: Frederick Ungar, 1972.

Scheibler, Rolf. *The Late Plays of Eugene O'Neill.* Cooper Monographs on English and American Language and Literature, no. 15. Bern: Francke Verlag, 1970.

Schickel, Richard. "The Cheever Chronicle." *Horizon,* September 1978, 28–33.

Schilder, Paul. "The Psychogenesis of Alcoholism." *Quarterly Journal of Studies on Alcohol* 2 (1941–42): 277–92.

Schulberg, Budd. *The Disenchanted.* New York: Random House, 1950.

Seabrook, William. *Asylum.* New York: Harcourt, Brace, 1935.

Sheaffer, Louis. "Eugene O'Neill and 'The Practitioner.'" *The Practitioner* 205 (1970): 106–10.

———. *O'Neill: Son and Artist.* Boston: Little, Brown, 1973.

Siegel, Ronald K., and Jarvik, Murray E. "Drug-Induced Hallucinations in Animals and Man." In *Hallucinations: Behavior, Experience, and Theory,* edited by R. K. Siegel and L. J. West, pp. 81–161. New York: John Wiley, 1975.

Sillman, Leonard R. "Chronic Alcoholism." *The Journal of Nervous and Mental Disease* 107 (1948): 127–49.

Simpson, Eileen. *The Maze.* New York: Simon and Schuster, 1975.

———. *Poets in Their Youth: A Memoir.* New York: Random House, 1982.

Snyder, Charles R. *Alcohol and the Jews: A Cultural Study of Drinking and Sobriety.* Monographs of the Yale Center of Alcohol Studies, no. 1. Glencoe, Ill.: Free Press; New Haven: Yale Center of Alcohol Studies, 1958.

"The Sodden Soul." Review of *Recovery,* by John Berryman. *Times Literary Supplement,* 30 November 1973, 1465.

Solomon, Philip, and Mendelson, Jack. "Hallucinations in Sensory Deprivation." In *Hallucinations,* edited by Louis Jolyon West, pp. 135–45. New York: Grune & Stratton, 1962.

Stefanik, Ernest C., Jr. *John Berryman: A Descriptive Bibliography.* Pittsburgh Series in Bibliography. Pittsburgh: University of Pittsburgh Press, 1974.

Stewart, David A. *The Adventure of Sobriety.* East Lansing: Michigan State University Press, 1976.

———. "The Meaning of Intoxication: A Dialogue." *The Journal of Social Therapy* 3 (1957): 130–40.

Stitt, Peter A. "The Art of Poetry XVI: John Berryman 1914–72." *Paris Review* 14 (Winter 1972): 177–207.

Strecker, Edward A. "Chronic Alcoholism: A Psychological Survey." *Quarterly Journal of Studies on Alcohol* 2 (1941–42): 12–17.

Sykes, Christopher. *Evelyn Waugh: A Biography.* Boston: Little, Brown, 1975.

Taylor, Dwight. *Joy Ride.* New York: G. P. Putnam's, 1959.

Thomas, Jackson M. "Alcoholism and Mental Disorder." *Quarterly Journal of Studies on Alcohol* 3 (1942–43): 65–78.

Thomsen, Robert. *Bill W.* New York: Harper & Row, 1975.

Tiebout, Harry M. "The Act of Surrender in the Therapeutic Process with Special Reference to Alcoholism." *Quarterly Journal of Studies on Alcohol* 10 (1949): 48–58.

———. "The Syndrome of Alcohol Addiction." *Quarterly Journal of Studies on Alcohol* 5 (1944–45): 535–46.

Törnqvist, Egil. *A Drama of Souls: Studies in O'Neill's Super-naturalistic Technique.* New Haven: Yale University Press, 1969.

Trapp, Carl E., and Lyons, Richard H. "Dream Studies in Hallucinated Patients." *Psychiatric Quarterly* 11 (1937): 253–66.

Twelve Steps and Twelve Traditions. New York: Alcoholics Anonymous World Services, 1953.

Bibliography

U.S. Department of Health, Education, and Welfare. Office of the Assistant Secretary for Health and Scientific Affairs. *First Special Report to the U.S. Congress on Alcohol & Health from the Secretary of Health, Education, and Welfare December 1971*. Rev. ed. Washington: U.S. Government Printing Office, December 1971.

Vaillant, George E. *The Natural History of Alcoholism*. Cambridge: Harvard University Press, 1983.

Vendler, Helen. "Poetry: Ammons, Berryman, Cummings." *Yale Review*, n.s. 62 (1972–73): 412–25.

Victor, Maurice, and Hope, Justin M. "Auditory Hallucinations in Alcoholism." *A.M.A. Archives of Neurology and Psychiatry* 70 (1953): 659–61.

Vidal, Gore. "Immortal Bird." Review of *The Kindness of Strangers*, by Donald Spoto, and *Tennessee: Cry of the Heart*, by Dotson Rader. *New York Review of Books*, 13 June 1985, 5–10.

Wain, John. "Here Lies Lower Binfield: On George Orwell." *Encounter*, October 1961, 70–83.

Waldeland, Lynne. *John Cheever*. Boston: Twayne, 1979.

Wasserstrom, William. "The Goad of Guilt: Henry Adams, Scott and Zelda." *Journal of Modern Literature* 6 (1977): 289–310.

Watson, James G. "The Theater in *The Iceman Cometh*: Some Modernist Implications." *Arizona Quarterly* 34 (1978): 230–38.

Waugh, Evelyn. *Brideshead Revisited*. Boston: Little, Brown, 1945.

———. *Decline and Fall*. 1928. Boston: Little, Brown, 1977.

———. *The Diaries of Evelyn Waugh*. Edited by Michael Davie. Boston: Little, Brown, 1976.

———. *Edmund Campion*. 1935. Garden City, N.Y.: Doubleday, Image Books, 1956.

———. *A Handful of Dust*. 1934. Boston: Little, Brown, 1977.

———. *Helena: A Novel*. Boston: Little, Brown, 1951.

———. *The Letters of Evelyn Waugh*. Edited by Mark Amory. New Haven: Ticknor & Fields, 1980.

———. *The Life of the Right Reverend Ronald Knox*. London: Chapman & Hall, 1959.

Whalen, Thelma. "Wives of Alcoholics: Four Types Observed in a Family Service Agency." *Quarterly Journal of Studies on Alcohol* 14 (1953): 632–41.

White, William F. "Personality and Cognitive Learning among Alcoholics with Different Intervals of Sobriety." *Psychological Reports* 16 (1965): 1125–40.

Wilson, Keith. "Jim, Jake and the Years Between: The Will to Stasis in the Contemporary British Novel." *Ariel: A Review of International English Literature* 13 (January 1982): 55–69.

Wolff, H. G., and Curran, Desmond. "Nature of Delirium and Allied States: The Dysergastic Reaction." *Archives of Neurology and Psychiatry* 33 (1935): 1175–1215.

Wolin, Steven J. "Hallucinations during Experimental Intoxication." In *Alcoholic Intoxication and Withdrawal: Experimental Studies*, edited by Milton M. Gross,

Bibliography

pp. 305–19. Advances in Experimental Medicine and Biology, vol. 35. New York: Plenum Press, 1973.

Wortis, Herman. "Delirium Tremens." *Quarterly Journal of Studies on Alcohol* 1 (1940–41): 251–67.

Zettler, Michael D. *The Bowery.* New York: Drake Publishers, 1975.

Zimering, Stanley, and Calhoun, James F. "Is There an Alcoholic Personality?" *Journal of Drug Education* 6 (1976): 97–103.

PERMISSIONS

Index